CW00572410

Return items to **any** Swin
time on or before t
and Audio B

WB
18/ "

09.

6 550 209 000

The Diary and Letters of a
World War I Fighter Pilot

The Diary and Letters of a World War I Fighter Pilot

2nd Lieutenant Guy Mainwaring Knocker's
accounts of his
experiences in 1917 – 1918 while serving in the
RFC/RAF

Christopher M. Burgess

Pen & Sword
AVIATION

First published in Great Britain in 2008 by
Pen & Sword Aviation
an imprint of
Pen & Sword Books Ltd
47 Church Street
Barnsley
South Yorkshire
S70 2AS

Copyright © Christopher Burgess 2008

ISBN 978 184415 741 9

A CIP catalogue record for this book is
available from the British Library

Typeset in Sabon and Garamond by
Lamorna Publishing Services

Printed and bound in England by Biddles Ltd

Pen & Sword Books Ltd. incorporates the imprints of Pen & Sword Aviation, Pen & Sword Maritime, Pen & Sword Military, Wharncliffe Local History, Pen & Sword Select, Pen & Sword Military Classics and Leo Cooper.

For a complete list of Pen & Sword titles please contact
PEN & SWORD BOOKS LIMITED
47 Church Street, Barnsley, South Yorkshire, S70 2AS, England
E-mail: enquiries@pen-and-sword.co.uk
Website: www.pen-and-sword.co.uk

To my family and all who knew my grandfather

Contents

Acknowledgements

I have only played a small part in compiling these memoirs; nothing would have been possible without the many others acknowledged here who have contributed to the task on and off over the past two decades or so! Sadly, several of those involved have now passed away, but this book is a tribute to their hard work and dedication to keeping the memory alive.

Thanks, firstly to Rosemarie Barnes of the Museum of Army Flying Ltd, Middle Wallop, Stockbridge, Hampshire, who typed the first drafts from the diaries to word processor as requested by Lieutenant Colonel Robert King-Clark, GMK's (Guy Knocker) nephew. Robert 'Rex' King-Clark started correcting these drafts before ill health and bad eyesight forced him to hand on the task in 1994. After I had sat on the diaries for some years we decided it was about time to complete the job. This would have been impossible without the hours spent by my late mother, June Mainwaring Burgess (GMK's eldest daughter), who was one of the few who could read my grandfather's handwriting, and also my father, Raymond.

About the same time, my brother, John Burgess, started to type up the volumes of letters, which was completed by the late Dr John Thackray (GMK's great nephew) who also added some additional memoirs from his great uncle's sister, May, and some biographical notes.

Thanks also to Roderick Suddaby, the documents curator of the Imperial War Museum, London, who is holding the original documents, and whose staff provided images of sketches from the letters and diaries.

Finally, my thanks go to John and Wendy Dowse, keen aircraft enthusiasts, historians and members of the Western Front Association, who encouraged me to get these accounts published, and who kindly helped integrate them into a suitable format.

Introduction

This is a firsthand account of my grandfather's experiences as a pilot in the Royal Flying Corps in World War I. While diaries and letters from service personnel survive in quite large numbers in World War I archives, they are less common from RFC/RAF officers, and so this series of letters and diaries represents an unusually regular and detailed personal record from that time.

The letters cover a period from April 1917, when GMK started his training as an RFC pilot in England, through his time in France with 65 Squadron, until April 1918, when he was injured and sent back to England. During this time he wrote virtually every day to his family, and often illustrated the letters with little sketches of aircraft and manoeuvres. My grandfather was a gifted artist, particularly with pencil and pen and ink, and also became an excellent photographer. The letters were transcribed by his mother into three exercise books at that time, and most of the sketches were pasted or copied into these volumes by my grandfather when he came home. The original letters, as individual documents, have not survived. Also included is a letter to GMK, from his father, on the day he flew out to France, and other letters and memoirs from GMK's sister, May, who was serving as a nursing sister in France.

Interpolated between the letters are diary entries while he was on active service in France from October 1917 – April 1918, but these also continue to the end of 1918 while he was in England convalescing, and then training other pilots. The diaries include other details of daily life, which help give a fuller picture of his personal experiences and emotions. Some additional material, provided by the Imperial War Museum, is included in the entries during the period while in France to help put some of the operational details in context.

GMK was a remarkable man. Unfortunately, I never got to know him as an adult, as he died in September 1971 when I was only thirteen, and he didn't talk to me about his war experiences. These letters and diaries put across a vivid account what it was like at that time through the experiences and language of a young seventeen – eighteen year old officer. They describe well the contrasts of dangerous offensive patrols, evening dinners, dances and theatre, and days of inactivity due to the weather ('too "dud" for flying'). GMK had a lovely sense of humour and never took himself too seriously. He didn't have much time for ostentatious bureaucrats, and named one of his Sopwith Camels 'Pooh Bah' – probably after *The Mikado* character of that name (Lord-High-Everything-Else).

The annotated photograph of 65 Squadron in the front cover of the 1918 diary is a poignant reminder of the many who gave their lives in that war. An almost identical photograph of the squadron, taken at the same time, is reproduced in a detailed history and account of 65 Squadron RFC/RAF in *The Society of World War I Aero Historians' Journal* by Norman Franks and Frank Bailey (1979), Cross & Cockade 10 (2) 49-58. This also gives a full listing of squadron casualties, aircraft serial numbers, victories and awards.

Other documents relating to GMK's World War I experiences include an article he wrote for the *Ex-Army Quarterly, July 1964 – An Airman Remembers. Vignettes from the Sketch-book of an undistinguished Sopwith Camel pilot in the winter of 1917-18.* This is reproduced in the appendices, together with a list of the many aircraft he flew in his RFC and RAF career between 1917 and retirement in 1946.

Text enclosed in brackets thus, [...], are transcribers' comments. Rank and initials of personnel are included where known. The letters and complete diaries have been transcribed verbatim where possible including the spelling, slang, or contemporary expressions and grammatical errors to preserve the originality of the documents. Some gaps remain, however, where the original handwriting was illegible or names crossed out. Some of the place names in Europe differ from the current ones or were spelt phonetically for ease of saying at the time and an explanatory sketch map and table of place names, compiled by John Dowse, is also included in the appendices.

The originals of the letters, diaries and some other documents are being held together in the Knocker collection at the Imperial War Museum, London.   Other documents are in the RAF Museum, Hendon.

GMK's relatives mentioned in the diaries

In January 1918, GMK returned to England on leave for two weeks and met various members of the family (see War Diary entry for 16 January 1918).

GMK was the youngest of eight children.   His only brother, Cuthbert George, died aged two months and is buried in Singapore.   The youngest of the sisters, 'Wee Janie' Bedingfield, died aged six and is buried in Barbados.   The remaining five sisters are mentioned in the diaries; all had family nicknames.

Elsie, GMK's eldest sister, was baptised Katherine Margaret Elizabeth Mainwaring.   She married Alexander King-Clark, 'King', and was Robert King-Clark's mother.   It is likely that the 'three kids' mentioned in GMK's diary are Robert King-Clark (then about five); one of his sisters, Jean, and Elspeth, his oldest sister (then ten).   Elspeth later became Lady Maclure.

Lieutenant Colonel Robert King-Clark MBE MC was in The Manchester Regiment and Glider Pilot Regiment. He was GMK's nephew and godson, and started correcting the first transcriptions of the diaries done by the Museum of Army Flying.   Robert (commonly known as 'Rex') served in Burma during World War II and later wrote a definitive account of *The Battle for Kohima 1944* (published in October 1995 by Fleur de Lys).   The sequel to this, *Forward from Kohima: A Burma Diary November 1944 – May 1945* was published in October 2003.   Robert died in December 2007.

May, his next sister, was born Mary Ethel.   It was she whom GMK met at the C.C.S. (Casualty Clearing Station) in France after he was wounded in April 1918. She later married American journalist Hugh McCaskey Love and remained in America. Cuthbert ('Cubby') was their only son. He became an oceanographer and lived in Seattle. He died of cancer in 1993.

Eily, was Eileen Agnes, also born in Singapore and never married. She was killed in the London Blitz in World War II when GMK was staying with her. GMK was buried in the rubble under a carpet and had to cut an air hole in the carpet with a penknife. He was later dug out relatively unharmed.

Gin or Ginny, born Winifred Victoria, also remained unmarried. My family knew her well as she was a frequent visitor at my grandparents' home, Brook House, Ashton Keynes, Wiltshire, where GMK and his wife Cynthia, settled in 1946, upon his retirement from the RAF. Auntie Gin served in the Land Army during World War II, was a fine tennis player, and later served as an umpire at Wimbledon.

Gal or Gally was the youngest (apart from Janie above). Not to be confused with a girlfriend mentioned in the diaries also called Gally! She was born Gladwys Mainwaring, and married Leon Acheson, Lieutenant Commander, Royal Navy. He became famous for action up the Yangste River in 1926. They had three children. Their second daughter, also Gladwys, was the mother of the late Dr John Thackray (died in 1999) who also contributed to these memoirs.

Underneath are the Everlasting Arms
GMK's alternative motto for the RFC – 25 April 1917

Chris Burgess
GMK's grandson
March 2008

Glossary

Some abbreviations and meanings of terms referred to in the diaries. See also the sketch map and full list of place names mentioned in Appendix 3.

archied	anti-aircraft fire
BEF	British Expeditionary Force
bus / busses	their own fighter planes. Included Camels, Nieuports, RE8s, SPADs, SE5s
C.C.S.	Casualty Clearing Station
C.O.	Commanding Officer
Dickebush	Dikkebus
drome	aerodrome
dud	used frequently – useless day / failed action / poor weather etc.
E.A.	Enemy Aircraft. Included Albatross (slang pl. Albitri), Gothas
H.C.	Holy Communion
H.D.	Home Defence
Kirk	Church (Scottish term, as part of the family came from Scotland)
M.B.	Medical Board
mags	magnetos – part of electrical ignition system
'napoo'	useless / no good
O.O.	Orderly Officer
O.P.	Offensive Patrol
Omer	St. Omer
Pat.	patrol
Plugstreet	slang for Belgian town Ploegsteert

Pop.	abbreviation for town of Poperinghe
R.P.	Reconnoitre Patrol
Sidcup	actually 'Sidcot' – flying suit
Tea party	dogfight or air-battle
Tripe	tri-plane

Biographical Note

by Dr John Thackray

Guy Mainwaring Knocker
Per Ardua ad Astra

Guy was born on 14 August 1899 at Saltash, the youngest child and only son of Colonel Cuthbert and Mrs Janie Knocker.

The Knockers were a fighting family. Guy's great-grandfather, John Bedingfield Knocker (1793-1861), saw active service with the Royal Navy from 1806 until 1814, when he was placed on half pay. He lived near Harwich until 1838 and in Dover until his death. Guy's grandfather, John Bedingfield Knocker II (1824-1900), served in the Indian Army from 1842 until he retired as a major general in 1879. Guy's father, Cuthbert George Knocker (1857-1928) joined the army in 1875 and served in India, Egypt and Singapore before joining the Army Service Corps in 1889. He rose to the rank of colonel before retiring in 1902.

Guy, his parents and his five sisters, lived at Barton-under-Needwood, near Burton-on-Trent until 1913, when they moved to Liberton, in Scotland, finally moving down to Dover in 1916. Guy went to Haileybury School and from there to the Royal Military Academy at Woolwich. He got his commission on 28 February 1917 and, having applied for nomination to the Royal Flying Corps, obtained it a few days later.

No 65 (Fighter) Squadron was formed in August 1916, initially as a training squadron, and flew to France in March 1917, in time to play a prominent part in the air operations during the Battles of Arras. In June 1917, the squadron moved to Calais for special patrol work in the Dover Straits area, to intercept enemy aircraft raiding England. After a short time, however, it returned to its normal duties with the Army. After a distinguished record of service it returned to England in 1919, and was disbanded.

The badge of 65 Squadron is a lion passant in front of fifteen spears with points downwards and the motto is *Vi et Armis* ('By Force of Arms'). The fifteen spears represent a notable occasion on 4 November 1918 when 65 Squadron shot down fifteen enemy aircraft in one day.

Training

7 April 1917 – 27 July 1917

*Extracts from Guy's letters written from his first Flying School at
Catterick, Yorkshire where he went after about three weeks pre-
liminary training at Reading, having joined there on March 12th
1917 . He got his Commission in the R.G.A. on Feb. 28th &
having applied for a nomination to the Royal Flying Corps while
at the Royal Military Academy Woolwich, obtained it a few days
later & after a short leave, spent with us at 8 Marine Parade,
Dover, he reported himself at Reading according to orders, in
company with three other young officers from "The Shop" & so
took his first step towards his Flying Career. The course at
Reading was supposed to last a month, but owing to the unex-
pected advent of a batch of Russian Cadets it was curtailed &
they got a sudden order on the morning of March 30th to report
at Catterick in Yorkshire that same evening at 8 o'clock. Guy had
just had his second inoculation for enteric the day before, he was
living in a "billet" & was glad of his landlady's help with his
hurried packing as he only had an hour to do it in. He had to
leave Reading before he had finished his exams.*

Mrs Janie Knocker, GMK's mother.

No 14 Reserve Squadron R.F.C.
Catterick, Yorkshire

7th April 1917 "Easter Eve"

At last my wish has been achieved! I went "up" last evening for
15 minutes. I was with the Flight Sergt who is a very good flyer.
I was in a dual control "bus" & sat behind. There are two sets of
controls, I rested my hands on one set & Sergt Gay worked the

other. We "taxied" into the open & faced the wind, then he opened the engine full out & we tore along the ground at about 60 miles per hour; then we rose in the air. You can't tell the exact moment when you "take off" but suddenly you look down & see the ground about 50 ft. below you & the sensation is perfectly gorgeous. For the first minute after leaving the ground I felt a little "seasick" but that soon went off & now it has no effect at all. The wind is rather cold on your face but otherwise I was perfectly warm as I was in a leather flying coat & wearing a safety helmet & big gloves which I borrowed.

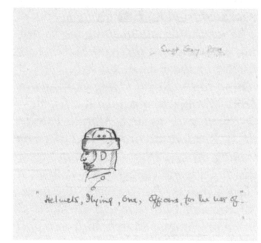

Helmets, Flying, One, Officers, for the use of.

We got up about 500 ft & then Sergt G. turned round, he put over the left aileron control & pushed forward his left foot. Instantly the "bus" tilted up to the left at an angle of about 40° & began to turn round to the left, this is called "banking"; it is rather a funny feeling as you think you are all "skew whiff" & leaving part of you behind! Then we went on straight & when we came over a farm, which looked very funny from above, he switched off, or rather throttled down the engine & put her nose down, at the same time doing a "banking" turn. This is a priceless feeling like going down a watershute! Then we glided down and landed beautifully with no jar at all. The aerodrome looked fine from above & you could see other aeroplanes on the ground & in the air.

Then Sergt Gay said he was going to let me work it, so we got off again & then he took his hands off the controls & put them on the sides thus I was working the "bus"! Then her nose began to get up so I put forward the joy-stick & brought it down but I put it forward too much & the "bus" started to go down again however I soon pulled her up, then we came down. We landed and went "up" three times running.

The weather was not very good but rather "bumpy" this means that every now & then as you went along the "bus" would bump & drop a few feet or perhaps would bump up. This is due to a kind of "air pocket" which always comes if the day is not nearly perfect, it is quite harmless but makes it difficult to feel what you are doing. I found it quite easy to breathe as we were only doing from 60 to 70 m.p.h. and there was absolutely no feeling of dizziness at all as the motion & wind prevents that, you never think of that & just feel that it is quite impossible to fall out. I just love it & there is no sensation in the world equal to flying.

This morning I was down again for early flying and got up for 10 minutes. This time I sat in the front seat where it is not so windy owing to having a wind screen. I tried a turn myself however it was a bad turn as I hardly "banked" at all & used too much rudder. I will know better in future, it was a bit "bumpy" too. The control consists of two foot plates which work the rudder, one stick in the centre which works the elevators and two handles at the top which work up & down for the ailerons – so it is really very easy. The engine is behind in these machines & they are termed "pushers".

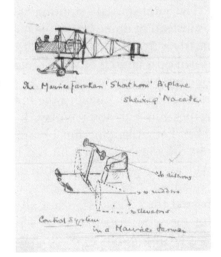

The Maurice Farman 'Short horn' Biplane shewing 'Nacelle'

Control System in a Maurice Farman

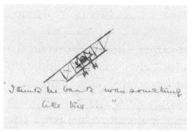

I think the bank was something like this.

No 14 Reserve Squadron. R.F.C.
Catterick

8th April 1917. "Easter Sunday".

I suppose you will by this time have got my letter describing my first flight; I had another yesterday evening lasting 23 minutes. It was just "topping" & not at all cold; I had complete control most of the time & took her off the ground & did several turns. I have got the "banking" all right & put on about the right amount. The Sergt who was instructing, told me to fly level at 500 ft, it is very hard to do this as you generally tend to climb or go down, however I managed it rather well & the Sergt was quite "braced" but he remarked it was probably a "fluke" as even the best pilots find it hard. We went over the surrounding villages & the view was gorgeous.

The Sergt started "stunting" once, he did a "turn" over a village & instead of doing an ordinary "bank" of about 40° he did a jolly nearly vertical one. I was scared blue & found myself looking down on a church & wondering when I would drop out! But that of course is quite imposs as going round a "turn" the centrifugal force keeps you glued to the further side of your seat. Well it was rather fun but don't worry, I shan't try any stunts myself yet. Then I tried landing but I wasn't very good at that as I flattened out too much & am a bit too heavy handed at present, still that will all come in time. (Both Mc Elroy & Maitland are in my Squadron. "Mac" is in my "Flight" & Maitland is in "B"). I passed the "Vickers" exam all right yesterday & got full marks for the sequences part of it. I played hockey this afternoon & it was great fun. No 14 & No 6 the latter won 7-6. Well I must stop this now.

R.F.C. Catterick

11th April 1917

Thanks very much for the parcel & cigs. which were very welcome. I haven't been "up" since I last wrote as the weather has been absolutely "dud" for flying & today the snow is thick. (I went to Middlesboro' on Monday & took a holiday as did nearly everyone else, I had quite a good time. I & four other fellows are going there to a dance this evening in aid of wounded Tommies as there will be no flying today & there is nothing else to do.) I passed in Artillery Observation yesterday in the written part & have yet to pass in the practical part in "sending" & "signalling". Well I have no more news to give you, thanks for the hockey stick & stockings also for your last letter. I am afraid your "last hope", that my nerves couldn't stand it, is gone as they are quite all right!

R.F.C. Catterick

15th April 1917

Thanks most awfully for your letters & parcels, the gloves were "topping" also the books – I have read most of them but still I will read them again! The dance on Wed. night was great fun but the drive home was jolly cold we got back about 2.30 a.m. There is not much news; there has been no flying since I last wrote as the weather has been a "dud". Yesterday I played "Rugger" for the Squadron against the H.L.I. We got badly beaten as we were two men short & had never played together before but it was a great game if a bit rough, the ground was rather stoney [sic] & we nearly all had cut knees. The Glasgow Highlanders were an awfully nice lot of chaps all broad Scots, we hope to play a return match against them some time soon.

  I went to church this morning but I don't think I shall go tonight as you can never tell if the wind will drop & if it does then there will be flying. I have some topping flying kit – a huge leather greatcoat lined with fleece, a pair of sheep skin thigh boots with the fleece inside going right up my legs – gorgeously warm, a safety helmet – padded – a fur-lined flying helmet like a leather Balaclava helmet; this is lined with beaver, a pair of goggles & a pair of fleece lined gauntlet gloves but these have no fingers and are most clumsy to grip the controls with so I think I am going to get a pair of fur gloves with fingers, they cost £1.1/- but are worth it. I am never strapped in flying because it is far safer not to be strapped in a "pusher" machine as in the event of a crash you are often thrown clear whereas if you were strapped in you would probably get the engine, which is behind, in the small of your back, if it carried through as it likely would, you can't fall out. Well I have no more news so will stop now.

The length of my course here depends entirely on the weather. You have to do altogether 3 or 4 hours in the air "dual" & then 5 hours "solo". With good weather I may get out in a month & if the weather is bad I may be here 3 months. You see a "Maurice" is not a very stable "bus" like a "Vickers" & I can't fly it in bumpy weather or at any rate it can fly but it is no good for "instruction".

The Safety or 'Hun' Helmet.

Fur lined helmet.

Catterick

18th April 1917

Thanks very much for your letter just received – also for the newspaper cutting. The Scouts' Machine which it refers to that can climb so well is S.E.5 (Scouting Experimental No 5). It flies level at a speed of 140 to 160 m.p.h. whereas a "Maurice" never does more than 60 to 65. Some difference! I have just this minute been up for 20 minutes with Sergt Gay. We had 4 landings. I was trying to land to-day & am slowly improving at it – my chief fault being that I am too heavy handed on the controls & a trifle too jerky. In landing you glide straight down for about 10 ft. when you very slowly pull back the joy-stick. This flattens it out, then you push it forward a trifle & then flatten out again about an inch on the stick & when she touches ground you put the stick forward gradually and hold her down. I flatten out rather too soon generally & am a bit jerky but I am improving. If you flatten out too much the bus will lose flying speed, the engine being off, & "pancake" the rest of the way & then exit undercarriage! The course of the landing is something like this

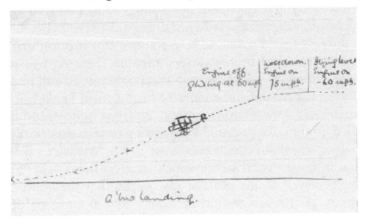

A 'bus landing; flying level, engine on – 60 m.p.h.; nose down, engine on 75 m.p.h.; engine off, gliding at 60 m.p.h.

I can "take off" & "turn" quite all right now myself but find flying level rather a problem as the "bus" always tends to climb a bit. I found today that going up hadn't the slightest effect on me; I might have been sitting in a chair at home! I don't think anyone would feel dizzy in an aeroplane; I just love it & am awfully glad I joined the R.F.C. The word "dud" originated in a shell which failed to explode on striking owing to a defective fuse that was called a "dud shell" – now "dud" has come to mean anything which is no good. "Dud" weather means no good for flying; it is not in parliamentary language! Well goodbye – please don't worry about me I am quite all right!

Catterick

22nd April 1917

Thanks so much for all your letters etc. Since I last wrote you will have got my epistle by this time; please will you send me some books to read as I can't get any here. There is really not much news for you in this letter; after I wrote my last to you I went down to the "sheds" & got another flight of 24 minutes. Yesterday I was up three times, it was too bumpy for instruction in the afternoon so I was taken up to let out the "aerial", this is a long line of copper wire with a weight at the end used in "wireless" from planes. I let it out 5 times & had a very nice joy ride as I was in the back seat & not doing any of the flying myself.

For the first time I managed to get above 500 ft & on that trip we got up to 1100 ft it was very nice up there & you got a splendid "view" & also the feeling you might just as well be 1100 as 500. Sergt Gay did some more of his "vertical banks" at that height, he did 3 or 4 turns on end & I got quite giddy being twiddled around like that, still I am getting used to these "stunts". It was so warm that I didn't even wear a coat & wasn't a bit cold without it, one feels far freer minus that great heavy coat. I tried strapping myself in for fun but discovered that the strap came undone when I was "up", that would have been a lot of use wouldn't it?

In the evening it got calm & I was sent for & got up again. This time the C.O. Major X – Y [Name erased, but "Major Ross-Hume" added in pencil on opposite page in Guy Knocker's hand], commonly known as Ping Pong, took me up, he is an expert flyer & a very good instructor. However on landing we broke a tail skid & so had to bring the "bus" in. Then I went up again with Sergt Gay & had a very nice trip. I did 4 landings, I do most of the controlling now including opening the throttle, taking off & turning & last night I landed all by myself – quite a good landing too! I flattened out a little bit too soon but not much. My chief trouble now is flying level; I find that my beastly left wing will insist on coming up & that I fly along left wing high instead of level. This means that instead of flying straight the "bus" is always side-slipping slightly to the right. This is my fault & not the machine's because the other day when "up" both the instructors & I took our hands off the controls & the bus flew quite level except that it tried to climb slightly being a bit tail heavy. I enclose a photo of the machine I fly taken by another man. I expect I will get up again today as the weather is excellent.

I am orderly officer today & have to conduct the "Church Parade". I also walk round breakfasts & say "any complaints?" The following are the latest R.F.C. songs:

(To the tune of "Another Little Drink" etc)

> When you're up alone "on solo"
> And you don't know how to land
> And you buzz around the aerodrome
> Your joy-stick in your hand.
> And you think of all the tales you've heard
> About "The Promised Land"
> Then another hour on dual
> Won't do you any harm!
>
> When you're out across "The Lines"
> And your ammunition's out
> And the "Archies" they are busy
> And you start "to swing about"
> And the "Fokkers" on your tail
> Will have you down without a doubt
> Then another thousand rounds
> Wouldn't do you any harm.

(To the tune of "The Tarpaulin Jacket")

> A stalwart young pilot lay dying
> And as near his crashed "bus" he lay
> To the frightened mechanics around him
> These last dying words he did say,
> Take the Gudgeon Pin* out of my kidneys
> The Con-rod** from out of my brain
> From the small of my back take the cylinders
> And assemble the engine again.

* Part of the piston
**Connecting rod

Well I shall be "on solo" myself soon as I have done 2 hours &
24 minutes "dual". However I feel quite confident & won't go up
"solo" till I am quite sure of myself. Jack Gilman has been made
a Flight Captain & has got the M.C. Jolly good!

Catterick

25th April 1917

Thanks very much for your letters & etc. I haven't written before this week as I thought I would wait till I had done my first "solo" & tell you all about it. The deed was done this evening!

The weather has been too "dud" for flying all day but this evening I went down to the sheds after tea on the "off chance" when for my special benefit the wind kindly dropped. Then Capt. Mardell told me to come up with him so up I went & flew the "bus" round & landed. We did this three times & then apparently satisfied with my exhibition Mardell got out & told me to go up alone! Gee!

I taxied right across to the furthest corner & turned her face to the wind & took off – she went up like a bird! The evening was simply gorgeous & nary a bump! I flew her round & landed & really made quite a good landing, this time I was a bit too flat so I went up again! next time on landing I lost my prop or in other words my engine stopped, still I landed quite well & waved for an air mechanic to come & start her up again then I couldn't resist the temptation of going up once more. This time I was 500 ft up & switched off the engine & landed rather far down the 'drome also rather fast but still it was a very good landing. Then I taxied in with some difficulty as "Rumpeties" are brutes to taxi!

Well my first "solo" is safely over & I am very bucked. The C.O. was very braced & said "A very good show, you took off well, flew well, & landed well – & you looked quite at home" – which I really did feel! That was jolly high praise from old "Ping Pong". he generally slangs you after you finish "solo" & sends you on dual again. Capt. Mardell said "Well done – you did well!" Ain't I a kink? I am most awfully pleased & feel just "ripping" flying alone. I was flying a 70 h.p. engine instead of an 80 h.p. I am down for early flying to-morrow at 5.30 a.m. Ye Gods! Well no more now. I am before Mac & Maitland in flying "solo". Thumbs up!

I think a good motto for the R.F.C. would be "Underneath are the Everlasting Arms".

Catterick

27th April 1917

Yesterday I arose at the grisly hour of 5.30 a.m. & went down to the sheds to take up a 70 h.p. machine which was a rotten "bus" into the bargain, it couldn't climb above 500 ft., & though the engine was doing 1900 revs. a minute the speedometer was registering only about 50 m.p.h! Well it was very cold & I was cold & half asleep & the engine was cold so it wasn't very nice flying & I took her round once & landed. I was so intent on watching the speedometer that I forgot about flattening out till a bit later & hit the ground a bit too steeply. The wheels hit the ground & the old bus simply bounced up & down & broke two wires in the under-carriage. However I soon got them put right & went up again for 25 minutes & did four landings – not very good ones but I didn't break anything more! I just wasn't flattening out soon enough. Then I came in & someone else went up.

At about 7.30 I went up again with the idea of flying over to Richmond (8 miles off) with another fellow in another "bus" but it was so "bumpy" that I made two landings, very good ones, & came in. I don't think I ever had such a bumping, side slipping, nose diving & all! Still I got in all right! I have now done 1¼ hrs solo & hope to have finished my time by Monday. If I can get a good excuse I may be able to get 48 hours leave, do you think you could find me one & send me a wire?! This afternoon was a great experience & I must admit I fairly "had the wind up", or in other words was in a blue funk! It was quite all right about my feeling dizzy that time with Sergt. Gay, & was only because I was being twiddled round! I shouldn't think of giving up flying I just love it. A Henry Farman "bus" crashed yesterday but the man was unhurt. It finished up nosedown – tailup.

The Henri!

Catterick

29th April 1917

Thanks so much for your letters both of which I received this morning. I expect you got my other epistle telling you of my second solo trip. The weather has been quite too "dud" for flying since. A steady N.E. wind has been blowing for 3 days which means no flying at all. If only I could get one really good day I would finish my time on "Rumpeties" & put in my remaining 2¾ hrs. & then would leave here. If you manage to find me an excuse for me to get 48 hrs. leave before I join my next Squadron I may get it! I am applying to go to Stirling as I want to fly Tractor Scouts. I am afraid however that I shall be sent to an Artillery Observation Squadron being a gunner. If I get Tractor Scouts I might be sent down to Dover as there are Martinsyde's Scouts there. Jack Gilmore at Dover. The Art. Obs. machines are all F.Es which are "pushers". I went to church today.

On Friday a lot of us went to Harrogate for the afternoon it is a very nice place with lovely hotels but it was very quiet when I was there. I won't get my "wings" after I leave here but I will get my "ticket" or Royal Aeronautical Club Certificate. I don't get my "wings" till I have passed through an Advanced Squadron & done 25 hours "solo". It is very warm indeed up here now wonderful to relate. Well you have all my news as I have done no flying lately.

Guy got his "ticket" on April 30th & at the same time 48 hours leave so he took the night mail to London & thence to Dover to find his Dad there alone, I having gone to Byfleet the day before. He spent the day & night at 8 Marine Parade and came up to Town on 2nd May & spent a jolly day with us all – Elsie, Gladwys & Leon & myself. We lunched at Gallards on Regent Street & then went to see George Alexander in "The Aristocrats" then the others went back to Byfleet. Guy & I had tea at the Regent Palace Hotel & then went to Putney for dinner. He saw me off at Clapham Junction for Byfleet & then went on to King's Cross to catch his own train back to Catterick. On May 3rd he was sent to join his advanced squadron at Tadcaster, about 50 miles from Catterick, so did not get up to Stirling as he hoped. We

had a postcard telling us he had been moved & his next letter, the
first from Tadcaster, was written on May 6th.

Mrs Janie Knocker, GMK's mother.

46th Reserve Squadron
Royal Flying Corps
Tadcaster, Yorks.

6th May 1917

Sorry not to have written before. This place is very nearly as
"dud" a spot as Catterick – 2½ miles from Tadcaster village & a
very rotten aerodrome very rough bumpy ground. The machines
here are all "pushers" viz. De Havilland 2-seater fighters
(D.H.1A) with 80 h.p. Renault engines. F.E.2Bs (Fighting
Experimental) very stable machines 120 h.p. Beard motor.
F.E.2Ds an improved 2B 250 h.p. Rolls-Royce engine.

At present I am on D.H.1s. I went up for 50 minutes dual
yesterday & did very well. I then went up again for 15 minutes.

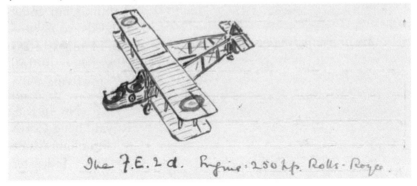

The F.E.2d. Engine 250 h.p. Rolls-Royce.

Then they thought I was fit for "solo" so up I went alone!
These machines are very sensitive fore & aft & "stall" at about
48 m.p.h. Well I was quite all right in the air – they are very nice
buses to fly. I went round & tried to land but I flattened out too
soon & put her nose up. She really "stalled" but I switched on
again. Then I tried to land again but a beastly F.E. came down
beneath me & right across my front. This put me off so I went

round again. By this time I was a bit "fed up" & it was getting "bumpy" so I tried to land. This time I thought I was quite near the ground & put her nose up to put her tail on the ground but I was really about 10 ft. up. I nearly "stalled" again so jammed down her nose & came down "bump" & continued to bump till the machine got "fed up"! I am now on dual again! I did quite well this morning & am quite confident that I have got the "hang" of landing now; I am going solo again next time. I won't hurt myself so don't worry. My course down was rather like this:

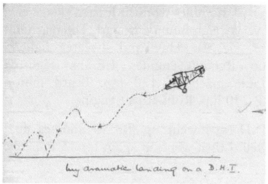

My dramatic landing on a D.H.1

I think I will pass out of this Squadron in about 3 weeks, most people do. Then I will go to Turnbury [Turnberry, Scotland] for a machine gun course & then "Wings"!

I think I am going to Leeds tonight – about 11 miles off as the weather is too "dud" for flying.

Nr. 46 R.S.
Royal Flying Corps
Bramham Moor
Tadcaster

7th May 1917

Thanks very much for your letters. This morning I went up again solo on De Havs, they are very easy buses to fly – but landing is as usual the trouble .The first landing was a perfect one with no bump. The next was rotten & on the next I broke a wing skid. However I didn't know this & went up again & did a very good landing. I am now beginning to get the "hang" of the buses. I have done 50 minutes solo in De Havs. Tomorrow I am going to fly on a cross-country to Catterick, it will be very interesting. I shall go via York & follow the river Swale etc.

I got to Catterick. I went to Leeds on Saturday & had a very good time – I went to see 'Three Cheers' which was excellent.

Today I went into York to buy a pair of goggles as I think I must have left mine at home & I must have a pair. I only got a cheap pair so if you find mine you might please forward them. After 2 hours on De Havs I will go on F.E.2Bs. I will probably get about two days' leave when I have finished De Havs, perhaps this week and I don't think I can run to another trip to Dover, what do you think? Of course I would rather go home than anywhere else! The wind is blowing & it is beastly cold there won't be any flying till it drops. I have managed to get the boss of a propeller which will make a ripping clock case. Well I must stop now as I have no more news. I didn't get to Kirk yesterday as we are 3 miles or so from the nearest.

Tadcaster

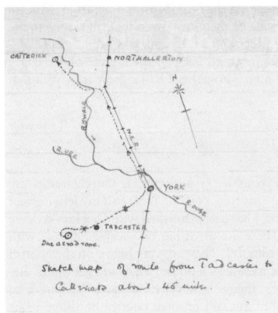

Sketch map of route from Tadcaster to Catterick about 45 miles.

10th May 1917

Thanks for your numerous letters & etc. I have finished my course on De Havs now having done about 4 hours solo. I am now going on F.E.2Bs. Today I went for a cross country trip to Catterick; it is about 57 miles away. Going there with the wind I took about 50 minutes, coming back against the wind I was 1¼ hours. On the way there it was rather bumpy & horrid but on the way back it was gorgeous. Going I could only fly about 3,300 ft. as the clouds were pretty low, coming back I got up to 4,500 ft. & volplaned down onto the aerodrome without using my engine. I did a fine steep spiral. I found it a trifle hard to breathe at 4,500 ft. but I will soon get used to that, not much good if I can't as I will have to get up about three times that height. It was lovely flying back & the old bus was going beautifully. I lost my way from York but managed to see the aerodrome away on my left & made for it. I travelled along the N.E Railway Line from York till I came to the River Swale & then I followed that till I came to the 'drome. I arrived at Catterick at 11.15 a.m. & stayed there till 7.0 p.m. as it was too bumpy to go back in the middle of the day. I arrived home at 8.15 p.m. Altogether I had a great trip. Well that is all for today.

Tadcaster

13th May 1917

Thanks so much for your letter and parcel, the cigarettes are "topping". I expect by this time you will have had my letter about my cross country flight. I have now finished with De Havs & have gone on to F.E.2Bs. These are great big two-seater Fighters with 120 h.p. engines (Beardmore). They are very heavy on the control & absolutely stable & as safe as a house. They will get out of any trouble or difficulties themselves & they can't be put into "spinning nose dives"! I am still on dual control but hope to be on solo soon. The front seat has no windscreen & so you get a terrific wind on you. Personally I don't like these machines as much as the little De Havs, as they are so heavy on the controls & are rather unwieldy but I expect it will be better "on solo". To-morrow Monday, I am going down to Reading to take that exam that I missed when I was there. I expect I will be at Reading for about three days. The Major here says I will be able to have a weekend on my way back so you will be having me at Dover again soon, I will wire when I am coming. I will get my trip to Reading free. I don't know anything about the work but have been "swotting" it up. I don't suppose they will let me fail as I have done so much flying! But you have to pass the exam just to get your "Wings". I enclose some photos I took when at Catterick; please send them back also my photo album. Don't show the photos of the buses all round as I really oughtn't to have taken them. I have got a chest of drawers & a spring bed in my room here so am well off. The huts are wooden & two men occupy one room. I went over to Harrogate lately & had quite a good time. The weather has been too misty for flying lately, good climate this! After I get my wings I may be instructing on De Havs, if I don't go "Overseas" I should love that. The messing here is very bad indeed, far worse than Catterick which was pretty poor!

Yesterday morning I spent cleaning wires on an F.E. an awful job! I went up for a short flip but it was very bumpy & the machine wasn't running well. Maitland has finished his Elementary & is now at No 6 R.S. [Reserve Squadron] Catterick learning to fly De Hav 2s Pusher Scouts. I'm afraid I won't be able to go to Church today either as I have to work for that exam this morning & then will probably be flying tonight. I am very sorry as I really wanted to go.

We don't get up till 7. a.m. A lot of Catterick men are here. No more news & so I will stop.

Guy went to Reading on Monday 14th May & had a three days exam. I went up to Putney to meet him as he wired asking me if I would. He got 24 hours leave on Friday 18th & I met him in Town. We lunched together & went to see "Daddy Longlegs" & greatly enjoyed our time together. We stayed the night at Putney & he went back to Tadcaster by the 4.30 p.m. train on Saturday 19th, I returning to Dover on the 4.20 train.

Mrs Janie Knocker, GMK's mother.

Tadcaster

20th May 1917

It was simply "topping" seeing you. I had a "ripping" time & enjoyed my short leave immensely. I had a very comfy journey back but on arrival at York found that there was not a train to Tadcaster till Monday morning. Net result a taxi! Net cost 19/- !!!
I found that another fellow had taken my room when I got back

so I promptly turfed his kit out! His expression on coming in about 1. a.m. & finding me in bed was a dream! I gently explained & he retired muttering imprecations, whereupon I chuckled & went to sleep!

I have been up 3 times to-day. The new goggles are "topping". The first time I came down & took a tyre off the machine, not my fault though. Then I went up again & landed amongst the sheep – one idiotic quadruped stood absolutely stock still while I ran over it with my left wheel, also I killed it but it wasn't my fault as you can't choose your ground & as a rule they run away. I shan't have to pay for it though!

Then I went up again & got up to 6400 ft when I was well above the clouds – a beautiful sight. When up I tried "stalling" with the engine on, I pulled her nose up till the speed fell to about 44 m.p.h. then the bus stopped & the nose flopped down to just below the level & we went on again, a very tame performance! I hadn't a coat on & was very cold so came down. This evening I went up again & as there were no clouds to speak of I managed to do my height test & reached a height of 8100 ft. I found that I had no difficulty in breathing there & it was lovely! I then tried "stalling" without my engine, a very different matter! I pulled her nose up with the engine on till she lost flying speed & just before she started to fall I switched off the engine. Down went the nose & the bus did a very steep nose dive for about 200 ft. till it regained flying speed when the nose went up. That dive is thrilling – you leave everything behind you for the moment! Oof! I did three lovely spirals down from 8000 ft. two right hands & a left – they were well over 45° of bank! I got back onto the aerodrome without using my engine at all & thus have passed the test! Thumbs up! I am very pleased with myself! To-morrow I am going to do my photography test & may be a cross country to Catterick again. Well no more now.

Tadcaster

22nd May 1917

Yesterday I did 3½ hours flying. In the morning I went up for 2¼ hours doing photography, I took 15 photographs but only two were of the proper spots & so I will have to do it again till I get my 6 proper pinpoints! I got up to 10,200 ft. some height! I had no feeling in my fingers up there through my gloves & all! The goggles are grand! I "stalled" at 10,200 ft. & came down without my engine in grand spirals, then I went up for 1¼ hours & did bombing – it's a ghastly job but I managed to pass in that. Well I will write again soon, I have no more news now.

Guy gave us a great surprise on Saturday May 26th by appearing suddenly & unexpectedly at 11 p.m. He finished passing all his tests on Friday night thus becoming eligible for his "Wings" & got leave till the 30th so came straight home. he managed to procure a pair of Wings in Town on the way through in a little shop & had them sewn on by the man who sold them so he was wearing them when he arrived. He got to London with 2/9d in his pocket & paid his taxi from King's Cross to Victoria by cheque! The man demurred but was told it was that or nothing so accepted a cheque for 5/- (double fare). Being Saturday afternoon every place was closed but Guy got into Cox's somehow & bullied them into cashing a cheque although they declared it was out of business hours & most irregular. They asked if he were off to the Front & he said "not now but I expect I shall be soon" so they cashed it! Guy had to return to Tadcaster but was in hopes of being sent up to Turnbury[sic] in Ayrshire for his machine gun course.

Mrs Janie Knocker, GMK's mother.

Tadcaster

30th May 1917

I had a topping day in Town yesterday & went to see "Zig Zag" at the Coliseum; it was priceless & awfully funny. I also did a Cinema & had dinner at the Maison Lyons & got the 10 o'clock train from King's Cross. I had a comfy journey to York where I had to change & wait three hours so I went to the Station Hotel & lay down in the Lounge till train time – they charged me 2/6 for that, swindle! I was met at Tadcaster by a "tender" & here I am.

I have been placed on the strength of 46 Reserve Squadron pro tem. & as the Flight Commander of "B" Flight is acting C.O. I am acting Flight Commander!!! I have to "instruct" & test "buses" & get people through, it is jolly hard work too! Fancy me a Flight Commander!! Nothing further about Tractor Scouts which I thought I might be put to learn. I had a ripping leave & enjoyed it awfully. Well my duties call so I must knock off. writing again soon.

Tadcaster

3rd June 1917

The other day I took the bus up to about 6000 ft over Harrogate & proceeded to delight that town with a few choice "stunts"! I managed to do the famous Immelman Turn – you pull the nose up with the engine on till the speed goes down to about 40 m.p.h. Then you kick on right rudder hard & switch off the engine, the bus "stalls" but instead of the nose falling straight down it falls over to the right, gets into the nosedive & comes out the opposite direction to that in which you started. I did a tail side also, that consists in "stalling" without pulling the joy-stick right in to you – on the stall the bus slides backward for about 30 ft before the nose goes down, however this is bad for the elevators & not to be recommended I have taken up several pupils on my flights for

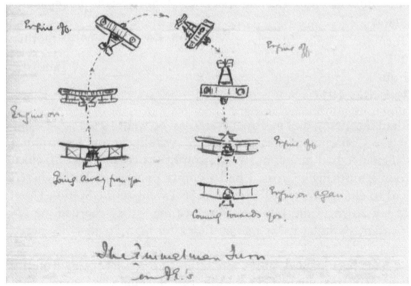

The Immelman Turn on F.E.s

"joy rides" & more or less "put the wind up them"!

I tried a new thing the other day (quite safe!) called the "Falling Leaf Flutter". It consists of coming down in a series of right & left side slips & is rather fun. Yesterday I went up & had an aerial "scrap" with another fellow in another "bus". I kept on his back nearly all the time & dived on him at 120 m.p.h. Some speed! The weather has been pretty "dud" lately & most unsettled. The other day I had a forced landing on an F.E.2B. My engine cut out at 3000 ft I looked for a good field, over judged my landing & came to ground at 80 m.p.h. – went slap through a hedge hardly feeling a bump & came to rest 150 yds the other side. I sent for A.Ms [Aircraft Mechanics] & they patched up the engine & I flew her home all right. I went to Leeds the other day & saw "Razzle Dazzle", jolly good. The other evening I went out to dinner with Burbidge to his home in his sidecar & had quite a good time. Three of my pupils got their "Wings" last night & did their night landings – very dark! I am afraid I can't get to Kirk today as being Flight Commander I have to stay here & fly! Well I will knock off now as you have all my news.

Tadcaster

6th June 1917

Thanks very much for your letters. I think I am going up to Turnbury [sic] on Monday next. I shall try to manage a weekend in Edinburgh on the way there if I can get it – won't that be nice? I am no longer Flight Commander as a fellow just home from France has come & taken over. I am just as glad as I now have a superlatively "cushy" time!

Yesterday evening I went up & took a man for a joy ride, I have never been up on such a gorgeous evening! From 5000 ft you could see for miles round & never a bump. Then above that you came into night mist. I got the bus up to 11,000 ft in 23½ minutes which is jolly good for a bus weighing something over a ton! I was just level with the top of the mist & in the light of the red setting sun it was lovely!

I did a perfectly vertical bank yesterday. On the way down last night from 11,000 ft I did every "stunt" I could think of. I started with an Immelman Turn & incidentally very nearly got into a spin (quite safe of course at that height) but it "put the wind up me"! Na poo! Then I did a spiral, then I stalled & did a vertical nose dive getting up the speed to 125 m.p.h. Next I did a very steep spiral then the "Falling Leaf" side slip stunt & then I S-turned onto the aerodrome & landed. The passenger said I was "some stunt-pilot"!

The other day we had "Formation Flying". The F.E.2Bs made a formation & the two F.E.2Ds were going up above to strafe them, we lost the formation & flew over Harrogate. It was very bumpy & thick above 4,000 ft & the other man was quite low & doing "stunts". I lost him & went home. At 3.30 p.m. he rang me up to say that he had had a forced landing at Redcar about 7 miles off! The other morning I went up to test a bus & the engine cut out just as I got up! I shoved her down to land in a field but she just picked up & crawled home! I had "wind up"! Thanks awfully for the bracelet it is topping & just right.

Tadcaster

10th June 1917

Thanks so much for your numerous letters & etc. Alas! Turnbury [sic] is "washed out". I am not going. A nil report went in & when our names went up it was too late – rotten, isn't it? I am now staying on here pro tem. The Flight Commander has gone away for a week so I am again acting F.C.! I have an assistant! isn't it priceless?! I have been having quite a few adventures lately. On Friday I went over to Catterick & took a passenger, I flew at 11,500 ft I stayed there a few hours. McElroy [later Captain G.E.H. McElroy, 40 Squadron] is doing awfully well; he has been "looping" on a Vickers. Coming back it was rather misty & I had some difficulty finding my way. On Friday night there was a Zepp. scare & flares were alight all night & patrol machines up. Yesterday morning I went up with a passenger & established my height record. I got up to 14,000 ft. It was very cold up there but I didn't notice that it was hard to breathe. The view was gorgeous; you could see the Humber nearly to the sea & all the mountains for miles round. I was over Harrogate; it took 20 minutes to come down. I had a little game with two clouds like this:-

I got a big cloud bump going under that one. I have been doing a lot of p r a c t i c e s c r a p p i n g with another machine, one gets on the tail of the other about 70 ft. behind & the other tries to get them off & get on his tail. You twist & turn a bit; it is great fun & splendid practice. Another machine passing you & going in the opposite direction seems to be going like a rocket. The other "bus" always seems to be "crabbing" sideways.

I nose-dived at 133 m.p.h. the other day. All these stunts are quite safe as I am always a good height up. Now I come to the incident for which I deserve about 14 medals for valour! Two of my pupils had gone up to scrap – one on the best & fastest bus in the flight – my own pet one in fact. Well they didn't come back. Then I heard that one had crashed at Northallerton – about 35 miles away & that the other had come down to see him – the poor chap was killed sad to say. I was sent over at 7.p.m. in sidecar to Northallerton – having had no supper! It took 2¼ hours to get there, I found the crash which was the best machine lying on its top plane & pretty well smithereened! The other was all right or looked so but I was told the lead from the main petrol tank was leaking. There are 3 tanks to a "bus". Service, Main & Auxiliary. The Auxiliary lasts about an hour – so the only thing to do was to fly it back on that. So I got it started up & "took off". The field was on an awful slope but I "took off" down hill & got up O.K. Then I flew back – I started at 9.10 p.m. & got back at 9.50 p.m. & it was getting rather dark. However I managed it all right though I was all the while expecting the engine to miss & splutter showing the petrol was giving out. The pilot of the "bus" wasn't there so I left him behind. I couldn't risk waiting as it was getting dark. He came back today – of course he had no right to go so far away. Such are the joys of a Flight Commander!

I went to church today but the service was awful. When I went to Catterick I left my pocket book behind with £8. in it – however

I phoned up & am glad to say it was found. Enclosed are some photos which my passenger took at 6,000ft – the one showing the wing tip was taken in a vertical bank – please return them.

Tadcaster

12th June 1917

I hope you got my Sunday letter, I am expecting yours tomorrow. There is not much to tell you, I have mastered the way to do pukka Immelman Turns & practise them! In one position you are more or less upside down but there is no danger of falling out as I strap in for them – they are great! I have discovered that a sort of half Immelman done with the engine on is the quickest way of turning round & so am practising that. McElroy came over here yesterday on his cross country from Catterick on a De Hav scout. However he made a "dud" landing and has damaged his tail skid & so is staying on till it is fixed up.

I flew over Harrogate today & dropped a message to a fellow there I know who was at College & who lives there. I don't know if it will reach him!

I hope you are all very fit – isn't this great weather? I never wear a coat flying these times!

A tragic thing has occurred, someone has "borrowed' my ripping "goggles" you gave me & has not put them back. I always leave them in my office & yesterday they were gone, they must have been stolen I am afraid. I have put up a notice & hope to get them back. Now please don't blame me it really wasn't carelessness this time!

Well I haven't any more news & so will stop.

Tadcaster

17th June 1917

Thanks so much for your letters which I received on Thursday – I was wondering what had become of you – I haven't been able to get to church today as there was flying all morning & I can't stand that preacher! It is swelteringly hot today & I sit in my office in my shirt sleeves & gasp!

I had a terrific adventure on Tuesday! A man had been on a

cross country & had had a forced landing at North Duffield near Selby. He had smashed his tail booms but they were patched up & I was sent to fly it back & at the same time as before so I naturally missed dinner!

Well we got off – I took the other man in the front seat in grand style – it was very misty however & I got above what I thought was the right river & followed it. After about ¾ of an hour, the distance from North Duffield to Tadcaster ought to take about 20 minutes if you know the way, there was still no sign of Tad so I came down to about 500 ft. & flew round. We then realised we had lost our way, we passed over a Cathedral Town & a large camp which we did not know but I saw a landing ground (a field with a white O on it) below & landed. It was an abominable ground all hills & hollows, sheep & long grass with no wind indicator. I kept my engine running & an ancient G.R. soldier came out of a hut so we asked him where we were – "Binsoe landing ground 6 miles N. of Ripon".

Ripon is about 25 miles north of Tadcaster. It was about 9.30 p.m. but we thought we would have a shot at getting back. We got in but the engine had stopped so I asked the ancient if he could swing my "prop".

"I be sure I can't" was the reply – so I got my passenger to help & we got it started. Then the fun began!

This is a rough sketch of the landing ground & the country round with which we came in contact. The dotted line shows our path in the air, the solid lead line shows the points our wheels touched. Well we took off & when about 150 ft. up the engine cut out! I jammed her nose down meaning to go over the wooden fence ahead of us. My wheels had actually touched the top of the fence when r-r-r-r-r-! roared out again full blast. I was going straight for those beastly trees! So I pulled the joy stick in as hard as I could, up went her nose & we cleared those trees by about 2 ft! At this moment the engine cut out again & I put her down to land in the next field but just as I was touching the hedge she opened out again with a roar so I pulled her up & hoped she would keep going, but no, with a despairing konk she cut right out this time so I landed in the cornfield – quite well – but pretty fast. The idiotic bus rushed like a mad elephant across that field, howled

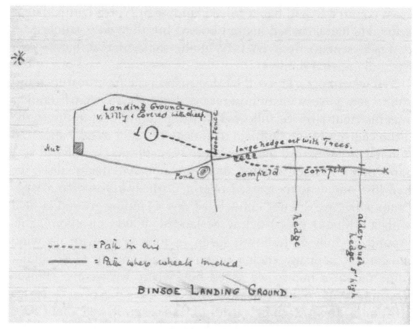

Binsoe Landing Ground

with joy when it saw the hedge & went slap through it! It was some hedge too! The bus cut a gap, of about 6 ft across, clean through it. The only damage done in that entire trip was a few cuts on the fabric of the planes made by bits of hedge! Some trip! I hadn't any time "to get the wind up"; all I thought of while it was going on was "Gee! This is some steeple chase!" When the bus stopped eventually we both stood up & howled with laughter! We then went to phone for assistance & having left a "guard" we spent the night at the house of a friendly solicitor nearby who kindly offered us hospitality. A very nice chap too, who kept us amused with his yarns till 12.30 a.m.!

Next day down in the village we were accosted by an old gentleman who turned out to be Sir John Templeton and he most kindly asked us to lunch, we went & had a jolly good feed; afterwards we went & sat awhile in the loveliest little riverside garden you ever saw.

Then the mechanics arrived & we got the bus started & took off from the cornfield – clearing the hedge at the end by about 6"!

However at 1500 ft. the engine again cut out – this time I made a good landing in the landing ground & got it fixed up. About 6.30 it was all right & we took off & followed the Great North Road home – you do see life in the R.F.C! It was some trip I tell you & steeple chasing in the air with a missing engine is most thrilling, rather too much so! I am not taking any unnecessary risks dear. I was ordered to fly the bus back & did so to the best of my ability – the engine did the rest!

A fellow was killed here on Monday in an F.E.2B which is very sad. Now don't get worried about me! I won't have it!

Well bestest love to you both, from The Bunsoy (some Aviator!!).

[The nickname "Bunsoy" is a Filipino name.]

46 R.S. Royal Flying Corps,
Tadcaster

19th June 1917

Thanks so much for your letters. I haven't much news of any interest this time but I made a very silly mistake the other day.

I took an F.E. off running on the little gravity petrol tank instead of the main tank with the result that she missed like six – banging & spluttering! I managed to crawl round at 150 ft. at about 55 m.p.h. Then I got it seen to & it was all right.

I don't think I shall go up to Turnbury [sic] for some while yet as I am an Instructor. Yesterday it rained hard & we all went to Leeds to see Harry Tale in his new Revue "Goodbye-e-e", it is awfully funny.

The F.E.2Ds were to have patrolled the Humber lately while the King was visiting Hull but as all the "buses" were temporarily unserviceable it was "washed out" which was a pity. I have been playing a good deal of tennis lately so please send me my racquet. Well I am very fit & enjoying life fine. Will write again on Friday.

In the Train

24th June 1917

Just a hurried scrawl to let you know that I was ordered this morning to report at No 40 T.S. Croydon. They have got Traction Scouts there, Rotary engines, so I have got my "Scouts" after all.

I will apply for leave as soon as I get there, so hope to see you before long. Nearly all the other fellows from 46 have gone to York for Home Defence. I will write fully later, I am going down to Croydon tomorrow & am staying the night at the Regent Palace Hotel [London], the two Russells are coming with me. I broke my height record on Friday with 15,000 ft! I had no feeling in hands or feet! I was medically examined the other day & passed as "fit & capable". Capt D [name erased] said I had done well & he was very sorry to lose me.

This move means more dual control so cheer up!

40 T.S. R.F.C.
Croydon

26th June 1917

Here I am again! The way they chuck you about in the Flying Corps! The day before yesterday at 10. a.m. I was told to proceed

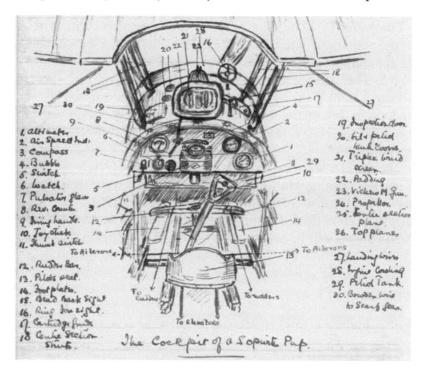

The Cockpit of a Sopwith Pup.

to Croydon together with the two Russells. We missed the 12 noon train at York & so stayed till the 4.50. We arrived in Town at 10.30 & stayed the night at the Station Hotel at Paddington. Yesterday morning I wandered round town had my hair cut & got a few things I wanted. Then we came down here by the 4.05 train. We are quartered in two empty private houses – very comfy & with lovely gardens. They are about 2½ miles from the aerodrome but tenders take you up & down. The aerodrome is very small & not very good – they never "wash out" flying & you hang about all day in the Y.M.C.A. Hut.

The buses here are Avros (with 100 h.p. Monosupap [*sic*] engines – rotary & "Sopwith Pups" with 80 h.p. Le Rhone engines – also rotary). The Avro's a fairly big two-seater tractor, on which you learn, & the "Sopwith Pup" is a tiny little single seater Scout. So I have got my "tractor Scouts" after all! They are very fast & can be looped & etc. The great stunt here is a spin! I haven't been up yet but shall probably have some dual this evening. The rest of the F.E. pilots have gone to Home Defence at York.

A Sopwith Pup looks like this:

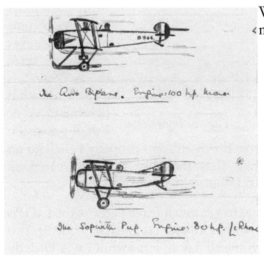

The Avro Biplane. Engine: 100 h.p. kronor

The Sopwith Pup. Engine: 80 h.p. [Le Rhone

Well no time for more now.

The Avro Biplane.
Engine: 100 h.p. Mono
[Gnôme Monosoupape].

The Sopwith Pup.
Engine: 80 h.p. Le
Rhone

No 40 T.S. R.F.C.

28th June 1917

Thanks for your last letters. I am sorry you didn't get mine sooner I posted it late on Monday night or Tuesday. I enclose a snap of me taken by a fellow in Tad. He had written under it, "Airman one intrepid, field service, Knocker". It is quite good. I have been up dual for two trips in an "Avro" & I can't fly the bus a bit at present as it is so wholly different to an F.E. It's fearfully sensitive on the rudder for one thing & has a rotary engine, it is also a tractor. It looks something like this. [No drawing.] It's a very nice bus & perfectly safe, you can "spin" them beautifully but they "come out" whenever you want them to. A "Spin" is an essential fighting tactic & I shall practise it

The Dawn Patrol – Sopwith Pups in Formation

when I get one! After I have flown an Avro properly I shall go on the Sopwith Scouts (Pups). They look like this. You can loop them. I expect I shall soon fall into flying them.

I don't think I shall be able to get much leave here, as the C.O. is an awful man! [Last six words almost completely erased!] You have to stay at the Aerodrome all day & it is awful! I was Orderly Officer yesterday & had to sleep at the aerodrome last night. My servant forgot to send up my camp bed & so I had to sleep in blankets on the floor! I slept excellently however!

Croydon

1st July 1917

Thanks awfully for your letters. I haven't much news to give you this time. I am afraid the lady who said her son had been up to 35,000 ft was romancing, as far as I know the record height up to date is 27,500 ft solo & 23,500 ft with a passenger – the former was created by an Italian & the latter by Hucks about a month ago. It is possible to get up to 20,000 ft without oxygen if one is used to great altitudes but you generally need it at about 18,000 ft. I found 15,000 ft sufficiently unpleasant! I fancy these Hun Raiders fly over at about 16,000 to 17,000 ft. In France the lowest layer of Scouts is about 16,000 ft.

For the last two days the weather has been very "dud" & there has been no flying. On Friday it was raining & we were washed out at 2.p.m. so I went down to Woolwich & had tea at "The Shop" with Dicky Sparkes – also dinner. Sparkes is a sergeant now & passes out in Sept. I saw Capt. L. [Note in Guy Knocker's hand: "Captain G. de L. Landon M.C. R.A."] second in command of 3 Coy. also his wife who is ripping. Altogether I had a great time & will go again. I am afraid I shan't be able to get up to Town to see you when you come unless the weather is "dud", however you must come down here instead. Choose an afternoon, any one will do, & let me know & I will get leave to come & meet you at the Station & will show you all round – it will be topping!

The C.O. [Note in Guy Knocker's hand: "Major Miles"] hardly ever washes out flying & the result is having to stick at the 'drome all day & you get no exercise at all as there is no tennis or anything. I haven't flown since I last wrote but expect to go "up" this afternoon & will probably go solo tonight.

The messing here is really excellent. Last night I went to the Croydon Empire but it was a rotten show. There are a very decent lot of chaps here. P. Mc L. Innes has been killed in France – He's the 4th Head of College who has "gone West" since the war began. I went to Kirk this morning & had a v. good service.

Well cheery ho! I am very fit & happy.

40 T.S. Royal Flying Corps
Croydon

3rd July 1917

Thanks for your letter. I think that the train arriving at Croydon 2.29 will be the best & most convenient for me to meet you which I will do if I can possibly get off. If not take a cab to the aerodrome & ask for me at the Guard.

I went solo yesterday, the first trip my engine was dud & I came down after one circuit. I got it patched up & went up again & thought I would get used to this "bus" so I looped it twice – some stunt! You put her down to about 85 m.p.h. & then pull in the joystick – up goes her nose & you look up at the sky. Presently you see the ground coming round again – it seems to go round you & you switch off the engine & out she comes! There is no real sensation like it; I only lost 100 ft. per loop. Don't worry – I won't make a practice of it! Then I had a scrap with another fellow – the Avro can turn very fast indeed & simply flicks round & doesn't lose any height on her turns.

Then I took her up to 4,000 ft. & did a "spin". Please understand that when I talked to you about a "spin" being unsafe I didn't know anything about it. It is <u>absolutely</u> safe as you can bring it out the minute you please. The way we do it is as follows. You pull up the nose till she stalls then switch off the engine, kick hard on the right rudder & pull the joystick right back into the right hand corner & hold them both there. She falls sideways out of the stall & down goes her nose & she starts to go round & round. Thus you are falling vertically down & spinning round. You lose height very fast but there is no sensation of giddiness at all as you don't "spin" very fast. Then to get her out of the "spin" you simply put the rudder central & she comes out in half a turn. I also tried a corkscrew roll but that wasn't a great success. I am always well strapped in & grab onto a strut when stunting, also I never stunt below 2,000 ft. I have done several loops & Immelman Turns. The Avro is a great "bus". Well Ta-Ta.

40 T.S. R.F.C.
Croydon

6th July 1917

I have been up twice today, it has been pretty misty but lovely above the clouds. I was up today in a bus with no air indicator & no belt, that was more or less all right but when the revolution counter conked I thought it was about time to come down which I did with great gusto.

Well na poo news – hope to see you on Friday.

Croydon

8th July 1917

We had quite a thrilling time in that air raid; we had been warned & had sent up Sopwith Pups on patrol. I went up in an Avro & thought I would just potter round & see if I could see anything. I got up to 9,000 ft but saw nothing except a Pup on patrol so I came down when I was told that I had been right underneath the formation of raiders. I wish I had seen them but I never ever saw any "Archies"! One of our fellows, Martin, had a thrilling time. He went up in a Pup & got up to 16,000 ft & saw a flight of 15 Huns above him at 18,000 ft in the mist – suddenly the whole flight came down on him. He got behind one & fired a few shots when he saw another machine diving on him so he pulled his nose up to loop & on the top of the loop jammed on hard bank & rudder. When he came out he was behind & underneath the Hun so he fired a burst of about 20 rounds & saw his tracers go into the bus & then the Hun went down in a spin! However I believe he got out of it & away. Rotten luck wasn't it? Then Martin, who had fearful "wind up", went round & round in circles firing his gun till the Huns buzzed off. Jolly good start!

I was up – flying "formations" yesterday afternoon & did a few loops (on a new & perfectly safe bus!). On Friday when you left I took up an Avro as high as it would go, I think the altimeter stuck as it wouldn't go above 11,500 ft.

I suppose the siren went yesterday – a lot of damage was done in Town – a bomb hit Swan & Edgars in Piccadilly Circus but it was a dud.

40 Training Squadron R.F.C.

11th July 1917

I had a crash last night & smashed my undercarriage & prop but wasn't hurt at all, so I went up again at once in another bus & did 2 loops & a spiral to prevent losing my nerve.

40 T.S. R.F.C. Croydon

13th July 1917

Alas Turnbury [sic] is once more washed out – only 4 are going, I not being one of them! I shan't believe any more Turnbury [sic] rumours till I actually get there – isn't it perfectly rotten?

I applied for leave today & the Adjutant gave it me till 2.0 am Sunday but my Flight Commander said I couldn't go as I had to complete my time flying. I am pretty fed up on the whole! I <u>may</u> get up to Town to see May but even that isn't certain.

I went solo on "Sop. Pups" on Wednesday evening & have done 2½ hrs on them so far. They are very nice busses [sic] but a bit tricky at first. They don't loop very nicely but fall out sideways at the top. (Quite safe but unpleasant.) But they spin beautifully & turn v.fast. I went over to Brooklands yesterday on one, they are beastly uncomfy things as there is a strut which catches you on the point of the shoulders when you lean back – mine are very sore today. I had a crash on an Avro on Tuesday! Just after I had taken off the petrol lead broke & my engine cut out, so I tried to land in a potato patch but struck a mound & the bus stood on its nose. I wasn't in the least hurt & went & took up another bus & did a couple of loops to keep from losing my nerve!

40 T.S. R.F.C. Croydon

14th July 1917

Just a line to tell you that I am really & truly going to Turnbury [sic] on Friday next. Yesterday was dud & flying was washed out. The two Russells & I went to Town & paid a visit to the Zoo in the afternoon & did a Revue in the evening. I was flying for an hour this morning & looped a few times on the new strong bus.

Well I must go & do machine gun drill now.

Croydon

18th July 1917

Just a line to let you know that I am kicking along all right & am feeling very "fit". I nearly had another mild crash yesterday. I was up in a "Pup" & had been flying round in the clouds. At 10,500 ft I shut off my engine & did a plain glide down – at 3000 ft over the aerodrome I tried to start my engine but she wouldn't start at all, so I just had to land without it! I wasn't going to overshoot the aerodrome so I did the next worst thing, I very nearly undershot it & cleared the hedge & some bushes literally by inches & going at a dropping 40 m.p.h. – she is supposed to stall at 45. I just got in however & landed all right. My Flt. Com. said "Do you know how near a crash you were?" I said "Yes, I guess I did". However when I said I had lost my engine he said it was rather a good show!

Croydon

22nd July 1917

I have been on Home Defence for the last week but came off today so don't worry! I was woken up at 8 a.m. today & informed there was a raid on, we sleep at the 'drome when on H.D. So I got up & crept into my flying clothes & got my bus ready, saw that the gun was loaded etc. However it was a wash out & we didn't have to go up. I don't mind saying that I was in a pretty good funk! but I was really quite disappointed when it was washed out! I went all round London the other day in a Pup & had a great trip though it was a bit cloudy. I got up to 16,000 ft which is now my height record, I didn't notice any discomfort except that it was most frightfully cold & I didn't have a coat on!!

I am very sorry about not having been able to get leave for this weekend but all leave has been stopped till pilots are ready to go to France. I may not be sent out yet as you say but I am not going to say anything about my age till they ask me!

I think I am really a fairly competent pilot now. My latest stunt (quite safe) is a roll. You put her down to 80 m.p.h. & then pull back the stick to the right hand corner, put on full right rudder & she goes right over, wing over wing, in a sort of corkscrew loop.

These Pups are lovely to loop now, you hardly pull back the stick at all & honestly you don't know you <u>are</u> looping! They go over with no strain at all & don't hang on top & don't lose any height. I have been practising fighting with my Flt. Commander & am improving. These machines come round so fast in a turn that you actually <u>get a bump in your own backwash!!</u> A roll is a very fast stunt but no good as a fighting one. I am getting to love Pups now.

I went to Kirk this morning & had quite a good service. I guess the Huns knew I was on H.D. [Home Defence] last week! Hence no raid!!

No 40. T.S. R.F.C.

25th July 1917

Well I am down to go to Turnbury [sic] on Tuesday 28th; I really think I will go this time as I have completed my tests for France. I had a topping Flip yesterday. I flew over the "Shop" at Woolwich & did a few spins, loops, rolls & etc. I then went to Thames Reservoir where they have a floating target & I came down to about 100 ft over the water & fired at it with my machine gun, great fun! Then I flew off again, I was right down low over the water & I felt like a hydroplane! Then I went to Brooklands & fought an R.E.8, I fancy he got me with his back gun (not firing really of course) then I flew back at 85 m.p.h. Suddenly whizz--boom – & a very fast scout (a Sopwith Camel) shot past me & whipped round onto my tail! I was rather bamboozled but eventually I did an Immelman turn & got him off. Then we circled round & I was in the centre & turning v.fast & he was on the outside of the circle & eventually I got on his tail then he buzzed off! I went up again later & did some beautiful stunts over the aerodrome & then – - – crashed landing. What a blow!!

I flattened out too soon & pancaked & my undercarriage conked with a sickening crunch & the bus stood up gently on its nose! I wasn't in the least hurt but I <u>was</u> sick at crashing! However I went up again today & did some good landings also rolls & loops to keep my hand in!! I went over to Hounslow & had a terrific scrap with an R.E.8 & then to Brooklands & flew over Surrey House [*sic*] at about 500 ft. My rolls are getting quite famous here & I am getting quite a name as a stunt pilot!! I saw the Sop. "Camel" again at Brooklands today but he just flew level with me & we waved to each other & then he did a ripping roll & hove off.

War Hospital, South Norwood

27th July 1917

Isn't this the limit? As you will see from above I am at present in hospital as the result of a crash on -- a --- push bike!! Here have I been flying for 4 months & never a scratch & then I go & get flattened out by a rotten push bike! After flying on Wednesday I was biking along the road & a fellow passed me on his motorbike & sidecar & offered me a tow. So I hung on to the sidecar & I think my pedal caught in the wheel & I swerved across the road! At this moment an old man, weighing about 16 stone, was roaring down the hill on another bike & -- we collided! I don't remember anything after that! The next thing I remember is being in bed with the doctor talking to me. I think I had slight concussion as I landed on my head! So I was carted down here & spent yesterday in bed with a splitting head & am staying in bed today but am much better. I am getting up tomorrow & the doctor says I will get 10 days leave! What ho! He also says I probably won't fly for a month which is just sickening! Just as I was getting expert on Pups too! Also na poo for Turnbury [*sic*]! I expect I will be home tomorrow or Sunday. The old fellow was also taken to hospital with no skin on his face poor chap. My ear is the only place grazed & I have a bump on my forehead & knee. I am some aviator – I can't even fly a push-bike! I am very fed up but it will be topping getting leave! This hospital is a pretty one horse show & I am not very comfy. I expect I will be better at home!! I may get a fortnight or three weeks but I don't know.

Training

28 July 1917 – 26 October 1917

Interval of 10 days sick leave at Dover.

40 T.S. Croydon

6th August 1917

Just a note to let you know that I arrived safely yesterday. I went up for an hour & 10 minutes in a Pup today & did some stunts & got on all right & felt fine. Then to my horror I was told to take up a D.H.5 and I did! I did fine in it really & landed quite well. You have to glide them down at 90 m.p.h.; they stall at 70, so you have to land very fast. However you have a good view being in front. I find them a bit awkward but will get into that soon. I rather like them as they are a bit like F.E.s. Don't worry!

40 T.S. R.F.C. Croydon

9th August 1917

This is just to let you know I am flourishing & am fit. I <u>think</u> I am going to a place called Turnbury [*sic*] on Tuesday or at least I am told so! – what do they do at Turnbury?! Well I am getting on A1 at D.H.5s. I like them awfully – as much as Pups now I am used to them. I did 6 landings this morning & all of them A1. I have now got the hang of flying & landing them, also I have looped and rolled them. They don't roll too well, still they do it, but they won't spin at all, I have tried them several times!

There is one other fellow on them & he & I are the first to try stunting them, as neither the C.O. or any of the Instructors have tried & the C.O. is the only other man who has flown them at all – we are rather dabs! I may go to France on them but don't think so – I wouldn't mind now if I did. The idea is that if you go out as a Pup or a D.H.5 Pilot they will put you on any Scout. The weather is very dud. I am on H.D. again but there will be no raids this weather. Being at present the Senior Pup Pilot I will lead the formation in a scrap. Wot ho!

40 T.S. R.F.C. Croydon

10th August 1917

Last night I was told that I was for Overseas & had to report at R.F.C. H.Q. at Mason's Yard at 3. pm. today. There were two more fellows from here. Well we reported & were then sent to the Hotel Cecil to find out particulars of our journey. I was down as a D.H.5 pilot & will probably go abroad as that -- not bad! The officer at the Cecil asked my age & when I said "18 on the 14th" he went & saw the General who said I couldn't go overseas till I was 18 & so I was sent back here! I was actually under orders to go to France by the 7.25 am train tomorrow – a near thing! I expect I will go to Turnbury on Tuesday & go to France immedi-ately after. I told the man I would just as soon go now as in a week but it was no good. I am not sorry except that I would like to have gone out with those 2 chaps. I had a scrap with a fellow yesterday in Pups & beat him easily – getting my sights on him a good many times. I have now finished my flying here & will just fly when there is a spare bus. Just before I went today my Flt. Com. said that he would be surprised if I didn't get the M.C. Nice of him wasn't it?

Princes St. Station Hotel, Edinburgh.

12th August 1917

I expect you have got my wire of yesterday. I got up here free & did want to see Edinburgh again!

Yesterday morning I went up in a Pup & fought Collingwood & beat him pretty easily as I got my gun on him pretty often. I got leave from the C.O. to come up to Edinburgh today as it is a holiday & there is no flying at Croydon. So I will join the train for Turnbury [sic] at Ayr with the others on Tuesday. I am having a topping time of it & it is just great to see Edinburgh, Liberton

& old Burnhead again. I will be at Turnbury [*sic*] if all's well on Tuesday night.

No 2 School of Aerial Gunnery,
Turnbury [*sic*]

15th August 1917

Well here I am at Turnbury [*sic*] at last. We are quartered in the hotel and are very comfortable & get very good grub. We are pretty hard worked 8 am till 8 pm. We were on the range today & flying in the evening. I went up in the front seat of a Vickers as an observer & used the camera gun on B.E.s, i.e. fired at a B.E. with a model Lewis gun which takes photos of your point of aim & shows where your bullets would go. I was just acting as observer. This is a lovely place. I expect I really will get to France after this; I will get some leave first if I possibly can.

Turnberry

19th August 1917

I am sorry that I haven't written lately but really I haven't a moment! We work from 8.am to 8.pm with very little time off all afternoon & we are working on Sundays just the same. My work consists in sitting in the front seat of an F.E. armed with a Lewis Gun & firing at rafts in the sea & flags towed 100 ft behind another machine. The latter practice is rather hard as a flag isn't much of a target. I am quite an expert observer now & stand up on the front seat of an F.E. with impunity, grabbing on of course jolly tight. I will try very hard to get a couple of days before I go. I guess I'll get it all right. When we are not flying we are generally firing on the range – a vile game! Imagine 4 machine guns in the space of 15 yds firing bursts of 20 rounds all together. It's a perfect inferno. I am a fair shot with a Lewis gun!

Turnberry.

22nd August 1917

The weather has been pretty dud lately & so there has not been much flying & we have been on the ranges much of the time.

Today we left the Lewis gun & are now doing the Vickers gun which is nice & easier to work. I think that on leaving here I will probably go back to my Squadron & will likely go abroad on the following Friday. I will apply for leave till then & will probably get it all right. I expect I shall go out on a D.H.5. I really shan't be very sorry to go out as there is none of this beastly red tape & hot air that fills all home squadrons! Besides it will be a great rag shooting down Fritz.

Guy to May (his sister)

No 2 Auxiliary School of Aerial Gunnery,
Royal Flying Corps,
Turnberry.

24 August 1917

Dearest

Thanks awfully for your topping letter. I haven't written for some time but will make it up now.

As you will see I am at Turnberry now at last. It is, I am afraid, not much of a catch & a great deal too like work! We are on from 8 am till 8 pm & working jolly hard all the time – chiefly shooting either on the range or from aeroplanes with machine guns at rafts in the sea or towed flags. It is great fun!

It is great sport standing up in the front seat of an F.E. & as the railing is only about 2 feet high you have to hang on pretty tight! I had 3 days in Edinburgh before I came up here & stayed in the 'Caley'. I had a simply top hole time all by myself! I saw Molly but I am afraid Molly is not much of a catch – she hasn't grown up a bit & has not much in her. However – I made up for that & my latest is Jane Hansen – the little Danish friend of Mrs Westergaard. She is not v pretty but quite topping! We had dinner together in the Caley & then I saw her home in a taxi! What ho! likewise 'Ow Snice'! I wish I had seen the 'little pedigree dawg'! Do you remember that! I went over to Troon & had a great time on Saturday. Jack's fiancée is a v nice girl. Cecil is quite impossible! He is I believe going into the R.A.A.S. He "thought of going into the Infantry but he didn't like the idea of that. If he can't get into the R.A.A.S. – oh they will have him in the R.F.C.!" He composes music & got an unfortunate lady to play me one of his waltzes! It was some waltz! 'Orrid! However – !

Yes, I had a near shave of going out the other day. I expect I shall go out as soon as the course is over. I shall be quite pleased to go out & I have no intention of getting picked off if I can possibly avoid it!

I am on a new bus now at Croydon called the D.H.5. (These details, please don't mention to anyone). It is a weird looking bus & looks like this – [No drawing available] –

If you compare it with my drawing of a Pup you will see that the wings are 'staggered' backwards instead of forwards like this – [No drawing available] – It is the only bus like this. The pilot has a grand view. They are pretty fast, & you have to land them at 90 m.p.h.! I have 'looped' & 'rolled' them but they won't spin.

I think I shall be on them in France.

Well cheerio dearest dear
  Brother Boy

P.S. Could you send me a <u>v. thin</u> pair of fur lined gloves to wear under my fur flying gloves for my birthday? I hope this isn't too much to ask. <u>If so please don't send it.</u>

Best Love G.M.K.

                                                         Turnberry.

26th August 1917

We had an exam yesterday & it was pretty easy & I think I did all right. We leave here tomorrow by the night train. I think I will go back to Croydon first & get leave from there as there is a lot of kit I want to leave at home. The weather has been very dud lately – rain almost every day & today has been the first really good day. I was up this afternoon.

                                                         In the Train.

29th August 1917

I arrived back at Croydon last night after a fairly comfy journey down on the Monday night. I discovered that I had been taken on the Staff at Croydon as Instructor on "Avros" & so I am not going abroad just yet! Aren't you glad?! I am really a wee bit sorry! However I am rotten at landing on "Avros". I took a pupil up this afternoon & made a simply appalling landing! At tea today I was sent for by the C.O. & told to take the first train to Norwich as there is an Avro there which is to be taken to Croydon, so I am going to fly it from Norwich to Croydon – What ho!! I will probably leave very early tomorrow morning as I don't get to Norwich till 9.30 pm tonight. If you see a machine doing stunts over Hounslow you will know it is me! It will be great fun! I passed all right at Turnberry.

Croydon

30th August 1917

I flew the bus back here all right from Norwich. I lost my way & landed 3 or 4 times. I was flying 4½ hours. I went from Norwich to Thetford then to Huntingdon where I had lunch & then to an aerodrome near the Thames. I started at 10 am & got here at 5.30 pm with only a punctured tyre. The distance was about 130 miles.

Croydon

2nd September 1917

I have been doing a good deal of Avro flying (dual control) trying to teach fellows to fly who can't! I don't like the old Avro very much but she is not a bad old bus. She is nothing like as nice as a Pup. I did two topping loops on an Avro yesterday with a pupil in the front seat!

Croydon

4th September 1917

I am now getting the hang of Avros. I took a man up today & showed him how to stunt & made him sick!

There was an air raid warning yesterday & I was all ready to go up but it was washed out. I was rather sorry as I am a bit fed up with doing nothing! I believe I shall be going overseas in about 10 days now!

Croydon

10th September 1917

Yesterday the C.O. went over to Dover in an Avro & took me to fly it back as he was bringing back a Pup. I asked if I could go & see Dad but he said I had to go back at once. However I did 2 beautiful loops & Immelman Turns right over the Parade which I hope he saw! I had a nice trip back at 12,300 ft. I hope to go up in a Camel tomorrow. I have done a good deal of dual today but it has been thick weather.

Croydon

13th September 1917

The weather has been pretty dud lately & today is the first flying day for a long while. I think my two months must be nearly up & it is time I went overseas. I am afraid I shall be on H.D. next Sunday so won't be able to come down home but will try to fly down to Dover to see "Dad".

In the Train

22nd September 1917

Herewith a few new experiences! Yesterday I had to fly a D.H.5 over from Croydon to Joyce Green; not far but I was blue with fear all the time as the bus was rottenly rigged & the right wing low. However I got there all right & came back in an Avro.

In the afternoon Capt. Trollope & I flew over to Staines to shoot in the Reservoir on Camels. Trollope landed & I landed to see what the matter was. His engine had conked & so being a Flight Commander he flew home in my bus & left me to look after his, which I thought was the coolest thing on earth! I waited by that rotten bus from 5 to 8 pm! Mechanics then arrived to take it away but I wasn't going back to Croydon at that hour as I knew we wouldn't get there till about 3 am! So I stayed the night at a neighbouring farm where there was a most topping little flapper daughter! I had a top hole time!

This morning a side car came & took me to Hounslow where I was flown back to Croydon on a B.E. As soon as I arrived I was informed that the C.O. & I were to go to Grantham & there we would find 2 Camels which we were to fly over to St Omer in France. We went to G. by the 2. train from King's Cross only to find that we were meant to go to Lincoln & we are on our way there now. We hope to fly over to the Aircraft Park at St Omer tomorrow & should arrive at about 11. am. We shall deliver the Camels & return at once possibly in a B.E. if there is one to fly home, if not by train & boat, so I am afraid Sunday at home is imposs! Won't it be ripping fun!

Lincoln

23rd September 1917

We arrived here last night & this morning we started but the clouds were very low so we landed again. This afternoon we had another shot but the clouds are at about 500 & so it is no good & we shall have to wait till tomorrow which is very annoying as Lincoln is a ghastly spot. This is an Aircraft Receiving Depôt & the Aerodrome is I think the worst in the country. Tomorrow we hope to fly from here to Lympne & then to St Omer, the whole trip should take about 2¼ hours. At St Omer we will probably fly back in another bus or will come back by train & boat.

7 Ravenna Rd S.W.

26th September 1917

False alarm again! Last night at dinner the C.O. casually informed me that I was for "Overseas" today. So I went & reported to the East Training Brigade this morning only to find that I wasn't needed & that I was to return to Croydon! However I phoned up & got leave to stay in Town till tomorrow so Jack & I went to see "Romance" which is topping & then we came down here to find Mum had arrived in answer to my wire!

I had a great trip over to St Omer. We tried to get off on Sunday but the weather was dud & we had to stay at Lincoln which is a simply appalling dull spot. The aerodrome is the worst in the kingdom all ponds & holes! I went to Lincoln Cathedral on Sunday night; it is a splendid old building & ripping singing.

On Monday morning at about 9.30 the C.O. & I got into our

buses & set forth. I didn't know the way down but followed the C.O. We flew mostly by compass & at about 80 to 100 m.p.h. all the way – we passed over Southend & arrived O.K. at Lympne having taken 2 hrs & 10 min to come from Lincoln, not bad going as it is about 160 miles & was pretty cold! We had quite a good lunch at Lympne 'drome & then took off again. We then flew across the water, crossing the English Coast at Folkestone & the French Coast between Cap Blanc Nez & Cap Gris Nez. About half way across my engine cut out! I was simply blue with fear! I saw there were some boats about which I determined to land near! However after frenzied fiddling with the instruments I managed to get it to start again to my intense relief. By this time the C.O. was miles ahead so I had to push along at about 105 m.p.h. to catch up. Then we took up the railway from Calais & flew on to St Omer. I saw a machine flying back from the Lines but couldn't see anything of the Lines. We landed all right at Omer. We then asked if there was a bus to fly back on & were told there was an F.E.2d with a 250 h.p. Rolls engine. As the C.O. hadn't flown the F.E. & I had, I flew back with the C.O. as passenger!! I came over at 13,800, the poor old C.O. shivering with cold in the front. I kept well away from Dover coming back as I didn't want to be "Archied" as a Hun!! Then I did a vertical spiral for about 5,000 ft & very nearly made the C.O. sick! I made an awful landing at Lympne! Then we had lunch at Folkestone & caught the 8.05 train to Town. On account of that beastly raid it took 4 hours getting up to Town so we stayed the night at the Charing X Hotel & went back to Croydon yesterday.

When I heard about going overseas today I was pretty "fed up" thinking I should have to go without leave but curiously enough the evening portion in my Daily Light [sic] read " Judge nothing before the time"!

The trip from Lympne to Omer took 45 minutes & from Omer to Lympne took 1 hr. & 10 minutes. Total there & back 2hrs 55m.

Guy to May (his Sister)

Homeland
Queen's Hill,
Hertford

28th September 1917

Dearest,

Thanks ever so, for your last letter. I am afraid I haven't written for ages, please forgive me.

Well, as you see I am at present on 48 hours leave prior to proceeding to No 65 Squadron, at Wye.

This Squadron is going overseas v.shortly & so I will be going with it I trust.

I had another false alarm on Wednesday & was informed at dinner that I was for overseas next day. So I packed up all my traps madly & rushed up & reported at H.Q. only to find that they didn't know who I was or what I was there for. Apparently it was just their little joke & they didn't want me! So I returned whence I had come & was transferred to Wye!

I had a great trip on Monday. The C.O. & I set off from Lincoln each on a Sopwith Camel – 130 h.p. engine & flew down over Southend & thence to Lympne, a spot about 2 miles from Hythe. We had dinner here & then set forth again. We flew over the water – my engine cutting out about half way! I screamed with fear & fiddled madly with the throttle & managed to coax her back to life! We crossed the French coast between Cap Blanc Nez & Cap Gris Nez & then followed the line from Calais to St Omer. Here we landed & then came back. This time I flew back in an F.E. with the C.O. as passenger as he hadn't flown the F.E. I did a vertical spiral down & nearly made him sick! Rather a shirt to have made your C.O. sick! Then we came back by train from Folkestone – 4 hours & arrived at 12.0 midnight! The times of the trip were as follows:

Lincoln to Lympne	2hrs	10 mins
Lympne to St Omer		45
Omer back to Lympne	1	10
Folkestone to London	4!!	(by train)

Day before yesterday Jack & I went to see 'Romance' – my second time! Isn't Doris Keane topping – I would like to kiss her! (and I will after the war if all's well!! Norraword!)

The other day I had a forced landing & had to spend the night out. I slept at a farm where there was a topping little flapper. Tres bon pour les soldats!

Well dearest dear, cheerio & write soon

Your own Brother Boy

65 Squadron R.F.C. Wye, Kent

1st October 1917

Here I am moved once more – this time finally I think till I go across to France. This is a simply topping Squadron – no hot air at all & an awfully decent lot of fellows here. My Flight Commander is a Capt. Higgins [Captain W.W. Higgins] whom I know quite well as he was a pupil at Croydon with me – a very good chap.

There are two O.H.'s [Old Haileyburians – GMK's school] here & two men from Croydon & I met another at Lincoln so I had quite a good reception. The Squadron is going out to France on the 22nd of this month & I hope to go with it. It will be ripping going out with your own Squadron! It is not an Instructional Squadron at all & the machines are all "Camels". We just practise stunts firing & formation flying all day & the hours are not long. I shall certainly be able to fly over & land at Dover. I will phone you when I am coming. I flew over there this afternoon & did some stunts, rolls & etc. I wonder if you saw me? The messing is excellent & the C.O. Major Cunningham was at The Shop & is a very good fellow. They are the most madcap lot of stunt merchants. Here & there are some excellent pilots amongst them.

I came down by the 7.15 train last night & was about 1½ hrs late on account of that air raid. We stopped outside New Cross & watched the shelling, several lots of "Archies" fell on roofs nearby – it was a great show! I hope you weren't bombed at Dover. The aerodrome here is small but good.

65 Squadron Wye.

7th October 1917

Isn't it topping all the Squadron are getting 4 days overseas leave & I expect to get mine this week! There is not much news, the weather has got simply beastly cold & it rains most of the time. I was up for a short time yesterday & it was terribly cold. It's going to be pretty awful in France if it is like this! However there will be only short hours in the Winter. We are in wooden huts here, very comfy with two to a room. I have one to myself as the other fellow is away at present.

I haven't been able to fly over to Dover yet but have often just flown over the Harbour, I will try to get over to land the first fine day, I will phone when I can. There is a most awfully nice lot of fellows here, all jolly good fellows & we all get on v.well together. We fight in 3s in France. My partners are Bremridge O.H. [Lieutenant G. Bremridge, Old Haileyburian] & I think Capt. Morrison [Captain K.S. Morrison], we practise flying together.

Guy to May (his Sister)

65 Squadron
Royal Flying Corps
Wye, Kent

7th October 1917

Dearest,

Thanks so much for your last letter. In accordance with request I am writing to tell you that I shall be going overseas with this squadron on the 22nd of this month! What ho! Isn't it annoy-ying. Pa – pa!

This is a simply ripping squadron however & there are the nicest lot of fellows in it I have ever come across. They are all most awfully decent man & we get on splendidly. I knew several of them before & two of them are O.H.'s. As I think I told you the machines are 'Camels'. I expect we shall go up in the North of the Line – where it is horribly energetic. I will of course try & get to Rouen if I can but I don't know anything yet. Perchance I shall come there with a 'cushy' one!

We are all now practising flying as hard as the weather permits – which isn't much as the aforesaid weather is pretty awful – <u>bitterly</u> cold & raining most of the time. The thought of 'Hun-punching' in this sort of weather doesn't attract me – not so as you would notice it! We had a simply topping dance here the other day – about 20 ladies came & we started at 9 pm & finished at 6 am! I met some ripping girls & rushed round the room in a way strongly suggestive of an intoxicated giraffe, but they were all too polite to say anything!

Two beastly officers from Dover who had come as guests got beastly drunk & began behaving disgustingly & there was nearly a fire fight. They offered to fight half of us! When the ladies had gone we laid out one & hove them out! They had brought a girl who was equally tight & so it was pretty awful!

I get 4 days leave this week as overseas leave! It is bon lour les trompers.

Well dearest dear, Cheerie ho?
    & the v.best love from the
    Brother Boy

Wye, Kent.

11th October 1917

I got back quite all right after leaving Dover & didn't even crash land. I choked the engine a bit taking off as perhaps you noticed but I managed to get it going fairly well after that. It didn't go very well all the time tho' I did one roll for your benefit, did you see it? It took about 25 minutes to get back against that wind! We aren't going out till the 26th so that means four more days. I tried to get to Croydon today but funked as it got so thick that I couldn't see at all & so I came back after getting pretty well lost!!

We practise formation flying at every available opportunity now

& are getting better at it. Today we did a formation to Lympne & fired into the sea, we also did some very "hot stuff" dives. I had a scrap with Capt. Morrison in the air the other day & I think I won it.

65 Squadron R.F.C.
Wye, Kent.

25th October 1917

All own kit has now gone & so I am living in what I have got on! I bought a very nice Haversack. I was down in Dover yesterday morning but couldn't get off. Two other officers & a lot of men & myself were doing an anti-gas course. I put on a filthy gas box respirator, you can only breathe through your mouth through a rubber tube & you breathe in air through a box containing potash permanganate, hypo and other diabolic compounds; your nose meanwhile being firmly held by a kind of clothes peg! Having put on this mask I had to go into a hut & shut the door & a man proceeded to turn on chlorine gas from a cylinder on the floor, we stayed in about 10 minutes & then went out. As a matter of fact you can't tell you are in gas & might be breathing ordinary air.

We are sleeping in billets at Wye now as all our kit has gone. I will try to get over again before I go. We have got that new windscreen on our buses & the cowling cut away which is a great improvement; there is less draught & much more room.

Bunsoy

65. Wye, Kent.

26th October 1917

We couldn't go over today as it has been raining all day at St Omer – very rotten! I can't get down to Dover as we have to be up at 7 am tomorrow & it wouldn't be worth it.

Enclosed is a Squadron photo, I am there. Also a picture of all 18 buses ready to start, mine is 5th from the end.

No more news – bestest love & Cheerie Ho!
From The Bunsoy

DIARY Friday 26th October 1917

Got up at 6.45 – at aerodrome at 7 am – Good weather. Weather raining at Saint-Omer. Hung about aerodrome all day – no flying as dud at Omer all day.

Went to say goodbye to London & Miss Pates with Pitt [Lieutenant G.H. Pitt] in evening after tea. Got a lift back in van. Dinner at Kings Head.

Bed early – v tired and bored. Phoned up Dad.

Letter from Colonel Cuthbert G. Knocker to his son 2nd Lieutenant Guy M. Knocker RA / RFC (born 1899 – aged 18) on the latter's departure to France from Wye Aerodrome, Kent, with 65 Squadron (Camels).

At the time, Colonel Knocker, aged 60 – late 21st Royal Scots Fusiliers, was OC Dover District as a retired officer – from May 1916 to the end of WW I. He was decommissioned sub lieutenant in the RSF in 1875; born in Madras in the year of the Indian Mutiny 1857.

[Supplementary information from Lieutenant Colonel Robert King-Clark, Cuthbert Knocker's grandson and GMK's nephew.]

8 Marine Parade
Dover

27 October '17

My very dear Bunsoy,

So you are across the water at last. We have all been on the qui viri since yesterday morning and have done lots of sky-gazing in that time. As you know we were up at Archcliffe at 7:30 am yesterday, and at 8:30 we went down to the beach near the Lord Warden Hotel. This morning Mother and I saw Eily [Daughter Eileen, a VAD nurse in France with the BEF.] off and then went on to the beach again and waited 'till 10 am thinking perhaps that you would be some little time getting away and that we might see something of your squadron, but were disappointed. When I got to the office I phoned to Wye to find out when the squadron left

and the answer came back 9:10 so we were probably at the
station when you crossed the coast or you were too far to the
West for us to see you. I am sorry we missed you but it could not
be helped. If you dropped a note I wonder if I shall ever get it!

Well dear son your active service has now begun and there is
lots of hard fighting yet in front of our Troops, in which you will
take your share. May God in His mercy keep you in safety at all
times, and may the Everlasting Arms be underneath and around
you is my earnest prayer. You have been a dear good son and
never occasioned your mother or father a moment's anxiety as to
your conduct. I have not the slightest fear that you will always
do your duty nobly and fearlessly. Whether you get rewards or
not I feel that there is no flying officer in your Corps who will
have a record for duty well and truly done more bright than
yours.

Your mother will have told you that we got you another pair of
gloves for you – they were not quite the same as the ones you lost
and were 10/- cheaper – 35/- instead of 45/- – but I think you will
find they are just as warm and the gauntlets are wider and deeper.
It was very bad luck losing the other pair. They were 'jumped' I
suppose – they had your name on them too so there was no
excuse. I suppose they never turned up as you didn't say anything
about them in your note received this morning. Many thanks for
the excellent photos of the Squadron and the 'busses' which I am
delighted to have and will get framed. I do hope the weather on
the other side will improve a bit. They seem to be having it worse
than we are.

We shall live now for your letters. I hope you will tell us all you
can about yourself and your life. If you want anything I am sure
you will let us know.

Eily was rather sorry to go back this morning to her hospital
work – but she will be all right when she gets back as she really
likes the work. It was very nice having her for a week and her
being able to see you. Winifred [Winifred, red-haired, 'Ginny' to
the family, Guy's favourite sister] is the next one for us to look
forward to seeing.

I have heard nothing yet about the numerous applications I

have put in for deployment and expect we shall find ourselves at Weymouth by the middle of next month.

Well dear son I must bring this to a close. I hear an aeroplane buzzing quite close and I should have rushed to the verandah to see if it was a 'Camel' from Wye a few days ago, but now I don't care if it is!!

May God bless and keep you, dear old boy, and with my best love

Your very affectionate Dad

Cuthbert G. Knocker.

P.S. When you meet the Hun give him one from me – he deserves all he gets and a good deal more.

Service Overseas with 65 Squadron

27 October 1917 – 31 December 1917

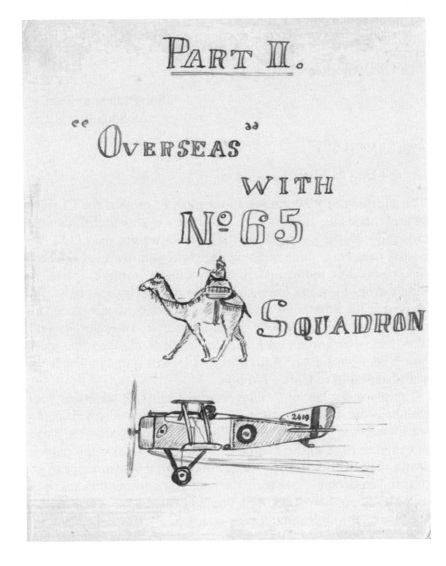

PART II.

"OVERSEAS" WITH Nº 65 SQUADRON

The squadron flew to France on the 27th October 1917.

The C.O. held a meeting of all pilots at Wye just before we flew across to France, and I remember he said that we were not going to France for the sake of our health, that casualties were bound to occur but that he wanted no mention of any casualties ever to be made in the Mess.

The Squadron equipped with 130 H.P. Clerget Camels flew to St. Omer on 27th Oct. and the transport under the command of Capt. Higgins and ground personnel went out by ship at about the same time.

The Squadron was later re-equipped with 160 H.P. Clerget engines.

Guy M. Knocker

"Somewhere in France"
65 Squadron R.F.C.

27th October 1917

Dearest Dad & Mum

This morning at 9.20 am we all set forth & crossed the Channel in great style. We flew over at 12,000 ft – it was frightfully cold crossing – this is a terrible war! However we got over O.K. We passed over Folkestone so I don't know if you saw us. I chucked out a note but unfortunately it got caught in my tailplane & didn't drop. I got my haversack inside my fuselage all right. We arrived at the Base at --- in about 45 minutes & we all landed all right but very cold. Then we got over here, put away our "buses" after which we got out an R.F.C. tender & were taken to a place North of --- to see our Aerodrome. It looked quite good but we shall have to have tents – No bon!

The place was about 9 miles from the Lines & we could hear the shells bursting. We saw a "formation" going across & could see them being "Archied" like billy o'! The roads are pretty bad out there – pavé in the middle & mud at the sides – the pavé is worse than the mud! Then we discovered that we were not to go to this Aerodrome so we took the tender to another one South of it. We shall go there by & by – you'll hear from me when we do. We passed through some towns which had been shelled but we were not near enough the Line to see much except Archies & kite balloons marking the line. We got to the other place & had a look round, there is no room there at present but one Squadron is moving before Nov 2nd & we are taking its place. Huts & a very good Mess I believe. Then we took the tender back to the base. I got out my haversack & we are now billeted in the town. I am in a brasserie & am very comfy with Mr Billy & some others. I had dinner in the town at an hotel, a very good one as I was pretty hungry! We are going to stay at this base till there is room for us at the Aerodrome. I am airing my French with much gusto! This town is bombed pretty often & there is a rumour of a raid being on at present but I have heard nothing & think it must be a false alarm. The aerodrome we are going to is in France <u>not</u> Flanders. We couldn't get away yesterday as it was raining all day over here, I am so sorry you went up to Archcliffe for nothing at that ghastly hour. It is awfully sickening about losing my gloves; I fear they must have been stolen. I rather wish I had changed my money in England as I paid for a meal here with £1 & only got 25 frs. for it! None of our transport has arrived yet! I guess we will rest here till we get up the line. I don't know when I will get your letters, not till we are settled down I suppose. I am writing this in my billet this evening & have been discussing the great sacréness of the Bosche with Mme la propriétaire who hates air raids! I wonder if you "got it" tonight at Dover. I am very fit & happy!

DIARY Saturday 27th October 1917

Up at 7. a.m. Got out machine and ran up engine. Got into air at 9.20. Major leading – very fast. Took 6,000 ft. to get into formation. Passed over Folkestone and crossed Channel at 12,000 – beastly cold.

Landed O.K. at St Omer at 10.05. Took tender from Omer to Poperinghe where we had lunch. Pop full of troops and a

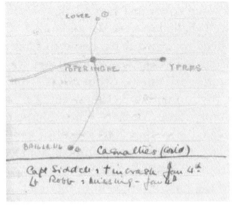

few houses had been shelled. Went to aerodrome at Lovée after lunch, 3 miles North of Poperinghe. Bad aerodrome. R.E.8s [21 Squadron] and Spads [23 Squadron] there already, only tents! No bon. Saw shells bursting and a formation being "archied". Took tender to Bailleul where we are going when the Nieuports [No 1 Squadron) leave. R.N.A.S.] Triplanes [No 1 Squadron R.N.A.S.] there. Went back to Omer via Cassel. Roads very bad in Flanders.

Dinner at Hotel de France. Billet tea at Brasserie 172 Rue de Dunkerque. Comfy bed – slept well. Talked to Mme [Madame] – Air raid at night – heard nothing.

[Note: Actually 65 Squadron replaced the Triplanes, No 1 Squadron R.N.A.S. and not No 1 R.F.C. as stated here.]

65 Squadron R.F.C.

28th October 1917

All this morning we just loafed about the 'drome at the base & did nothing in particular except have a look round as we had no orders. After lunch we were told to fly our "buses" up to the aerodrome at the place we went to first yesterday – not the one we are eventually going to as there is no room there. We had orders to leave them there as there is apparently some danger of them being bombed down here.

So we flew up. I had a very nice Pup as my engine was running beautifully; it took about 25 minutes to get there. When we got fairly far up I could see the flashes of the guns & also a line of grey smoke marking the Lines. I also caught a glimpse of a well known town just behind the present line which has been pretty well shelled to bits. We all landed all right & put our buses in the sheds to wait till we come to fetch them by & by – you'll hear from me when we do so. Then we had tea with a Squadron of Stationary Engine Scout pilots – one of them I knew as he was at Croydon with me. They seemed a v.nice crowd & they had a very comfy little Mess & huts. Shaped like this – [No illustration available] – they had a wall of sandbags all around them as the place is sometimes bombed. Some of them had just come back from "Patrol" & told various yarns. Then we took a tender back to the base (there is nothing like the R.F.C. for motor trips!). On the way we passed a column of troops coming up to the Trenches

& a long line of lorries full of men going back to "rest camps". From the aerodrome I could hear the guns fire on the front v.plainly, there was a good deal of it tonight, we got back here in time for dinner about 8. p.m. I am writing this in my billet before going to bed, we have to go up to the aerodrome tomorrow at 9 a.m., that is as far as I know of our future doings! I don't think we shall go up to the Line till our kit etc., arrives which ought to be some time yet. I don't think we are actually to commence hostilities till Nov 15th but I don't know yet for certain.

Well I'm awa to ma bed so good night!

P.S. I caught a glimpse of a Bosche [*sic*] machine over our lines today being "Archied" like fun! I couldn't get to church today as I had no time at all – I was rather sorry.

G.M.K.

DIARY Sunday 28th October 1917

Brekker at 9.00 at Hotel de France. Tender to aerodrome at No 1 A.D. Loafed about all morning and looked round aerodrome.

After lunch flew 'buses' to aerodrome at Lovée to prevent them being bombed at St. Omer. Saw gun flashes and the long grey smoke of the lines and also part of Ypres. Could hear heavy gunfire all along the front, specially at Ypres and south of it, after landing.

Had tea with Spad Squadron, just back from offensive patrol. One had got a Hun. Took tender back, v.slow as they didn't know the way and a bad driver – v.cold. Home via Hazebrouck – why I can't think. Took 2 hrs – beastly cold. Dinner with Weedon, O.B. & L.W.

Back to billet – air raid warning – washout. Formation to Lovée was excellent and much slower than yesterday.

65 Squadron R.F.C.
B.E.F. France

29th October 1917

This morning after brekker at 9.30. a.m. we went by tender up to the aerodrome where we left our machines yesterday. We took off by flights & "A" Flight went for a sort of tour round the Lines. The weather was pretty thick & so we didn't see very much but what we did see of the ground was wonderful, you can form no idea of the ghastly state of it up to the Lines. Imagine huge stretches of brown grey mud – no grass to be seen – simply covered with great shell holes half full of water. I don't suppose there were more than 10 yds between each hole – just like a tennis lawn would be if, after heavy rain, 50 people in high heeled shoes trampled over it. A lot of wooden huts could be seen among the shell holes & now & again flashes of batteries firing from out of the mud. I also saw a couple of large mine craters like small ponds full of water. We landed at the aerodrome at the place we are going to bye & bye – you'll be wanting to know the name – [Bailleul]. We had lunch here – a v.comfy little Mess hut. After lunch I found some trifling thing wrong with my "bus" & so I couldn't get off with the rest. They went further down the Lines keeping our side of course & I believe they got "Archied"! I waited till my bus had been patched up & then set off home alone. I kept well our side of the Lines! By this time the weather was quite clear & I could see v. plainly all that is left of a certain very well known town – it is a pretty awful sight! Absolutely shelled to pieces & it looked as if it had been gutted by fire, there were heaps of shell holes round it. I was not "Archied". To the north of this Town could be seen huge flooded areas, the flashes of guns & bursting shells could be plainly seen; I landed at the original aerodrome. I watched some of our buses over the Lines being "Archied" & they appeared to get it pretty thick, it looks something like this [Here follow three blank lines, where the drawing would have gone...]

After we had all landed we went & had tea at the Squadron, then – the Major [Major J.A. Cunningham DFC, CdG] being in our tender – we went down to the Wing H.Q. to receive orders for tomorrow, from there back here to the base. Tomorrow I believe we are to have another of these Comic Cook's Tours to the Battlefields of France! It is most frightfully interesting, we aren't allowed over the "Lines" as yet & so it is quite safe. There is a comic Air Raid on here at present but the firing has stopped so I guess it is all over. It is a lovely night & I expect London is catching it in the neck. Our kit hasn't arrived yet but I think it is on the road. I hope you have got the other letters I wrote. I haven't had any yet but I don't expect to till we settle down. The "all clear" has just sounded.

Well no more now. I will write every day if I possibly can.
Bestest love to you both from the Bunsoy.
P.S. I met Dunkerly from Tadcaster here today. G.M.K.

DIARY Monday 29th October.

Up to Lovée by tender at 9.30. Flew by flights round Ypres, Dickebush
& Claor [?] to Bailleul, visibility poor. Ground simply covered in shell
holes – mud awful.

Landed o.k. at SPAD aerodrome at Bailleul, lunch there. Guard -----
shorn off pressure tank by A.M., after lunch flight left without me. I
waited till it was fixed up and then got off, looped once. Flew N. Scholer
Mont Rouge and Kemmel to Ypres – Pop. road. Went down as far as
Ypres – Ypres in an awful state – saw batteries firing. Landed at Lovée
o.k. Watched 'Archie'!

Tea at R.E.8 Sqdn. poor mess. Tender to Liting H.Q. and then to
Omer; strafe coming off tomorrow. More tours round lines. Dinner at
Le Commerce. Air raid at night – heard guns etc. Lovely moon. Expect
London got it badly in the neck.

65 Squadron R.F.C.

30th October 1917

Another day's adventures – Quite thrilling this time! We left here
as per usual at 8.30 a.m. by tender & went up to the place where
we left our air ships. There was a howling gale blowing & as we
saw on the aerodrome a machine, which had been doing contact
patrol, completely crashed on landing the Major deemed it wiser
for us not to fly today – v.nice too! I am sure half of us would
have crashed if we had! So we took the tender down to the place
we are going to bye & bye & had lunch there in the town. Before
we had lunch "Old Bill" & I were strolling down a street when
suddenly – Boom – Wheeee – Crump!!! A huge cloud of black
smoke & a house about 200 yards further down the street simply
dissolved into brick dust! A hefty great Bosche [sic] 9.2"
Howitzer shell simply wiped it off the earth. No one was hurt but
it made me jump about 20 ft into the air! We thought that part of
the town rather unhealthy, so we hove off & had lunch.
Afterwards we strolled down & had a look at the mess – the
whole frontage had just fallen flat! As we were watching them

clearing away – Boom – Wheeee – another one went over us but as we did not hear it go off it must have been a dud. By this time it was raining hard so we took the tender round to the R.N.A.S. Aerodrome, where we shall be going as soon as they move out & waited for the Major, who was visiting another Squadron. Several more shells went into the town while we were at the 'drome but none near us. Then we "tendered" back here for tea which I had in the Y.M.C.A. Officers' Club – a very comfy place. There were two tenders of us coming back & we had a race – we passed the other one going at about 40 m.p.h. along a narrow road – it was great fun!! At dinner this evening I met Critchley from "The Shop", he has just come out in the R.H.A. & at present he is wandering round France trying to find his Battery! We are going up to the Line to fly round again tomorrow I think if all's well & weather permits – I am getting a bit fed up with tender trips on bumpy roads! No kit as yet! Altogether it has been rather an exciting day – being shelled is a trifle unpleasant mais c'est la guerre! I am very fit & happy but have had no letters from home so far. I hope you get all mine, I have written every day since I came out & posted them where & when I could. I believe there was a small "push" up North this morning & v.successful.

Well cheerieho & the bestest love to you from the Bunsoy. G.M.K.

DIARY Tuesday 30th October

Left by tender at 9.00 am, went to Lovée – very windy. R.E.8 crashed v badly, Observer killed, pilot badly injured. No flying on a/c of the wind. Push took place early this morning – very successful. As far as the outskirts of Passchendaele.

Took Tender to Bailleul. C.O. lunched at 170 Squadron, Lovée. Lunch in town, Bailleul shelled! House struck 200 yards from me by a 9.2" shell – dissolved in smoke! 2 other shells over the town.

Raining hard by lunch. Went to No 1 R.N.A.S. Sqdn Mess – C.O. v late – v fed up. Turned up at last – Tender back to St Omer. Raced other tender and beat it! Great fun v.cold and wet.

Tea at Y.M.C.A. Club. Read after tea. Rain off. Bought socks. Supper in town – Bed.

65 Squadron R.F.C.

31st October 1917

Dearest Dad & Mum,

Just a wee short letter tonight as I am very tired & will have to be up early tomorrow. This morning we flew from our aerodrome all up & down "The Lines" around. There were 11 Hun machines above us one time but they did not trouble us & as we aren't allowed to scrap just yet unless attacked we left them alone. I saw them but didn't know they were Huns 'till I got down. This afternoon we did another short patrol. There was a smart "push" going on in part of "The Lines" & we watched the guns firing. We could also see great clouds of smoke, either a gas attack or a smoke barrage – I don't know which. I saw those mine craters which we were told about some time ago at ----; huge things full of water. Our transport has at last arrived! Well no more now as I am going to bed.

DIARY Wednesday 31st October

Tender at 8.30 to Lovée. Flight formation to Ypres, Bailleul, Armentières, "Plugstreet", Dickebusch, Houlthulst Forest. 11 Huns above us! No scrap. Lunch in Pop. Formation of 3 after lunch. Ypres, Bailleul. Pump fan seized up in morning o.k. in afternoon.

Rolls & loops over aerodrome at Lovée after return. Transport arrived with Higgin etc. at Omer for dinner.

Gas attack in afternoon at Polygon Wood. Saw Sop. Dolphin at Omer in morning – four guns, 200 h.p. Hispano slight back stagger. 5000 in 4½ mins. Excellent view – as fast as a 180 hp S.P.A.D. Top plane level with fuselage.

Got to get up at 6.00 am tomorrow. Feeling rotten inside all day.

DIARY Thursday 1st November

Up at 6am. Guided all the transport convoy from Omer to Lovée! Awful! Took wrong road at Arques and had to go back – 12 lorries! Wrong road at Pop. took transport down switch road marked NO LORRIES arrived at aerodrome after 4¾ hours! V.thick day. Two patrols (B & C) due but washed out. 'Camel' from No 7s spun into ground and man killed.

Heavy firing in afternoon and evening. Staying with No 21 R.E.8 Squadron for the night. They seem alright. Transport arrived at last!! Bon. Going to Bailleul tomorrow probably, Très Bon.

Still feeling rotten inside but better than yesterday.

2nd November 1917

Awfully sorry that I didn't write you yesterday but I was pretty busy. I got up at 6 am. I was told to guide the convoy of our Squadron Lorries containing our kit, which arrived at the base on Wednesday night, up to the place where we have left our airships. In all we had 12 heavy lorries, 3 Crossley tenders & 3 motor bikes! Imagine this on a narrow road full of other lorries! Well we set off but just outside the base of course I must go & take a wrong turning & the whole caboodle had to turn round! All went well till we got to that town near the lines & also near our 'drome which is rather unpopular with the Huns as it gets shelled. Here I again took a wrong road & had to take the convoy down a switch road marked 'No Lorries' but I told the Traffic Corporal to go & boil himself when he tried to stop us. We arrived at last after 4¾ hrs, a ghastly trip! The weather was "dud" & so there was no flying. We had lunch in the Mess & stayed the night with an Art. Obs. [Artillery Observation] Squadron on the same Aerodrome. Bill & I had the beds of two men on leave – they however turned up at 4. a.m. I was awake & heard them swearing at finding us in their beds. To all outward appearances however I was asleep & remained so!

This morning "A" Flight was to do a Defensive Patrol at 10,000 ft. We were not to cross the lines but were to attack any Huns who came over – however the clouds being at 500 ft. it has been "washed out". This place is within sound of the guns & they were going pretty well all last night. Today the Transport Convoy has moved down South to the aerodrome we are going to occupy by & by – you'll hear when we do. I think we are going to fly over there & settle down today, I shall be jolly glad when we do as I'm sick of going round to other Squadrons. Well no more news today.

DIARY Friday 2nd November

Spent last night in bed of an officer on leave. He turned up at 4am and cursed like **** to find me in bed. I was officially asleep! Got up at 7am and he went to bed!

Raining all day – no patrol. Transport and all my kit left for Bailleul, v bored and fed up – Mess here v rotten, good fellows tho! Am v.sick of a Nomadic life.

65 Squadron

3rd November 1917

Yet Another Billet!

Dearest Dad & Mum,

There is very little to tell you today – the weather still continues dud. As soon as it is fine enough an R.N.A.S. Squadron on the coast goes to England while the one in our future aerodrome takes its place & we in turn will occupy its vacant place.

This morning – as all yesterday we just loafed around the Mess we were staying at last night & felt very bored! This afternoon we watched a Rugger match No 21 v No 4 played on the aerodrome. In the journalistic style I may say it was played within sound of the guns at the Front about 10 miles away. Philip Gibbs would have loved it! After this we bade the Squadron goodbye. "A" Flight has taken up its abode pro tem in a Convent in the town (Oh no! The nuns have departed!) I am writing this in a comic little nun's cubicle. The beds are the worst part & are of doubtful cleanliness. I only hope they are extinct!! I had a very comfy night last night in the bed of a poor chap who has gone west. The guns are going pretty hard again tonight but it's just an Evening's Hale [sic] I think. Well no more news I'm awa tae ma bed!

Bestest love from the Bunsoy.

P.S. I went to a very good Cinema in the town today & saw Charlie Chaplin – a good fellow C.C.!

DIARY Saturday 3rd November

Spent night in bed of fellow who has gone West R.I.P. Slept v.well. Dud all day. Getting v.fed up with this. Lunch with 21. Rugger match in afternoon 21 v 4, 4 won 8-5. Within sound of guns – what price Philip Gibbs!

Down to Pop. in evening. Tea at Aprils – rotten. Cinema – v.good after tea. Dinner – with difficulty – at Skindles – v.good meal – v.amusing drunk Canadian. Billeted for night at Convent! Beds pretty unhealthy! Slept well however. Guns going hard – a hate on!

Bosch counter-attack in morning – & Bosch guns going all day. Various rumours current about our going to Italy.

65 Squadron R.F.C.

4th November 1917

Settled down at last! Yesterday morning we went up to the aero' but the weather was dud so we just loafed about. I had lunch at the Officers' Club in the Mess & afterwards from 2-3 stood by for a defensive patrol over ---- at 10,000 ft but no orders came so I didn't go up. At about 4 p.m. orders came that "A" & "C" Flights were to go to our own 'drome at By & By – you'll be wondering where that is! Well we set off & it was as thick as pea soup & I could only just see the man in front of me through the mist. We got pretty well lost & wandered around Flanders till we saw some Verey Lights going up out of the fog, we headed for there & found the aero'; they had been sending up the lights for us to see. It was nearly dark when we landed but no one crashed. Two of "A" Flight machines didn't turn up & we heard they had landed at a farm further South – tears of joy from us all to hear they had got down O.K. They turned up this morning! The Mess here is unfurnished at present but quite nice – two huts joined by a passage. My hut is very nice, it is one of three little round ones. Inside it is partitioned off as follows [No illustration]. Corrugated iron outside & wood boards inside, v.warm. I am sharing my room with Marshall [2nd Lieutenant L. Marshall] – the lad from Wellington. Well "A" Flight is going on Defensive Patrol at 12 &

it is nearly that now so I will close – – – Confusion to the Huns!
I am awfully glad to get my things again.

Bestest love – I am very fit & happy – Bunsoy,

No mail yet. 2.30 p.m. Back from patrol O.K. saw nothing.

DIARY Sunday 4th November

Up to Lovée after brekker. Messed about all morning – v.thick weather.
Cleared up after lunch stood by for patrol from 2-3. Na poo, at 4.00 pm.
'A' & 'C' flights set forth for Bailleul. So thick that I could only just see
O.B. ['Old Bill' – Lieutenant G. Bremridge]. Completely lost! Saw Verey
lights and landed – a v.bon landing too! Higgin & Little Willie [2nd
Lieutenant A. Rosenthal] landed at Armentières. Found kit here.
Topping to be in ones own mess. Bed early – very cold.

DIARY Monday 5th November

Slept poorly. Got up at 8.15, ran up engine. Fairly cloudy. Up on a
Line Patrol at 11.15 – all present except L. Willie, v.rotten formation – 5
is a beastly number. Patrol at 11,000 over Ypres. One Hun seen. No
scrap – v cold. Lost on the way back. Down to Bailleul at 3.30 – Bought
some things. Lecture by Major in Mess afterwards.

Straightened out room a bit. Dinner in Mess. Bed. Slept excellently.
Pretty cold.

65 Squadron R.F.C.
B.E.F. France

6th November 1917

The mail has at last arrived & I had two letters from Mum & one
from Dad, the gloves & your other letters have not come yet but
I expect they will "roll up" all right in time. The letters were
dated 2nd & 3rd Nov (Mum's) & 31st Oct (Dad's). You appear
to have had a warm time of it with the Gothas! I have had no
experience as thrilling as being bombed. I am in a room with
O.W. (Old Bill) now. I have changed my hut as all A Flight is in
one line now. I am getting my room made comfy & went to the
town & bought some pictures, a basin & a few oddments. The
Mess is getting put right & we have now some chairs! I will try
& photo my hut. This is a sketch of my corner of the hut (more
or less). [No illustration] That's as near as I can draw it looking
from my bed to the door. I was up on a defensive patrol at 7.15

a.m. today but saw no Huns. However we saw a v.big show on the ground – it will be in the papers you see! The whole ground was dotted with the flashes of the big guns going off & the wreath of smoke barrages. I write in pencil from choice – it looks well from the front!

Bestest love & write often!

DIARY Tuesday 6th November

Up at 7am Line Patrol with O.B. & L.W. [Little Willie] Formation Good. Ypres and Houthulst Wood. Saw no Huns. Watched the battle for Passchendaele – gun fire terrific and smoke barrage clouds low – pretty thick. Up 1 hour. Passchendaele taken.

To Bailleul in evening, bought things for room, dud all day. Bailleul shelled at ½ hr intervals. Mail arrival.

Guy to May (his Sister)

On Active Service in the Field

Passed by Censor No 5308

65 Squadron
R.F.C. B.E.F.
France

7th November 1917

Dearest,

About time I wrote to you, what? Well here I am settled down at last, thank heavens. This Squadron has been wandering about ever since it came out, waiting for the Squadron who had this aerodrome to clear out. We came in here on Sunday.

We are in little Nissan huts – v.warm & comfy. Before we came here we were staying with another squadron north of this place. It was North West of a v.well known town – perhaps the best known in the war. This place is about 12 miles south of it & about 7 miles from the Lines – within sound of the guns. The town near this place was shelled with 9.2" shells all yesterday at half hour intervals. It was being shelled when I was in it about a week ago. I was strolling down the street when suddenly "B o o m !! whe e e e! Crump!!" – & a house about 200 yds further down the street literally dissolved into brick dust! Gee, but I jumped some! I have been up on several defensive patrols at 10,000 but have not been across the lines yet. I saw some Hun machines the other day but we left them alone!

You have no idea of the awful state of the ground around the lines. There is not a square inch without a shell hole – that town I mentioned is in an awful mess – hardly a standing wall! I was up yesterday morning & watched a v.big show on the ground. The gun fire was terrific & the whole ground was glittering with gun flashes.

It will be topping if you can get up the line & see me. Let me know all about it. I think we shall be going over the lines pretty soon now! Wotto!

Well, bests & love dearest
   from the Brother Boy

DIARY Wednesday 7th November
Dud all day nearly. Rain in morning v cold. Went for joyride in afternoon in L.W.'s bus looped etc. Went over Armentières. Nearly got lost.

To Bailleul in evening. Got some things. Gotha raid at night at 3.a.m!

65 Squadron

8th November 1917

Another mail hurrah! This time I got your 3 early letters. Mum & Dad's first one – one from Elsie, one from May, also from Uncle Jack Cox [? last part illegible] & one from Carrie! I also got the gloves & etc., the former are very nice but not so warm as the others. Thanks awfully for your two first letters – I am keeping them both. Yesterday was dud nearly all day but I went for a "flip" in a borrowed bus, as my engine was being taken down & cleaned. I went over [a] small town & nearly got lost! In the evening I went down to the town & got some more things for my room. I haven't used my hot [water] bottle yet. Last night there was an air raid all round here by Gothas at 3 a.m. I heard the engines & "Archies" but it was much too cold to get up & look.

The weather today is fine thank goodness. This morning at about 11 a.m. a Hun machine came over & we were ordered to go up after it at once so I hove off first in my bus which is now running toppingly. I got up to 16,000 ft. & I think I saw him far off but lost him again. Then I joined some other "Camels" & did an ordinary defensive Patrol – we saw some Huns across the Lines but none near us. I was jolly cold I can tell you! We are getting the Mess in order now & my room looks v.bon!

Bestest love to you both from the Bunsoy.

DIARY Thursday 8th November
Lovely day – Bath in morning – v cold day. My bus ready. Tested it – v nice. Looped etc. Hun came over and O.B. and I went up after it. Got to 16,000 but missed it – Line Patrol – awful cold.

Read in afternoon and played bridge – lost 4f 25c! Bed – v cold.

65 Squadron R.F.C.

9th November 1917

Dearest Dad & Mum & Joe

Thanks awfully for your two letters, also for "Flying" & "Ashore & Afloat". There is not much news to give you this time. We didn't fly yesterday afternoon as it was raining & as it continued all evening I stayed in Camp. We played Auction Bridge & I lost 4 francs 50 cts! By the way you remember I said yesterday that some Huns had come over – well "B" Flight met one of them. He got the wind up & dived away from them at a great pace, in fact he over dived himself & his wings folded back & he was slain. One Hun the less! The other day, I think it was Tuesday – it was very cloudy & we sent up some patrols – defensive of course, anyway 3 of our fellows – Harrison [Lieutenant W.L. Harrison], Cutbill [2nd Lieutenant E.H. Cutbill] & Gordon [Lieutenant E.G.S. Gordon] failed to return & are still missing. I guess they must have got lost & landed in Hun land. Rotten luck – wasn't it? Three new pilots have just arrived from the Base. This morning

I stood by for early patrols but didn't have to go up. How topping Joe coming home, give him my bestest love. This morning from 10.45 – 12.15 we went up on Line Patrol but it was very cloudy & we couldn't see anything – we saw no Huns. I guess we will be crossing the Lines soon now! Wind up! We have got some blue curtains for my hut also a table made of a board – it looks great! We also have some mats on the floor & pictures on the walls. I wore the new fur gloves today – they are great! The weather is very unsettled & rains on & off. I had a shot at censoring Mum's letters, rather an amusing game! "The roar of the guns made one man's blood go cold."

Well na poo now. Bestest love to all three of you from the Bunsoy.

DIARY Friday 9th November

Fine morning. Patrol at 11am. Clouds all the way up. Formation poor – Engine dud. Contour chasing with O.B. in afternoon. Put the wind up troops on parade! Went to Armentières – v.knocked about & deserted!! Watched a communication trench being shelled. Saw kite balloon being archied – too close to be pleasant! Engine went 'wonk' and cut out at intervals all way home. Ignition wire broken. Shorting on another cylinder. Got it fired up o.k. now.

To Bailleul in evening, not quite so cold.

10th November 1917

Just a wee note as there is not much time before the post goes out. There is no news at all to give you this time. Yesterday afternoon Bill & I went up & had a practice scrap. I beat him I think. We then put the wind up troops on the road then I went over a town S.E. of this & quite near the Lines (Armentières) it has hardly a whole roof in it & looked very deserted. I watched the Huns shelling Communications trenches about 300 yds out of the town – v.good shooting.

Then I saw a kite balloon about ½ a mile away from me & my own level getting "Archied" so I thought it was time to go! My engine started cutting out on the way home & I thought I wasn't going to get back but just managed to. An ignition wire had gone & was short circuiting other cylinders; it's all right again now tho'. I went into the town yesterday evening & got a few things.

Today it's raining hard – I have just lost 4 francs 50 cts at Auction! I shall never gamble, I haven't the luck! (N.B. by Mother good thing too!)

No time for more.

The Bunsoy.

Guy to May (his Sister)

On Active Service in the Field
Passed by Censor No 5308

65 Squadron

10th November 1917

Dearest

I hope that by this time you will have had my last (& first letter). I have had two from you so far I think.

I am afraid there is no immediate prospect of my getting down to Rouen to see you but when I get my leave – in 5 or 6 wks if all's well, we must arrange a meeting somehow or other.

Well, we have been out on patrol at 5000 ft over the lines pretty nearly every fine day for the past week & I have had one scrap. I haven't done in any Huns yet! The first day we were out was rather unfortunate as we had two missing & 1 wounded.

I was out with 'A' flight – 5 machines – & we dived on a couple of Hun L.V.G. two-seaters. They at once hove off for their own lines & we lost them. I fired my guns at one of them & the observer fired at me but to no purpose.

They were v.well camouflaged & looked something like this [No picture available]

I was most awfully excited while it lasted.

The worst part of going over the lines is the "Archie". That is simply awful! You are sailing along quite peacefully when suddenly you hear a "Woo-ourf!" – you simply spin your head round & see a black blob just behind you. Then you see two or three more little blobs all round you & a second after you hear more "Woo-oofs"! It is most alarming till you get used to it. The other day you could trace our path by the trail of "Archies". Fritz is a harmless little chap but apt to be peevish when irritated. He is a jolly good shot too!

I saw an albatross scout fairly close the other day. Having been shot he went down in a kind of floppy spin.

Well, the post goes -

Bestest Love my dearest
  From your Brother Boy

DIARY Saturday 10th November
Rain, Rain, Rain all day. No flying. Down to Bailleul in afternoon. Got a stove. Played bridge and lost 4 fr 50c! Rotten. Wrote letters in evening to Eily, Mrs Russell Taylor, Joy, Carrie, Chris. Major Cross in for Supper. O.B. orderly officer. Not so cold. Bedroom warm from the stove.

Guy to his sister, Winnie.

11th November 1917.

65 Squadron R.F.C.

Dearest Joe,

Congraggos on your safe return to civilisation after having the [?] terms of the Alps, I do wish I was at home to see you, however when I get some leave – ah! that will be très bon. Well I am lurching along all right & am so far unpunctured & in one piece. I haven't been over the lines yet but have often been up on defensive patrols up & down one side of them. The ground in this part of the lines is a ghastly sight. Imagine a tennis lawn after heavy rain – clay soil. Then reconstruct your ideas after ten dozen ladies in high heeled shoes (the kind that "give such a good grip you know") have been trampling all over it for about half an hour & after a puppy has been digging holes in it (mine craters) – then shove a few heaps of broken bricks about it (towns) then arrange a series of electric flash bulbs all over it & light them on & off at intervals (guns). Then flood half the lawn & imagine more rain. Then go up a step ladder & survey the whole effect & you will have an accurate impression of what the Lines look like from the air. The effect will be improved if you choose the coldest day & arrange for a band or something noisy to give the proper noise of the engine! I saw a Push from the air the other day – a wonderful sight. The gun flashes were multitudinous. We have the cutest little huts here; they look some thing like this: [No illustration]

DIARY Sunday 11th November

V. thick most of morning. Short line patrol washed out – because of clouds, v.cold. No E.A. seen. Up for a flip in afternoon. Huge scrap with Keller [Lieutenant C.F. Keller]. Beat him once and was beaten once.

To tea at No 1 with Moore, v.good tea. Not to church all day – must go next week. Read in evening.

65 Squadron R.F.C.

12th November 1917

Dearest Dad & Mum

Across the Lines at last! The weather is lovely this morning & at 11 o'clock 6 machines of "A" Flight went up on an "Offensive Patrol" – about 6 miles over the Lines. Then "Old Bill" went home with a missing engine & we five carried on. At first it was all right but then we started getting "Archied" & that really put the wind up me. You are flying along when suddenly a black blob something like this:

'A' Flt on Offensive Patrol. Signed in lower right corner: G.M.K.

suddenly appears near you & then you hear a "woof" & probably several more "woooofs" all round you. They got the range almost exactly so we dived & lost height. Peace for a bit till they got the range again & so on – we went along doing turns all the time. The shooting was too jolly good for us! No one was hit tho'. Then suddenly our leader dived & we all saw two Hun L.V.G. two-seaters. The leader went for one but didn't get it & I went diving down at the other one but my Aldis sight was oily so I just fired blindly, then he stuck his head down & hove off home.* [Asterisk refers to note in Guy Knocker's hand]

I followed for a bit & I heard his old observer pooping off at me like 6! But as I was only 3000 ft & 5 miles behind [the Lines] I thought I had best chuck it, I don't think I hit him. Gad – I was excited! Then I joined the formation & went home! Pitt in "C" Flight was wounded in the leg this morning & got his bus badly shot about – he is in hospital. No one got a Hun. Last night I went to tea with No1 Squadron with Moore – a man I knew at Croydon. I didn't get to church but must try to get next Sunday. Am v.fit.

Bestest love,
  Bunsoy.

*Capt Morisson [*sic*] was missing after this scrap. I learnt from him in 1927 that he had followed this Hun over as far as Lille & had shot him down. On his way home he was himself wounded & shot down, remaining a prisoner till the end of the war.

DIARY Monday 12th November
Lovely day. Up at 11 for South line patrol over the lines – 'Archie' awful! [Dadezele?] to Quesnoy. Dived on 2 L.V.G.'s at Armentières. Indecisive. Wind up! Great fun the scrap. Pitt wounded, Scott [Lieutenant D.H. Scott] got a direct hit from Archie, Morrisson [see above] missing. Up on S.O.P. again at 2.00 pm. 'Archie' round Comines simply awful. Saw some Scouts. 1 L.V.G. no scrap. V.misty on the ground. All returned o.k. Only 4 on this patrol.

Headache in evening. This game is not at all safe. 'Archie' is awful!

[2nd Lieutenant W.H. Hemming?] crashed taking off. Broken legs – awful smash. A very unfortunate day on the whole! 4 buses written off completely.

13th November 1917

Thanks for your letter dated 11th. I have written to you every day & will try to continue to do so. I am getting quite good now! Yesterday afternoon we went up on another show across the Lines. This time we got "Archied" very badly. When they got our range we dived to lose height. On one occasion the wily Hun anticipated this move & we dived into a perfect nest of them! I was simply scared blue & crouched down in my bus & looked as small as poss! No one was hit at all but after that we didn't fly in a straight line for more than 10 seconds. "Fritz" is a playful little chap but apt to be peevish when irritated. "B" Flight fired a lot of rounds into a town behind the Lines, this annoyed Fritz terribly & they got well "Archied". We saw two or three Albatrosses [*sic*] well above us & one two-seater below us which we dived on but he hove off at once! Those two L.V.Gs which we fought in the morning were a white livered pair for as soon as they saw us they turned for home flying as hard as they could & made no show at all. I think Higgins killed the observer in the first one, anyway we frightened them badly!! Pitt was wounded in the leg yesterday morning & is now doubtless on the way home to Blighty – lucky beggar! Balfour [Lieutenant B. Balfour] had an explosive bullet in his petrol tank which fortunately did not light it. *Morrison in "A" Flight was with us when we dived on the L.V.Gs & has not been heard of since; I guess he must have landed in Hun Land as I don't think he was shot down.

Scott [Lieutenant D.H. Scott, M.C.] in "B" Flt was killed. "Archie" really doesn't worry you much but is a bit annoying at first.

[The German aircraft referred to above and frequently in these letters, is the "Albatros" – with one "s". Guy Knocker consistently misspells it as "Albatross". He occasionally uses the plural form "Albatrii". He is not alone in this!]

The following is my first impression of the L.V.G. & about as I saw it first. He was well camouflaged & painted all colours – they nearly all have swallow tails. I am not on patrol at all today &

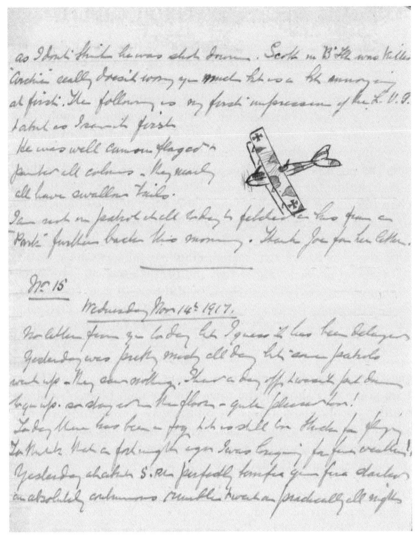

fetched a bus from a "Park" further back this morning. Thank Joe for her letter.

DIARY Tuesday 13th November

Misty nearly all the day. I went down to Serny in morning with C.O., Cox & Balfour to collect 4 Camels. Got back o.k. not on patrol all day – thank Goodness. Terrific gun fire in evening at about 5pm and all night especially at 11.30pm – towards Armentières and "Plugstreet".

Cummings in for dinner and another from No 1. Read and talked to T.E.E. after dinner. Bed at 11 – slept excellently.

First impressions of an L.V.G.

Morison shot down one of the L.V.G.'s from
himself shot down later previous

14th November 1917

No letter from you today but I guess it has been delayed. Yesterday was pretty misty all day but some patrols went up – they saw nothing. I had a day off & wasn't put down to go up, so stayed on the floor – quite pleased too! Today there has been a fog & it is still too thick for flying. To think that a fortnight ago I was longing for fine weather! Yesterday at about 5. p.m. perfectly terrific gunfire started an absolutely continuous rumble & went on practically all night increasing in intensity for about ¼ of an hour about 11.30. We don't know what it all meant but guess it was Fritz being playful & having to be suppressed! I think I am going to a show in the town this evening. I haven't got my muffler yet but guess it must be on the way. I hope you have had all my letters up to date. I have written every day except one a long time ago, I hope Joe gets the one I sent her. Well I guess I'll stop now as I can't think of any more to say!

DIARY Wednesday 14th November

Thick fog nearly all the day. No patrols at all. Read in morning. Up for a short flip in afternoon. Contour chasing and looping. Nearly all the Squadron went mad.

Down to Bailleul in evening. The Tivoli full up. Talked to Madame for ½ hr. To Club with Cox [Captain G.M. Cox] and Withington [Captain T.E. Withington]. Back in tender. Played bridge in evening lost 1 Fr 50c.

15th November 1917

This morning I was on Dawn Patrol. At 6.15 six shivering & bad tempered mortals crept into their airships & leapt forth into the very air! It was a lovely blue sky but misty on the ground with a strong west wind. "Archie" was not v.good today & we didn't get much of it – for which I was truly thankful. In fact he didn't worry me at all – I was much too busy watching 9 little black specks above & behind us! These were the wily Albatrosses. "B" Flight was also up & the Albatrosses dived on them & I think "B" Flight brought two of them down. They didn't worry us at all. Then at 10.30 a.m. we went up again. This time it was very reassuring as "B" Flt. joined us making 10 buses & there were some Nieuports & S.Es about too. The air over the Hun Lines was simply black with our machines, it was pretty cloudy & we only had about half a dozen "Archies". It was a priceless sight to see our machines dashing up & down, completely demoralizing Fritz for we hardly saw anything of him. We saw some Nieuports scrapping with two Albatrosses & one two-seater even dived down to join in the fun! This completely put the wind up the Hun for he immediately hove off. I didn't get a shot in as there wasn't time but I saw the Albatross scout – He looked something like this:

Very well camouflaged – in fact you could hardly see him against the shell holes. He had a paint brush tail with a one piece elevator, you will see the difference if you refer to my sketch of the L.V.G. I was just  starting to get excited when the scrap broke off. We are now using explosive bullets in our guns – the Huns always do so I don't see why we shouldn't. It's pretty well na poo Hun if one hits home. Well no more now. I am very fit & well. Thanks so much for No10 [letter]. The muffler has arrived & it is topping!

DIARY Thursday 15th November

Up on dawn patrol – 6.30 am! Lovely morning, hardly any 'Archies' – on Northern Patrol. Saw Huns behind, did not attack us at all. 'B' Flt had a scrap. Cocks [Captain G.M. Cox?] & Symons [Captain H.L.

First Impression of the albatross Scout

Symons] got a Hun each – v.good too! Up again at 10.30. Cloudy – no 'archie' at all to speak of. Acting with 'B' Flight – stacks of our machines. Huns kept well away! Came in for the finish of a scrap. Nieuport and 2 albatrosses and 1 L.D.G. Indecisive. Did not fire. For [?] flip to Armentières at 3pm. Saw no Huns but got 4 archies a time. Hove off! To the 'Tivoli' with Tiplaft in evening – v.good. Dinner at the club. Had some Beaune!

Major Nethersole [Major N.H.B. Nethersole] in to dinner and also Gorringe. Quite warm, Bed.

16th November 1917

Thanks very much for your letter dated Nov 11th I also heard from Gally, Elsie & Dorothea.

There is not much fresh news. Yesterday afternoon I went for a short flip up to the Lines at a place South of this famed of Bairns father to see if I could catch any old Hun twin-seaters doing Art. Obs. [Artillery Observation] but there weren't any. However I fired a few rounds from my guns over the Hun trenches (just to show there was no ill feeling) & went on. I was well behind our lines when suddenly Woof! Woo-oof! Wuff! Woo-oof! up came 4 "Archies". I hove off!

Just heard I am for Patrols <u>now</u> & the post goes out at once.

Bestest love, Bunsoy.

DIARY Friday 16th November

Dud all day, thick fog. I was a duty officer. 'B' Flt on patrol, nothing seen. In camp all day.

Slept in squadron office – warm & comfy. Nothing of interest.

65 Squadron R.F.C. France

17th November 1917

Sorry I had to break off my last letter so abruptly but I was told that I was wanted at once for patrol as the weather had cleared up & "C" Flight being short of pilots I was to go with them. However one of "C" pilots took a bus up for practice & took one wheel off when taking off, he knew nothing about it so of course crashed landed – but he wasn't hurt & the bus went onto its back. This left "C" with only 3 machines & so the patrol was washed out & I didn't go up after all. But the post had gone by that time.

Yesterday I was Orderly Officer & spent most of the time censoring letters, quite an amusing job, most of the men romanced horribly! However armed with a large pencil I cut out any place names. I had to sleep in the Squadron Office near the phone but was very comfy. We are getting another stove for our hut.

Thanks for your letter of the 12th. I went to a very good sort of Music Hall in the town the other evening – it is run by the Canteen Committee. The Squadron has amassed quite a menagerie of pets, one tiny little terrier pup, one French police dog pup, 3 pigeons & a goat. The latter got on the table in the Mess the other day & started to devour the sugar. There has been thick fog here all day & consequently no aviation – tant mieux! We are playing the "Ack Gunners" of the Squadron [at] "soccer" this afternoon as we can't get anyone to play "rugger".

DIARY Saturday 17th November

Dud – Got up early! Did stunts on the parallel bars. Had a bath. Played soccer v the A.M.'s in afternoon – 2-2. Played v.badly indeed! Moore over to dinner in evening. Watched him playing poker from 9 – 11.40! Fearfully bored! Invited to dinner at No 1 tomorrow with Withington.

Got a new stove in our room. o.k. Played Auction & Cut Throat before dinner – did not lose for a wonder! No flying all day.

65 Squadron R.F.C. France

18th November 1917

Thanks for your letter of the 15th also for the gloves & photos which are both excellent. I played "Soccer" yesterday afternoon <u>very</u> badly. I can't stand "Soccer". We drew with the men 2-2. I had a man Moore whom I knew at Croydon in to dinner last night & I am going over to dine with him tonight. This afternoon we are playing No1 Squadron at rugger, I am playing, I think. I know this is Sunday but you can't waste the opportunity of getting some exercise on a "dud" day. I went down to the town to go to Kirk this morning at 11 but there was no service, so I think I am going this evening at 6 if poss. Sundays out here are just the same as other days as regards the work. This morning at 9 am. I went up on patrol but it was very thick – clouds at 3000 ft so we did a patrol up & down the trenches, just our side of them at about 2000 ft.

We went over the scene of the recent activity – there is no distinct trench line & the troops appear to be holding shell holes full of water to boot. We saw no Huns & they only put up a couple of shells at us which were nowhere near us. You can find your way by compass all right when it's dull – fly due West & you are bound to come to the Lines. I played Auction again yesterday before dinner & won for a wonder alas not heavily enough to see the colour of my francs again! There is a Capt. Fullard in No 1 Squadron who has got 40 Huns he broke his leg yesterday at Soccer. Rotten luck wasn't it? Crump!! Something has just gone off with a hut-shaking crump! The wily Gothas me thinks depositing eggs! Well na poo pro tem.

Bestest love from the Bunsoy.

As I have said, I will write every day whenever poss. but if I should miss one day occasionally through not being able to write before 2 pm when the post goes, please don't be alarmed! G.M.K.

DIARY Sunday 18th November

Fairly thick. Up on patrol at 9am, did a Line Patrol at 2000! A couple of Archies. No E.A. seen. Over the trenches at Passchendaele – awful mess they are in.

Rugger v No 1 in afternoon v.good game – lost 6-0. I played fairly well. To dinner with Moore in No 1. To Church in Bailleul before v. good dinner indeed.

65 Squadron

19th November 1917

Thanks most awfully for the "topping" bag, it is most beautifully made & is just the thing to hold my belongings which are at present higgledy-piggledy in a box, (which is what you would expect from me!) This morning we went up for a practice patrol & tried to teach a new pilot to fly in formation! He simply terrified me by dashing madly about the sky – apparently trying hard to run into everybody. We went up to the Lines & fired our guns & saw an old Hun two-seater which hove off at once. I went up again at 12.30 to see if I could get him but he was not to be seen. I saw two lines of trenches & fired my machine gun at the Eastern ones. I hope they were Hun trenches & not our own!

I went to church last night in a sort of hall in the town where they have concerts, quite a nice little service; I went with Withington & Wigg [Lieutenant V. Wigg]. Then Withington & I went to have dinner with No 1 – Moore from Croydon is there, they are in the same aerodrome as we are. Moore is the man who went out to France the time that I reported as a D.H.5 pilot.

I am hanging my bag on the wall between the foot of my bed & the window. I see in the paper that John H. Russell (the one with the medal) was killed at Croydon in a collision, I was awfully sorry to hear it. The weather is still too dud for us to do offensive patrols so <u>we</u> don't care if it snows ink! I do hope Dad will get a job in the Air Service – we want some old soldiers to stiffen up the R.F.C. We have heard no word of our missing pilots.

Bestest love to you all from the own. Bunsoy.

DIARY Monday 19th November

Thick all day. Up on formation practice in morning. [?] a danger to the state! Over Armentières – saw 1 Hun two seater which hoved off at once. Did nothing in afternoon – played bridge and won 2 francs! Up alone to Armentières to see if I could get the Hun! Na poo. Major borrowed my bus in afternoon. Back o.k. Feeling rotten in evening. Bed v.warm.

65 Squadron.

20th November 1917

Thanks for your welcome letters & the photo which is jolly good. I guess this is going to be the most thrilling letter yet!

This morning the clouds were at about 4000 ft. & so we did a Line patrol – in pairs – I went with "Old Bill". After flipping round for some time I saw a Hun fairly low on our side of the Lines – just over --- Forest. I also saw about 12 Hun Scouts above, I thought I could get that low Hun so I dived onto him. Then suddenly I heard pop-pop-pop-pop-pop – behind me, I looked round but saw nothing so I did a steep climbing left turn. Then I heard the popping behind again & saw a stream of red tracer bullets going in front of me. (These are dummy bullets which are fired off first as sight shots to show the direction of the firing.)

That "low two-seater"!

Then as I climbed I saw a Hun Albatross Scout diving straight at me so I went straight for him & said to myself "Get out of the way you swab"! Sure enough he turned away to avoid hitting me. By this time about six of them were on me. So I just stunted as I have never stunted before! One went just below me & I clearly saw his light yellow flying cap. Then another dived in front of me so I said "I'll get you, you blaster!" so I dived like smoke at him – I was so excited that I didn't care if I collided or not! I fired at him but he went under me & I missed him. Then I saw another above & in front so I pulled up my nose as far as I could & blazed off at him. All the while the others were shooting at me! Then another dived away from me & I got my sights on him & saw my tracer bullets going right at him but I

9.30 a.m. 20th November 1917

don't think I got him. By this time I thought I had just about had
enough & I was expecting a bullet in my back at any moment –
so I just shoved my nose down & went down in the fastest spiral
dive I have ever been in – in fact I thought I was going to pull a

wing off but I didn't care so long as I got away! I found odds of 12 to 1 a trifle steep! Anyway I dived down to about 20 ft of the ground & then turning due West hove off as fast as I could. I think I was doing 110 m.p.h. just above the shell holes. The Albatrosses followed me for some time at about 500 ft & then left off & went away. Gee! I <u>was</u> glad! Then I climbed through the mist which was now about 1000 ft & rejoined "Old Bill" who had lost me & wasn't in the scrap.

I kept well away from that part of the Lines for the rest of the time I can tell you! I saw an R.E.8 shot down by "Archies" – it was a ghastly sight & it just fell over & over with one wing flapping loose. Then I went home!

I had 11 holes in my bus – mostly through the tailplane & rudder & 3 in the wings but none very near me – I guess "The Everlasting Arms" were around me that trip all right. I have never been so thankful that I could chuck a bus about. If I had flown straight for one minute they would have got me! As it was I think it was a pretty rotten show on the part of the Huns, I am sure 12 Camels would have got one Albatross!

Anyway it was some show.

Bestest love from the very own
Bunsoy.

DIARY Tuesday 20th November

Some Day!

Fairly clear – clouds at 4000. On Line Patrol in pairs with Old Bill. I went for a Hun low over Houthulst. O.B. did not come. Then I got about 12 Albatross on top of me – all shooting like mad! I splitarsed like ****! I shot at two or three of them but did not hit any. They were all round me! Then I thought it was high time to heave off! So I did the **** of a spiral dive down to 20ft and then hove off due W. and got away! Thank God! Eleven holes in my bus.

[These Huns had black and white checked planes and black and white hoops round the fuselages. They were probably a 'circus' led by Von Bulow from one of the Roulers aerodromes. They were well known in the Ypres salient.]

65 Squadron R.F.C.

21st November 1917

Thanks for yesterday's letters; I haven't heard from you today so I suppose you didn't write. No further news of interest to report – I didn't go up again yesterday as I had had enough "scrapping" for one day! I have drawn a beautiful picture of the scrap & will enclose it in this. [See letter dated 20th November]. Last night I walked down to the town & had dinner there with a man Tiptaft [2nd Lieutenant C.P. Tiptaft], whom you don't know by name, we had a very good meal at a café down there.

This morning it is raining & blowing with much vigour & gusto & I don't care how long it keeps on! We are playing No 1 again at "Rugger" this afternoon I think which will be good fun. I am going to ask Northwood, who went out with Moore, from No 52, to dinner tonight but don't know if he will be able to come. I am afraid I shan't be able to send you a photo of my room as it is a case of "Verboten photographen" out here.

About the Aldis sight being "oily" – the Aldis is a kind of telescope tube which sticks out along the top of the gun as far as the cowling & sometimes oil is splashed on it from the engine.

No more news.

Bestest love. Bunsoy

DIARY Wednesday 21st November
Dud all day, played bridge in mess most of the time. Out to dinner with No 32 Northwood, Jones there, v.good time. Weedon [Captain L.S. Weedon] came too. Drank gallons of Creme de Cacao. Back at 1.30!

65 Squadron R.F.C. France

22nd November 1917

Dearest Dad & Mum,

So sorry that I can't post this letter in time, however I have a good reason for it. It was pretty "dud" this morning however we were sent up on Line patrol – that was all right & we met neither Archies or Huns. Coming back however the formation dived down through the clouds to get below them & we didn't come out of the clouds till we were only about 50 ft from the ground. As I had got separated from the rest in the clouds on coming out I saw no other machine, moreover I had only a very vague idea of where I was! I then espied another "Camel" – "Hurrah!" said I, "he probably knows the way!" However when I saw the letter of his "bus" I knew it was Rosenthal who is rather a "dud" & I was quite sure he knew no more than I did! So we both wandered round at about 100 ft for ¾ of an hour but couldn't see the 'drome anywhere as it was very thick. At last I hit upon a town which I recognized as the one near which we stayed before we came here, so I landed at our old aerodrome & had lunch. After lunch we set off again & by this time it was like flying in pea soup – so we contour-chased at about 50 ft! By pure luck I managed to hit this place & landed O.K. I am jolly glad we found the way all right. Last night I went out to dinner with No 32 Squadron to see Northwood & had a very good time. They are about ¾ of an hour by tender from here & we got back at 1.30. Thanks for your two letters & also for Win's epic! Thanks awfully also for the books & the baccy & the fags & the piece of lava from G which is great! No more news.

Bunsoy

DIARY Thursday 22nd November

Brekker in bed: Up on patrol at 10 am v.thick, line patrol. Got lost with L.W... After wandered round for ¾ hr & finally got to Pop. Lunch there. Back after lunch. Thick as pea soup! Nearly lost. Bridge in evening. Lost 3 fr. Bed early, read in bed.

65 Squadron R.F.C. France

23rd November 1917

More thrills for you!

This morning "A" & "B" Flights went up on Offensive Patrol. It was pretty misty & the two Flights came past each other in the mist & Rosenthal [2nd Lieutenant A. Rosenthal] & Keller [Lieutenant C.F. Keller – but see later] collided, it was a ghastly sight, I am afraid both "went West". Then Old Billy [2nd

Lieutenant Bremridge] got lost but he came back afterwards all right. That left only 3 in "A" Flight – we saw two Hun two-seaters – one a green one, "B" Flight had fired on that & I got onto his tail about 100 yards behind & simply pumped lead from both guns into him – with no result – he simply flew on. I am quite sure he was armoured! I fired at the other & he went down in a dive & then a spiral, I think I got him.

Then about 8 Albatrosses came up & we had a messy scrap! They fired at me & I felt a bullet fly past my leg! Another inch & it would have been a "Blighty" one! Rotten luck!

I may have got an Albatross but was too excited to notice it. He went down after I had fired about 50 rounds into him! I then got lost but looking up I saw what I thought were Nieuports. "I'll go & join them" said I, & I was just getting into Formation with them when I saw they were Albatross Scouts which are very like Nieuports! I simply hove off!

Then I picked up Higgins [Captain W.W. Higgins, O.C. "A" Flight] & we came back. I had 11 bullets through my bus & enclose the shell of an explosive one which stuck in a strut. Pilcher was wounded in the hand, lucky beggar! Marshall, (the young Wellingtonian), is missing from "B".

Well the post goes. Bestest love from
     The Bunsoy

[2nd Lieutenant L. Marshall was in fact killed in the above mentioned collision with 2nd Lieutenant A. Rosenthal. (See below.) But Lieutenant C.F. Keller was not involved in this accident; he was taken prisoner on the same day.]

DIARY Friday 23rd November

N.O.P. at 11-12. Wigg did not come. Rosenthal collided with Keller. Both killed – an awful sight. [Rosenthal actually collided with Marshall in a cloud. Keller missing and I think a prisoner. – later note by GMK in diary.]

Dived on 2 two-seaters & scrapped 8 scouts! Fired like 'stink' at them! I think I got one! Bus shot about. Thank God again. 11 holes thro' my airship. Diagonal strut gone and one in fuselage. One missed my left leg by about ½ an inch!

No more pats in afternoon, Marshall missing and Tiptaft wounded in the foot, landed behind Passchendaele. Pilcher [2nd Lieutenant T.F. Pilcher] wounded in the hand and both legs, lost his thumb. Got down o.k.

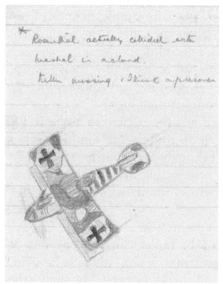

65 Squadron R.F.C. France

24th November 1917

Thanks so much for your letter of the 19th. I didn't go up again yesterday & was quite glad. My bus needed a new left bottom plane [wing] & two new fuselage struts so it was pretty well shot about.

I went to see Pilcher today, he is in the C.C.S. [Casualty Clearing Station] here & is going home shortly – he has lost his left thumb but is otherwise very fit. It was a very stout effort of Higgins yesterday. He had gone off having broken off the scrap but he looked round & saw me all alone fighting about 4 Albatross Scouts so he came back to help me & shot one off my tail & we both got away. I am nearly sure that I got one of the Hun two-seaters but as it wasn't verified by our Archie gunners I can't claim it officially. Anyhow I simply pumped bullets into him & he went down in a dive & then flattened out & got into a spiral which I believe is how they sometimes go down if the pilot is killed. There is no further news at present – we were due for patrol this morning but there is a howling gale & the clouds are very low so it is washed out. Three loud cheers & applause from everybody.

Bunsoy

DIARY Saturday 24th November
Howling wind all day, no patrols for us. Rugger match No 1 & us v No 19 & No 53. Very good game we won 8-0. Northwood & Jones to dinner. Pearson and some others from 32. Very merry. Played Cardinal Puff, sang and drank in evening. Great time. "Naval No3" a good song. Bed at 12.00 – quite warm.

65 Squad. R.F.C.

25th November 1917

Thanks awfully for Tuesday's letters. I just love getting them; the Mail is the great event of the day out here! "Nothing of importance to report in this communiqué"

Yesterday there was no flying as the howling gale lasted & it still howls today & so there is no flying today either – loud & prolonged applause from all concerned! Yesterday a combined team of No 1 & No 65 played a similar team of No 19 & No 53 & we beat them 8-0. I was playing & it was a great game! Two fellows from Croydon whom I "instructed" have arrived to fill up gaps in 65. V.nice chaps too. Our mess is just the same as at home, quite civilized! Well the post is off so I will stop.

DIARY Sunday 25th November

Gale continues. No Patrol all day – to church in evening at 6 v.good service – electric plant and no lights! Good sermon on the fall of Jerusalem. (Jerusalem captured Nov 11th).

To dinner with No 1 with O.B. and McKinnon [2nd Lieutenant J.F. McKinnon] after church – good fun.

65 Squad. R.F.C.

26th November 1917

Thanks for your letters & "Flying" & Books of Today. I went to church yesterday evening & had a topping service & some v.nice hymns. "O God our Help" & "Abide with me". The sermon was about our Crusade in Palestine. There were no lights as the plant had gone dud so we did it all from memory.

I had dinner again at No 1 & had a v.good time indeed. The wind still howls & I haven't been up but am going up to teach some new fellows formation flying. This dud weather is great & can last as long as it likes! There is no news of any importance except that it is very cold! I expect we shall be having snow soon. Wot ho! I expect you are at Weymouth by this time so am writing there. My room is fairly tidy now & very cosy. Well there's really no news so I will stop.

Bunsoy.

DIARY Monday 26th November

Wind still high, loud and prolonged cheers! No patrol, Dyer [2nd Lieutenant H.A. Dyer] and Matthews arrived yesterday – very bon! Took up Matthews [Lieutenant C.D. Matthews] for a practice formation in afternoon. Very cold. Up to Ypres and back. Did a few loops. Mess under repair – down to show in Bailleul in evening – "The Optimists" – Excellent show. Musical evening – Dyer played and I sang "A Wee Deoch and Doris". Bon!

Had a hot bottle at night.

[2nd Lieutenant H.A. Dyer was reported as "Missing, reported killed." on 7 December 1917. Dyer was a famous orchestra conductor and learned to fly Camels at the age of 38.]

65. R.F.C.

27th November 1917

The gale continued all yesterday but I went up for a short flip in the afternoon & taught one of the new pilots' formation, we did not go across the Lines tho! In the evening I went to a concert party down in the town a most excellent show & we all thoroughly enjoyed it. A man Dyer has come to the Squadron whom I taught on "Avros"; he is an excellent man & plays the piano beautifully. Last night we had a musical evening & after much thought I sang "A Wee Deoch & Doris" amid loud applause! I guess I am the only man, who, if pronouncing the last line is any test, was "a richt ye ken", it was great fun. The Squadron is having some Xmas cards done & I believe I am to design them. Suggest a suitable design!

This morning it was raining but it held off at 11 so we went up on patrol. Just as we got to the Lines however it became very thick & started to rain & so Higgins fired a white Verey light & came home amidst shouts of applause from the entire patrol. "Old Bill" is taking up some new fellows to practise formating, I am not going up & one of the new blokes is flying in my "bus". I hope to goodness he doesn't crash it, I think I should weep if I lost my own ship as I just love it & know all its little tricks.

I see from the papers that Cavalry Major Baron von Richthofen is back at the Front again, I hope I don't meet him though I would dearly like to bring him down – I'm afraid it would be vice versa though!

The mail hasn't arrived today. Rotten! Na poo maintenant--

Bestest love from The Bunsoy

DIARY Tuesday 27th November

Rain early. Stopped at about 11. Up on patrol at 11.45. Went up to Lines but it came over dud and started to rain and so we hove back. Bumpy as **** landing but all landed o.k. No more patrols today – applause. To "Optimists" at night.

As the papers would have you imagine a pilot – An intrepid birdman.

What the aforesaid 'birdman' really feels like when over the Lines!

28th November 1917

No news & so excuse a note. I fetched a machine today from a Base about 20 miles W. of this & flew it here. I am not on patrol today. I went to a show again last night. We are doing a new kind of stunt now for the present but I can't say what it is. I think it is a bit safer & therefore much preferable to the ordinary patrol. Well goodbye.

Bunsoy.

65 Squadron.

28th November 1917

Thanks for your 24th letter. There's very little news to give you this time yet – the wind is still blowing hard from the West (it is extraordinary how the weather persistently works for Fritz). One or two Huns have been over here but did nothing; I don't know why they aren't over today because with a wind like this they would be home in two ticks. I was up with "Old Bill" & two other men on an Offensive Patrol this morning. The clouds are pretty low but above them it is lovely. We didn't go very far over the Lines as it takes so long to get back against the wind. We saw two Huns miles off & had no "Archies" so it was quite a nice trip on the whole. I had dinner down town with Matthews yesterday evening & a v.good dinner too! There are some very good shops down in the town & it is not much knocked about – only a house here & there has been shelled. The "Bus" is running very nicely & was not hurt yesterday by the pilot who borrowed her. A good bus Pooh-Bah! I expect O.B. was jolly glad he was out of that scrap I had – I wished <u>I</u> was out of it! I was our side of the Lines over the shell holes all right; I don't think anyone saw it.

Bunsoy.

DIARY Wednesday 28th November

Went to fetch new bus. Strong wind. Got back o.k. McKinnon missing. No Pats in afternoon.

Dined in town with Matthews.

DIARY Thursday 29th November

S.O.P at 12000 in morning clouds low. No E.A. seen – wind strong. O.B. leading – quite successful. No more pats.

65 Squadron

30th November 1917

Thanks so much for your two letters – the one written in the train especially. Now you are not to worry about me, I am perfectly fit & happy & I hope fairly well able to mind myself! I am afraid I am not such a fearful hero as you make out as the sight of a Hun inspires me with most profound terror & "Archies" make me scream with fear! After all one <u>has</u> to fight – & even a worm will turn! Today I stood by to go up from 7.45 to 9 a.m. but did not go up. I am down for patrol from 3 till dusk to prevent Hun two-seaters indulging in machine gun practice at the expense of the P.B.I. [Poor Bloody Infantry!] in our front line trenches, but as it is now raining I don't suppose I shall go up – I don't care if it snows ink for the rest of the Winter! Yesterday I went to pay a visit to the Archie Battery which is quite close to this place. I had tea with them & discussed the best way of putting the Hun "Archie" off his aim! Of course, as I suppose you know, when we are over the Lines we never fly straight for more than a minute or two at a time but are always swinging about – if you fly straight you give "Archie" time to work out your height etc & the first shells are generally the nearest. Leave starts a week on Saturday; I expect I shall get mine in about 6 weeks if all's well. Well cheeri awfully oh! & don't worry – "It's just like bein' at hame"!

Bestest love from The Bunsoy

DIARY Friday 30th November

Stood by for Interruption not up. Wind howling gale. Up for a flip in afternoon, looped and rolled. Soccer match in afternoon. We won 3-1. A lot of Warwick officers to dine. Binge after dinner. Sang a "wee DD"! Bed at 1.30! Gee v.tired – cold. On early show tomorrow!

65 Squadron.

1st December 1917

Thanks for your letter received today, I have written to Weymouth for the last 5 days. Yesterday was dud all day but I went up for a short flip in the afternoon for the benefit of a number of the Warwicks who were playing us at "Soccer". The Colonel of the Warwicks came and there were 3 Majors for dinner. We had a very merry time & sang songs till 1.30. I sang "A Wee Deoch an Doris" amid loud applause! We all felt pretty dud this morning & to cap it all I was down for the early show at 6.30! In spite of all my prayers for dud weather it was fine & so at that grisly unchristian hour I crept into the air – so dark that I could hardly see my instruments – & proceeded to patrol a section of the Line at 10,000 ft to drive off Huns shooting at our Trenches, I was with Matthews. Presently I saw two shapes over the trenches – the Wily Hun two-seaters! Taking my courage in both hands – I had jolly little this morning – I climbed up & opened fire at one of them at about 150 yds. My right gun jammed but I kept my left one going – then the Hun waggled his tail to let his observer get his gun on me – which he did, I then thought I had better go so I swung away! Matthews then dived on the Hun but did not get him & both Huns hove off & returned not. I then went back to brekker. Dud so far. I am going to collect a machine from further back this afternoon.

The Bunsoy.

DIARY Saturday 1st December

Up at 6.45! Feeling like a wet rag! With Matthews, very tired too. From Hollebeke to Vlamertinghe – saw two-seaters. Engaged one but did not get him. One thro' my bus. My Buckinghams jammed. Very thick with rain after. Sent down to Audrique to get Eaton's [Lieutenant E.C. Eaton, Canadians] bus. Awful trip! 3½ hrs.

Night at the R.E. Mess. Topping fellows. Played bridge.

65 Squadron.

2nd December 1917

Thanks so much for your last letter the last from London.

Yesterday two of our fellows got lost & finally landed at a place near Calais! I was sent to fly one of them back – good old Instructor form! The other had crashed. It took 3½ hours by tender to get here & as I arrived at 6.30 I stayed the night at an R.E. Wagon yard at the Officers' Mess. They were nearly all

Captains & they were most awfully kind to me – the C.O. is a ripping man. I was treated as a sort of honoured guest – leaving the room first after mess – all the officers, including the Majors, standing aside to let me pass! They gave me tea & bread & butter in bed this morning before breakfast – altogether I had a ripping time!

I left this morning before brekker – the bus was in a pretty rotten field & there wasn't much petrol left but there was an absolutely howling gale blowing. I got the A.M's to hold back my bus till I had got my engine full out – & then they let go. The old bus simply gave one hop & was off the ground – the bumps were truly awful but I got back here all right in about 15 minutes with the wind, some going that!!

There was, I believe, considerable activity up on the Front this morning so "A" Flight had to go & do an offensive patrol at 3000 ft over the Lines with a 60 m.p.h. W. wind blowing! As it happened there were no Huns & hardly any "Archies"! This way we wandered about at 3000 ft right over the Hun land was a fine proof of our Aerial Superiority! I got one bullet through the main spar of my left plane – a lucky shot from the ground but that was all – that makes my 24th hole – poor old Pooh-Bah, always gets shot up. No more patrols today – 'ooray!

Bunsoy.

DIARY Sunday 2nd December
Beautiful day. Up at 7.30, before brekker, tea in bed! Left at 8.55. Bus in dud field. Perfectly shrieking wind. Got off in 5 yds came home on Gravity – in 20 mins. Landed o.k. Up on low N.O.P. [North Offensive Patrol] (3000) at 11am. No E.A. seen, hardly any 'Archies' no M.G. – no signs of a push. Got blown far over the lines. Complete master of the front. – Good show!

65 Squad. R.F.C.

3rd December 1917

Thanks very much for the first letter from Weymouth – yesterday morning I did nothing except read. I went to Kirk in the evening & had a v.nice service – Higgins, Matthews, Wigg & Baker [Lieutenant E.J. Baker] went with me. I read again in the evening.

It was a very cold night. This morning at 11 a.m. "A" & "B" Flts went up on a 10,000 ft offensive patrol but as there was a strong N.W. wind blowing we didn't get very far over the Lines – it was a lovely morning but pretty cold. The result was that both my guns froze up hard & I couldn't fire them at all! In the event of Dad's dream coming true I hope I shall defeat one Albatross [sic]. I wouldn't mind one so much but 12 – no! No more patrols for me today thank goodness. No more now. Bestest love from

The Bunsoy

DIARY Monday 3rd December

Strong w wind n.o.p. in morning 3 E.A. seen which hove off at once – both my guns froze up hard.

Read in afternoon and evening.

65 Squadron R.F.C.

4th December 1917

Thanks awfully for the Xmas Card Design I think it is simply priceless. Thanks too for the pound of tobacco which is most excellent. I am even now smoking it. Did you ever get the little piece of explosive bullet which I sent you?

This morning Higgins & I arose at 6.30 & leapt into the atmosphere to patrol the trenches at about 500 ft to keep the Hun two-seaters from shooting at our troops. It was pretty thick up in the North of the Line & there were no Huns so we went further South where the trenches are clearly marked & not obliterated with shell holes. I did a little shooting on my own account! I fancy we must have annoyed Fritz quite a lot as we shot a good few rounds into his trenches. The West wind has at last dropped thank heaven. It is quite nice & warm today. Last night I was awakened by the aerial Hun indulging in one of his comic little air raids. I don't think he dropped any eggs but the "Archies" near here kicked up a vile row! I have not been up on patrol today but am going Hun punching again on a dusk patrol!! Well the inexorable post waits for no man & so I guess I'll stop.

Bestest love from   The Bunsoy

DIARY Tuesday 4th December

Dawn Patrol, no Huns seen very thick up at Ypres – went down south & shot up trenches at Armentières – Pretty chilly – wind N. On Interup: call came thro but my engine was dud. Tested it. Loops etc.

To show with Matthews in evening – very good spy play. Miles in to dinner – musical evening.

65 Squadron

5th December 1917

Yesterday & today I have been standing by to go & drive off. Hun two-seaters doing Art. Obs. but have not had to go up yet. I was just going up yesterday but my engine was "dud" so I stayed down. It is a lovely cloudless day here & very cold & freezing hard.

Last night we had several guests including Major Miles from Croydon who is now O.C. 43. We had a musical evening & quite a merry time. Old Bill is at present in hospital. He was turning his prop when the engine suddenly started & the prop smote him on the legs – only bruised them though – he is all right & will be out again in 2 or 3 days. The aerial Hun has been over quite a lot today & has been duly "Archied" – taking photographs I suppose as he dropped no bombs! Well no more now – best love.

DIARY Wednesday 5th December

Very cold. Stood by in morning and just missed going up.

Dusk Pat; Passchendaele to Hollebeke. No Huns but lots of our busses. Ypres Salient a fine sight at sunset – quite enjoyed the flip. Orderly officer – slept in office, very cold too!

65 Squadron.

6th December 1917

Thanks awfully for your last letter. This morning I was on a dawn patrol 6.45 a.m. It was very cold & clear with no wind on the ground but it was warmer in the air. As before I had to prevent Hun two-seaters shooting at our Trenches so I went to a spot in the Lines where the Trenches are very clear & where I have been before & thinking the Huns in the Trenches must be beastly cold

I warmed them up with my machine gun from about 500 ft. then he started shooting at me from the ground so I hove off for a second & then came back & gave him about 100 rounds.

At 10.40 this morning Higgins & Matthews & I went up to drive off a Hun two-seater doing Art. Obs. There was no Hun to be seen in the spot named so we did a patrol for an hour. There were 5 Albatrii over their side & we tried to lure them over to our side. I was at the back some way behind & we flew back to our lines. I saw one Hun diving at me a long way off – so I dived away watching him the while. Presently I saw a stream of white smoke coming from him & heard pop pop pop – pop – pop ---- I guessed I had bested him so I did about half a climbing turn. You should have seen the Hun! He did the deuce of an Immelman turn & made for his own lines in a nearly vertical dive and was seen no more! Wind up!

Last night I did a "dusk patrol" which means from 3 till as late as poss. There were no Huns but the Lines were a wonderful sight in the Setting Sun. The two new men in our Flight are Matthews & Peacock [Captain E.F. Peacock].

Bestest love from

The Bunsoy

DIARY Thursday 6th December

Beastly cold but no wind. Dawn patrol! Ugh! Warmer in air than below! No Huns seen but shot up trenches at Armentières & Houplines. Got m.g. from ground – strafed him! Up on wireless at 10.30. No Huns near Berselere. Air full of our machines. Dived on by Albatri and fired at but on turning round the Hun hove off in a vertical dive!

65 Squadron

7th December 1917

Thanks for your letters. I am glad you didn't pass a day without getting a letter from me; I have only missed one day I think.

I didn't go up again yesterday afternoon but just sat & read. Today the frost has gone & the wind has got up a bit & the sky is cloudy. I had a morning in bed. At 9.30 I went up to H.Q. for a machine gun exam which you have to pass before you can get leave. I knew nix about it & don't suppose I passed, but still I shan't be going on leave for a bit yet & will have another shot – of course I <u>may</u> have passed! I stood by ready to go up after two-seaters from 12 to 1 but didn't have to go up. I am off for the rest of the day but will probably go & cheer up the Hun Infantry with a few rounds from my guns this evening! We have taken to carrying bombs now. Two buses in each flight have them – mine hasn't!

Today we are going to try & bomb a particularly pestilential Archies Battery across the Lines. I can imagine the Hun "Archie" gunners speaking: "Ach! Hier komm der Camels. Ve vill let zem come over & zen shoot zem as zey go back! Zey nevaire do no 'arm! Zey vas no goot at----!" Woof---! Boom! -Woof!--Boom!- (Exit Hun amid fragments!) "Curtain falls"!

DIARY Friday 7th December
  Bill still in hospital. Wind all day – no patrols.

65 Squadron R.F.C.

8th December 1917

So sorry that I couldn't write home in time for the post today but I had to rush away to an Aircraft Park further back to collect another "Camel" to replace one of ours. I got it back all right.

This morning I was up on an offensive patrol, it was pretty "dud" at the start but it was quite clear afterwards. We wandered up & down about 5 miles over the Hun Lines at about 10,000 ft. quite peacefully. Once we got "Archied" rather badly but we all swung about for a bit till we passed out of the area. There was not a Hun machine to be seen at all except a two-seater very low which hove off at once. I don't know where the scouts were! They can stay there anyway! I was out on a "dusk patrol" last evening – there were no Huns but I shot up the Hun trenches. They shot at me from the ground but missed me of course!

I went out to dinner at No 70 last night & had a very bon time indeed. Matthews is in "A" Flight & replaced Morrison.

Well na poo now thanks v.much for day's letters.

Bestest love from The Bunsoy.

DIARY Saturday 8th December

Bill came out of hospital. Patrol in morning.

65 Squadron R.F.C.

9th December 1917

Thanks very much for your letter of this morning. Last night a lot of fellows from 70 & 32 came to dinner, it was great fun. I'm afraid I must have got a bit of a chill as I am feeling rather funny today. I stayed in bed till 1 pm. We are now starting Winter training which means a great deal less over the Lines & a lot of practice in formation flying, shooting, & etc. rather a good scheme on the whole. We only do one show a day now.

Well no more now, please excuse the scrawl.

Bestest love from The Bunsoy

DIARY Sunday 9th December

Awful pains all day. In bed until 12.45. Up for lunch. Bilious I think. Dud all day thank heavens. Bed early before dinner at 6.30. Good sleep.

65 Squadron.

10th December 1917

I am afraid I missed the post today as we were on "Offensive Patrol" from 2 – 3 and my hat – it was an awful show. I don't know what Higgins our leader could have been thinking about! To begin with we first came across 2 Albatrii which Higgins didn't attack – then we struck 3 more. I couldn't attack as I was well behind trying to catch up – & we never attacked those, we were 5 mind you. Then to finish it all 6 Gothas went past just above us – they had been over the Lines & we didn't recognize what they were till too late & so let them go. I am no fire eater myself but hang it all – not attacking 2 Albatrii. We are all as sick as we can be! And missing the Gothas! A Gotha is a certain M.C. [Military Cross] if you get one! I suppose I ought to have gone for the Albatrii but I wasn't also certain which they were & when Higgins turned away I didn't like to break formation. I really don't know what Higgins was thinking about! I guess "A" Flight had better do something desperate tomorrow! Jack Gilmore [*sic* –

Captain J. Gilmour] is coming here as a Flt. Com. isn't it topping!
I am quite all right again today as I had 11 hours sleep last night.
I am going to dinner with 70 tonight.

Bestest love from the Bunsoy.

DIARY Monday 10th December

Dud in morning h.o.p. from 2-3 – dud show. Saw 2 Albatri and then 3
and did not attack them – why? Lord knows! 6 Gothas came out of the
sun and we did not recognise them and they hove off. What a chance to
miss.

Dinner with No 70. Vinter ill. Got a bit squiffy! Home at 1.30! Very
tired.

65 Squadron.

11th December 1917

Thanks awfully for your letters, thank Joe for her excellently
typed epistle. Today the weather is dud – low clouds very cold –
no flying at all. Last night I went down to No 70 for dinner &
had a topping time, they are an awfully good lot of fellows. I did
no more flying after yesterday's show! Higgins goes on leave
today, I guess I ought to get mine in about 6 or 7 weeks if all's
well – What-Ho!. I think I am going over to 25 squad. this
evening as the C.O. there is Major Duffus [Major C. Duffus] who
was my Flt. Com. at Tad [Tadcaster]. Jack Gilmore [sic] has
arrived here; he has been at home for 6 months. He is taking
Weedon's [Captain L.S. Weedon, Royal Fusiliers] plane as O.C.
"C" Flight. It is ripping having him here. I guess we will do well
with him as he has had such a lot of experience.

Pooh-Bah has got a new engine in her & is going quite well –
not quite so well as it did at the first – but still – a good bus!

I couldn't get to church last Sunday as I wasn't feeling very fit,
must go next week if all's well.

G.M.K.

DIARY Tuesday 11th December

Dud all day and beastly cold. Jack Gilmour arrived – Higgin went on
leave. Took tender to St Omer and there got tender to Bois d'Hain.
Dinner with Major Duffus. Tender late at Omer – 12.30!

Tyre burst on way home – arrived at 3.15! Very cold in bed! Feet frigid.

65 Squadron

12th December 1917

Thanks for your letters ----!!!!---- huge commotion outside! Yells
of "Gothas!" I rush outside in time to see 5 "Gothas" in a gap in
the clouds. I then spring smartly behind my sandbag wall – a
second later a 112 lb bomb falls with a crash about 150 yds away.
This is followed by two more, then they heave off. I rush down to
the Hangars with some others & leap forth into the atmosphere!
I climbed to 9000 ft & saw the Hun heaving off well over his lines
so I came down & wrought my vengeance upon the Hun trenches
firing 200 rounds into them; I only hope I hit someone! No one
was hurt <u>here</u>. I now carry on with the letter having missed the
post! Last night I went down by tender to the Base I was originally at, from there took a tender to No 25 Squadron where I had
dinner with Major Duffus – who used to be my Flight
Commander at Tadcaster, it was topping seeing him & I had a
very good time. Then I went back to the Base, the tender was very
late & didn't arrive till 12.30. On the way back from the Base we
had a puncture & didn't get home till 3.15 am!

This morning – just my luck – I was on the early show & at 8
a.m. we went out on a 2 hours line patrol. The clouds were very
low but eventually we climbed above them & saw 6 Hun Scouts
well over the Lines. We flipped round & presently saw these
Albatrii [at] about 5000 ft. (we were at 8000 ft) playing about
happily above a gap in the clouds – waiting to dive on an R.E.8
below! However it was not to be! We manoeuvred & got the sun
behind us & then dived straight out of the sun on to the Huns oh
the joy of diving on an Albatross! – he generally does all the
diving! They didn't see us till we were right on them. I was behind
& didn't go right down – however Wigg, the leader, shot one
down. Then I saw another level with me, I was alone so I dived
away wondering if he would follow & meaning to turn on him.
But Wigg was above me & he & another attacked him & I
climbed up. he went down smoking & the others all dived away
hell for leather! Pretty good "A" Flight getting two. This
afternoon we were on patrol & got badly "Archied". One shell
burst about 15 yds in front of me. Gee! I was scared, a bit went
through the cowling (the covering of the engine).

We dived on a couple of Hun two-seaters & drove them off – then we came home at about 100 ft – great fun! Wigg is leading in Higgins' place & is a stout man! Jack Gilmore [*sic*] got lost today & landed in a field behind the Hun Lines. Some Hun soldiers rushed up! When Jack saw they were Huns he opened out his engine & hove off again & got back all right.

Bestest love from The Bunsoy

DIARY Wednesday 12th December
Up on Res. patrol at 8! Clouds at 3000 – archied over Houthulst. Climbed above the clouds and <u>dived</u> on 6 Albatri from 8000! Damn good! Wigg got 2 Huns; I funked and had wind up S.O.P. at 12. Archied like hell over Comines – nearly hit! Drove off 2 two-seaters near Moorslede. Gotha raid after lunch! Three 1 lb bombs, up after them, saw them. Strafed trenches at Hollebeke Chateau. Dinner with No 1. Rogers got a Gotha.

65 Squadron.

13th December 1917

Thanks for both your letters. Both the Huns Wigg got yesterday have been confirmed by "Archie". One fell behind our lines in flames. It was saved & taken to No 23. Wigg & I went up to see what was left of the Albatross – there was nothing left except the tailplane & elevator & the radiator marked "Daimler Mercedes" & the joy-stick with gun triggers. The tail was painted yellow. I got a little door off an inspection hole near the tail. Wigg is going to claim the tail skid & joystick. The rest of the bus is buried in the mud. The pilot jumped out before it came down to the ground. The joy stick is rather a comic affair & has two handle grips to hold onto & thumb pieces for firing the guns – like a Camel.

I went up to the funeral of one of our chaps who crashed & killed himself one day when coming back from patrol, rather depressing ceremony.

The weather has been dud for patrols all day & I just went up for 20 minutes to fight Matthews but it was very thick.

I was out to dinner with No 1 last night but got back early. A fellow – Capt. Rodgers – in No 1 got one of those Gothas which bombed us yesterday. He was straggling & one of his engines was dud & Rodgers got on his tail & fired a couple of bursts into him. He glided down with his fuselage smoking for quite a long way & then at 2000 ft he simply blew up & came down in pieces. I guess the fire must have fired his bombs. Jolly good work, isn't it?

Well no more news now dears. I am afraid I missed the post today as I was at the funeral this afternoon.

DIARY Thursday 13th December
Dud all day and no flying – trés bon. Did nothing – flew and fought Matthews. To Cory's [sic – Lieutenant F.M. Corry] funeral in afternoon and tea at No 23 – saw the Albatross Wigg shot down – nothing left but the tail plane.

65 Squadron.

14th December 1917

There is no more news – today the weather is beautifully "dud", low clouds mist & rain! No patrols at all – bon for troops! I am playing rugger this afternoon against No 53 C.C.S. [Casualty Clearing Station]

I am going to get an ashtray made from a propeller boss & a piece of the Albatross & send it home to you. Did I thank you for the woolly gloves – they are simply ripping & keep my hands topping & warm.

DIARY Friday 14th December
Thick and low clouds all day, no patrols at all. Played No 53 C.C.S at Rugger in afternoon. Lost 11-3 – poor team. Were on early patrol tomorrow – hope it is still dud!

65 Squadron.

15th December 1917

Another strenuous day over. In accordance with the usual luck of "A" Flight, we having two shows to do today, the weather is at once beautifully fine! Thus we arose at the grisly hour of 6.30 & did leap into the atmosphere to be offensive! We were on a Southern Patrol & our friend "Archie" was particularly hot – we got shelled the whole length of our beat & back! Also I got up in a hurry & didn't put on my chin piece – result that my chin is frost bitten! Not badly though & I have greased it. We were on patrol again from 1 till 2 but my engine went dud – to my secret joy! & I returned & took up another bus & tried to find the Formation but couldn't & so did a Line patrol – no Offensive for me alone! I guess we'll have a slack day tomorrow. I'm afraid I missed the post again today but I may catch it yet! No more news so I will stop.

DIARY Saturday 15th December

No such luck! A cloudless day! Up at 7.15 on S.O.P. strong west wind as per usual. No E.A. seen but archied all the way from Hollebeke to Armentières and back! The villain 'archibald' at Comines. Very thick in afternoon S.O.P. [Southern Offensive Patrol] from 2-3. Ignition wire went on my bus and so I turned back. Took up Higgins bus but could not find formation for sure – did a Ypres patrol!

Bed early. Gee! but I do dislike Cocks. [*sic* – Captain G.M. Cox?]

65 Squadron.

16th December 1917

Thanks most awfully for the topping parcel of Xmas things. The pipe's ripping & so are the cigarettes & I am sure the books will be most interesting. The crackers & cakes I am keeping till Xmas, the cake looks "topping". Thanks also for "Liebestraum" the bother is to get someone to play it now that Dyer [2nd Lieutenant H.A. Dyer] is missing.

Cousin Aggie sent me a fine parcel too, wasn't it nice of her? I hope you will get my presents for me as I asked last time – now do get something really decent for yourselves & the girls.

We have a new scheme now to go out on offensive patrol in 2 lots of 3 & working independently – the idea being to catch the Hun two-seaters by surprise. I was up this morning above the clouds & over the Lines. We had no scraps as the only Huns we saw were right across the Lines. There was a strong South wind blowing & we got blown up North & finished up about 10 miles from the sea! My frost bitten chin is much better & with my chin piece I can fly in perfect comfort. We are getting new flying suits instead of leather coats. Jacket & trousers combined made of waterproof cloth & lined with fur – they are fine & warm & less cumbrous than a coat.

Well no more news.

Bestest love from The Bunsoy.

DIARY Sunday 16th December

Cloudy, on N.O.P. in two lots of 3 – I with O.B., strong S wind blowing. Went well over the lines at 10000 above the clouds and got blown up as far as Dixmuide. Saw the sea! Came home along the Canal. Saw 7 Huns well East. Did not attack! Went below clouds, saw 5 Huns over Roulers. Shot up Hollebeke Chateau at 1.15 – no sign of Cocks the rotter! Very thick on way back. No more patrols.

Read and wrote letters in afternoon. Got 3 parcels for Xmas. To Church in evening and stayed to H.C. very nice service. Tender driven into the ditch on way back – Bitterly cold.

65 Squadron.

17th December 1917

There is snow on the ground today – it is jolly cold & I am on a Reserve Patrol for 2 hours in the afternoon! Gee! This does not mean crossing the Lines though but still it will be some chilly! It was dud this morning but it has cleared up in time for "A" Flight's show – it always does! I have read "The Airman's Outing" it is a topping yarn & absolutely realistic, you ought to read it. The writer has a profound respect & lasting hatred for the "Villain Archibald" – he says the only [two] "marked cards" you have to contend with in the gentle game of War Flying are the Ace of Clubs – as representing the Hun Aircraft & the Knave Archibald. He used to be an "Observer" in No 70 when they had Sopwith two-seaters & mentions Trollope in the book, referring to him as the "Tripe Hound". The bombers he refers to are No 27, Jack Gilmour's old Squadron. My chin is quite all right now. I have just been looking over my "bus" & testing the adjustments of the sights & etc. All my three mascots are going strong & have so far been very efficacious! I went to Kirk last night & had a very nice service & stayed to H.C. [Holy Communion] after, that has always proved a very sure safeguard to me & I am sure it always will.

Bunsoy.

DIARY Monday 17th December

On Res: Patrol from 2 till 3.30. Dud all morning. Beastly and vilely cold! 2 hour show, 6 E.A. seen, we retired! Joined in scrap – Nieuports v Albatross. Kelsey shot him down in flames West of Houltem near Ypres Canal. I didn't get down.

To tea with No 1. The Hun fought jolly well and was Lt Voss who had got 17 of our machines. Lecture na poo. Read in evening. Great show tomorrow.

65 Squadron.

18th December 1917

I am afraid I missed the post again today. Some more thrills!

Yesterday we did a Reserve Patrol; this does not incur crossing the Lines. It was a two hours show & most frantically cold, everything froze – the breath on my face mask & chin piece – & my guns, but they got all right again. Just at the finish we saw some Nieuports scrapping some Albatross Scouts. We dived down but I couldn't get a shot in. Then I saw the Hun do a roll & then go down in a spin firing his guns all the way – the Nieuport followed him & then I saw the Albatross go down in flames. Then we returned about frozen stiff. The Hun was a jolly good sportsman & fought jolly well, he looked something like this going down:-

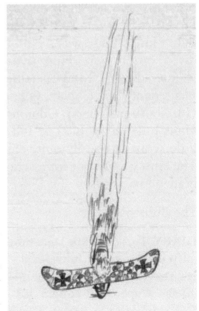

Then today – a translucently clear day – as is usual when "A" Flight has a show <u>and</u> cold as cold! I was on another R. Patrol from 10.30 till 12.30 another 2 hour show! About frozen again! No scrap this time but we saw a few Huns.

Then the great show this afternoon. At 2.pm every available Camel in the Squadron under the leadership of the C.O.

went out on a pukkah offensive patrol over a big town about 4½ miles over the Lines. We chased 3 Albatrii, evidently decoys. Then about 6 came down from above & there began the very deuce of a scrap! The whole sky was a tangled mass of Camels & Albatrii, Tracer bullets & Archie (who was determined not to lose any of the fun!). The first thing I saw was a Camel who afterwards turned out to be a man Sage [2nd Lieutenant D.M. Sage, G.L.] – going down in flames. Enter Albatrii with tumult! I shot furiously at anything with crosses on it. Then I got two on my tail & turning round saw 2 Huns simply streaming with tracer bullets apparently destined for me! So I swerved off! The Camels were now all split up so I went back to the Lines & joined the C.O. Presently Old Bill joined us & we went back. Turning again for the Lines I saw O.B. suddenly do a sharp turn (I was just below him) and then I saw an Albatross dive on his tail. So I shot him off his tail. Then he turned onto my tail but I turned round & faced him & let him have it as hard as I could. His nose tipped down & he went down in a vertical dive. O.B. followed him down & finished him off when he came out of his dive. Meanwhile the C.O. had sailed on obliviously. I followed him & presently another Hun dived on me & let drive but he shortly turned back owing to the presence of other "Camels". The C.O. didn't know there was a Hun there. Then we wandered round & dived on 3 more Hun two-seaters who hove off. Then we wandered back. Total casualties Sage in flames & 2 missing [2nd Lieutenant R.H. Cowan, G.L. and 2nd Lieutenant J.D. Cameron, G.L., both prisoners]. Gilmour shot down 2 Huns, the C.O. two Huns (one fell to bits) & Bill & I one. Gee! It was some merry little scrap & I really quite enjoyed it. I got 2 holes in my plane. The Hun was all out for a scrap today & he jolly well got it! Well bestest love from

The Bunsoy.

DIARY Tuesday 18th December
Up on Res: patrol from 10.30 – 12. Very cold. Huns seen well east a few two-seaters over the lines. No scrap – archied near Didmal. 17 machines upon O.P. at 2pm. led by the C.O. Huge scrap with Albatri. Sage shot down in flames, 2 missing from "C" Flight. The C.O. got 2

Guy Mainwaring Knocker and his father, Cuthbert, at Haileybury School.

Guy in Royal Military Academy uniform photographed with his father.

Guy in Royal Military Academy uniform, 1917.

Guy, his mother and father, at Dover during 1917.

Guy with his sister, May, and father.

'A' Flight, 65 Squadron, RFC. Wye, Kent, October 1917. Left to right: 2nd Lt. A. Rosenthal, 2nd Lt. V. Wigg, 2nd Lt. G.M. Knocker, 2nd Lt. G. Bremridge, Capt. W.W. Higgins and Lt. K.S. Morrison.

...ots of 65 Squadron RFC at Wye, Kent (or Wyton, Cambs?), September 1917, in preparation for ...ng to France. Standing, left to right: 2nd Lt. L. Marshall, Lt. B. Balfour, 2nd Lt. G. Bremridge, ...G.H. Pitt, 2nd Lt. E.H. Cutbill, Maj. J.A. Cunningham (OC), Capt. L.S. Weeden, Capt. T.E. ...thington, Lt. W.L. Harrison, Lt. D.H. Scott MC. Seated, left to right: Lt. C.F. Keller, Lt. E.G.S. ...rdon, Lt. G.M. Cox, Lt. K.S. Morrison, 2nd Lt. A. Rosenthal, Lt. H.L. Symons, 2nd Lt. V. Wigg, ...d Lt. G.M. Knocker. *(Courtesy of the Imperial War Museum, London. Q67792)*

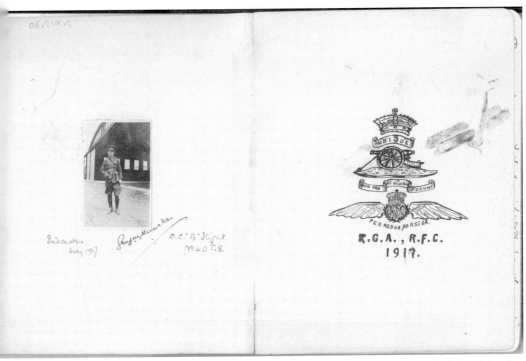

...he front of the first volume of letters. A photograph of him as OC 'B' Flight No. 40 Training School, ...adcaster, taken in 1917 faces his drawings of the RGA and RFC badges.

Sopwith Camels of 'A' Flight, 65 Squadron, RFC. The aeroplane nearest, B2419, was Guy's aircraft which he named '*Pooh Bah*'.

Pooh Bah at Wye, 1917.

Guy with his Sopwith Camel.

Lieutenant Douglas Shanks and Camel from 65 Squadron. He was injured in a flying accident on 31 January 1918, although the photograph is dated January 1919.

A pen and ink sketch by Guy of a British Scout aircraft.

Another sketch by Guy of a German Albatross DV.

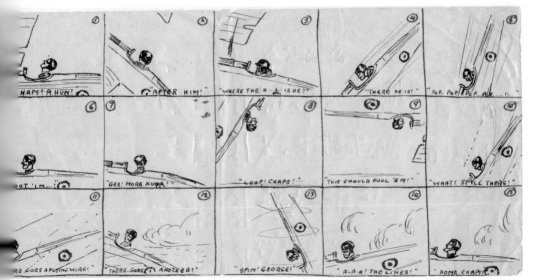

A cartoon strip by Guy depicting an encounter with the Hun (date unknown).

A caricature of Guy, dated 1934.

Guy with his Merlin – he kept two ('Jenny I' and 'Jenny II') in his later RAF career.

Guy with his wife, Cynthia (left), and his sister, 'Ginny', in 1960 at their home in Ashton Keynes, Wiltshire.

A post-war photograph of Guy (date unknown).

Group Captain Guy Mainwaring Knocker dressed for inspection of Oakley House School Cadet Corps, 23 July 1962.

Huns, Gilmour got 2 Huns, Bill and I got one between us. I shot it off his tail and it went down vertically, Bill followed it down. The C.O. never saw it at all! Dove on four two-seaters but they got away.

Moore & Kelsey in to dinner bearing trophies of the Hun. Starry night. Standing by tomorrow at 6.30! ****!!

Albatross Scout D.Va and R.E.8

65 Squadron

19th December 1917

I do have rotten luck, after doing 2 shows yesterday I was down for a standby at 7.a.m. this morning & so got up in case one of their machines went dud & wouldn't start. They nearly always do start – but of course this morning one didn't! Freezing hard on the ground but it wasn't very cold upstairs! Then I was up again after Gothas this morning but saw nothing. I am going up again on an Offensive Patrol this afternoon. I seem to do nothing but fly!

Jack Gilmour is in our Squadron & is O.C. "C" Flight. Weedon [Captain L.S. Weedon, Royal Fusiliers; ex-O.C. "C" Flight] has got Jaundice & has gone home. I have been transferred to "C" Flight as they are short of old pilots [GMK is just 18!]. They nearly made me leave Pooh-Bah in "A" & have another "bus" but I simply stuck at that! I am rather fed up at leaving "A" Flight but still Jack Gilmour is a jolly good leader.

That Hun the Nieuports brought down the day before yesterday which I saw going down in flames turns out to have been a Lt. Voss brother of the famous "Voss" & he had brought down 17 Allied "buses". Yesterday a R.E.8 brought down an Albatross. The pilot was slightly wounded & he landed in our Lines. They got the Albatross intact & I went to see it today. It's a lovely machine beautifully streamlined. The fuselage is all covered in 3-ply wood & has a 160 [h.p.] Mercedes engine & 2 Spandau machine guns – but rotten sights. O.B. is out of hospital & quite all right again now.

Bunsoy.

DIARY Wednesday 19th December

On Reserve for "C" Flight at 7.30. An engine wouldn't start and I had to go up! I was fed up! Vilely cold, no scrap. Up after Gothas in morning. Cloudy, no Gothas seen. O.P. in afternoon. Whole squadron. No Scrap, went into 3's. Some E.A. seen but not attacked. I in 'C' Flight now! ****!

Jolly tired and fed up in general. Bed in office taking Balfour's place as O.O.

65 Squadron

20th December 1917

I did that last off: pat: yesterday afternoon under Jack Gilmour's leading. We saw 5 Albatrii well above us but they didn't dive on us & we couldn't get up to them so we let things be. It was pretty thick low down with a thick mist & we nearly got lost coming home. I enclose a Brigade Xmas card, <u>not</u> my design!

I was jolly tired last night having done nearly 10 hours in the last three days including one massive battle! Today we were down for another comic Squadron Formation but praise be to Allah! – there is such a fog on that you can't see 50 yds so we got a day's rest. I am pretty glad of it too! This is the coldest day we have had yet but there is no wind & it is quite pleasant. Well this letter will be to wish you dear people the very happiest Christmas & the best of New Years – let's hope that 1918 will see the end of this beastly affair! I will write to all the sisters & hope you will choose some decent presents for them from me, I haven't had time to go down town lately – mind you get yourselves decent presents.

Another man Symons has gone on leave – I guess I ought to get mine at the end of January. Well dears it is time to knock off. I am very fit & happy. The very best of Xmas wishes & God bless you all, from your very own

Bunsoy.

DIARY Thursday 20th December

Thick fog all day. No flying at all. Freezing hard. The Warwicks in to dinner and 5 M.A.C. and the Bedfords Col. Huge night! I sang "Annie Lawrie" and a "Wee Deoch and Doris" then we had "Naval No 3" & "The 'Arf Pint" & "The Muffin Man". Everyone got tight; it finished up with the Col. of the Bedfords lying flat on his tummy in the middle of the road at 12.20, armed with a light imitating a machine gun!

65 Squadron

21st December 1917

Thanks so much for your two letters, also for Dad's!

It was dud all yesterday for which many thanks! We had a great guest night last night. I went to the concert in the Town before dinner; it was quite a good show. Then I came back & found 3 R.A.M.C. Captains & 2 Colonels of other regiments in to dinner. After dinner we all sang songs & most people got a bit merry. I sang "A Wee Deoch & Doris" & "Annie Laurie" amid loud applause. Then we sang "Do You know the Muffin Man that Lives in 65?" One man goes up to another & sings that line, then that man sings "Yes I know the Muffin Man" & he links arms with the first & the two go round to someone else. Finally the whole room has joined up & I found myself with one arm in the C.O.'s & the other in a Colonel's capering madly round the room all shouting – "We all know the Muffin Man that lives in 65." It was simply priceless. Then they left. Just outside the gate Colonel --- proceeded to drill the others. Then I & some others marched along the road – the Colonel then yelled out "Take cover" & all the comic old Captains madly ran to the sides of the road – the sight of Col. --- lying flat on his tummy at 12.30 a.m. armed with a flash light & making a noise like a machine gun in the middle of the road struck me as being the funniest thing I had ever seen.

Fortunately today was absolutely dud – thick fog & very cold. I was sent down to No 1 A.S.D. [Aircraft Supply Depot?] to collect a Camel but we had lunch in a town half way & as it was very dud in the afternoon we came back. I had tea with No 1. Please always pray for an East wind, that means it blows you back towards your own lines. A West wind is the one we all hate. The fog is still thick & there is every chance of a dud day tomorrow Wot Ho!!

Well bestest love from the Bunsoy.

DIARY Friday 21st December

Freezing hard all day. Fog still pretty thick all day. Sent to Serny to collect. Lunch in Ami [?]. Got very thick in afternoon and so we came back. Moore came with us.

Tea with No 1. Major Carter in to dinner. Bed 11.30. Very cold.

22nd December 1917

Enclosed is cheque for £3 for the Xmas presents; I am afraid the ash tray won't be ready for a while yet but I will send it along when it is. By the way will you please send me that pair of "Issue" flying gloves – leather outside sheepskin within – there is a new issue of very warm ones & I have got a pair but I have to return the others.

The cowling of the "bus" is the round tin guard which goes round the engine in a rotary engined bus. Yesterday as I told you there was no flying at all & it was freezing pretty hard all the while. Today the frost is gone & it is fairly clear with a layer of clouds at about 5000 [feet]. I went down to No 1 A.S.D. [Aircraft Supply Depot?] which is 15 miles West of this at 8.a.m. this morning & collected a Camel. I then went up on a Reserve Patrol from 11 till 12.30. I saw a good few Huns but as I lost the rest of the formation in the clouds I didn't attack any. There is another Off. Pat. from 3 – 4 this afternoon but I am not going up as I have done more flying lately than most people! Loud applause!

Jenkins my best friend at Croydon is coming here, isn't it topping. O.B. came out of hospital about 3 weeks ago, didn't I tell you? I don't think Wigg will get anything for his Huns.

Will you please write & ask Cox how my accounts stand; I have given up keeping them in French money as a bad job!

Bunsoy

DIARY Saturday 22nd December
Up at 7.15 and by tender to Serny to collect 'Camel'. Thick at first but cleared up. On Res: Patrol 11-12.30. Lost Formation. Saw some Huns – no scrap. O.P. from 3-4. Rumoured Hun push on! No E.A. at all save one 2 seater, no scrap. Shot up trenches at Hollebeke. Jack got lost and crashed at Hazebrouck.

Read after dinner. Another 'tea party' tomorrow. Heaven send 'dud' weather!

65 Squadron

23rd December 1917

Thanks so much for your ever welcome letter. Another cold day. Morning mist & no early show. We are down for a show this afternoon & as it has practically cleared up I think there will be one.

We love going to do another whole Squadron show – commonly known as "tea parties" but I don't think there will be one of those as we haven't got a full complement. I went up on the Patrol from 3 – 4 yesterday afternoon after all as there was a rumour that a lot of Hun two-seaters working but we only saw one & he hove off & there were no Scouts & so we didn't have a scrap after all.

We ought to have a pretty merry time here on Xmas Day – I hope Heaven sends dud weather!

We have a pond near the Mess which is frozen hard & we amuse ourselves by sliding & giving the puppies slides! By the way with reference to our mighty scrap on Tuesday General Webb-Bowen the Brigade Commander sent the Squadron a wire "Your fighting today was splendid, congratulate all pilots". Pretty good, what!

The fellows in "C" Flight at present are Capt. Gilmour, Balfour [Lieutenant B. Balfour], myself, Eaton [Lieutenant E.C. Eaton], Darlington & Boyd [Lieutenant J. Boyd, Scottish Rifles].

"A" Flight: Capt. Higgins, Bill [2nd Lieutenant G. Bremridge], Wigg, Matthews, Capt. Sydall [Captain C.B. Sydall, Canadians], Peacock.

"B" Flight: Capt Withington, Cocks, Hall [Lieutenant W.H. Hall, G.L.], Baker, Symons [Lieutenant, later Captain H.L. Symons, Can. Eng.], Shanks [Lieutenant D. Shanks].

Well no more now – as the hour for Patrol draws nigh!

DIARY Sunday 23rd December

Dud weather in morning, no patrols. Up on Squadron O.P. in afternoon – very quiet. Balfour leading my 3, no 'tea party'. One two seater seen and 5 Albatri – no scrap. Gorringe [Lieutenant F.C. Gorringe] shot down Hun in flames at Hollebeke, shot trenches at Armentières from 50 feet.

[Note: This aircraft had observed the 11/Warwicks concentrating on the Reserve Lines before relieving the Front Line but fortunately Gorringe got him before he could lay on the batteries. The Warwicks were much relieved.]

Church in evening. Saw Madame.

65 Squadron.

Christmas Eve 1917

"Marley was dead to begin with – dead as a door nail" – & so on!

I wonder if you are reading that this year – I hope so – carry on the good work! I couldn't get a copy out here I wish you would send one.

Well the gods have decreed a dud day with low clouds & fog &

no flying – loud applause! I hope it stays like this tomorrow!

Yesterday from 3 – 4 I was on Off. Patrol with two others we saw 5 Hun Scouts above us but they didn't attack us. One rash Hun two-seater ventured up to about 200 yds of the Lines & nearly every formation in the sky dived on it – eventually it was shot down by Gorringe of No 70 – it fell crashing & then burst into a large sheet of red flame – & that's that! These little things teach the Hun not to come near the Lines. At about a quarter to 4 I went off to shoot up the Hun front line trenches. I went very low, lower than I have been before, in fact just above the wire, & fired both guns at the trenches hard, I don't know if I hit anyone – I hope so!

No news of any import so I guess I'll stop. I wish all you dear people the merriest of Christmases.

Bunsoy.

DIARY Monday 24th December

Dud all day. Thick clouds and mist. Nothing doing at all.

Down town with Cocks in afternoon. Saw Madame and Marie! Kissed the latter! To dinner at the Club. All 70 Squadron there – Huge show! Stood on table and sang songs – A.M.'s [Air Mechanics] sang carols at 12.30 till 2! Awful noise. Cold and thick at night.

65 Squadron.

Xmas Day 1917

Thanks awfully for the wrist watch curl [?], it is a wee thing too big & I am getting it altered at the Flight Workshop.

Well I hope you dear people are having a jolly good time at Home today. I guess we are going to have a pretty merry time. Some people are beginning now! This morning we were all horrified to see a beautiful day as we were down for two Squadron Offensive Patrols – we went up in the morning but to our huge joy it came over very dud & so we came back & it has stayed dud ever since. Last night Cocks & I went down to dinner at the club & there we found all 70 Squadron having a dinner, we joined them & had no end of a time! Most people finished up standing on the table singing songs. Then when I was in bed about 12.30 a lot of fellows started singing carols. Please excuse more as the Mess is in an awful state everyone crashing about singing! Bestest love to you all dear folk at Home & the most ripping time & luck to you all from the very own

Bunsoy

DIARY Tuesday 25th December – Christmas

Clear in morning. Up on patrol at 10.30 but came over cloudy and it was washed out. <u>BON!!!!!!</u> To lunch with No 1 and in afternoon slid on the pond.

To sleep in afternoon not revving very well. Dinner in evening, not much of a show, nearly everyone, except me very tight. Too tight to be amusing. Snowing. May it be dud tomorrow!

65 Squadron

Boxing Day 1917

Thanks so much for your letters received today.

Well it was very dud all yesterday with no patrols after the effort in the morning. I had lunch with No 1 & congratulated Capt Rodgers – who got the Gotha – on his M.C. We had a very successful dinner last night but I went to bed fairly early as I was rather tired & most people were a trifle too merry to be amusing! It snowed most of the night & the snow is thick on the ground now. We were due for patrol this morning but this was washed out as there was more snow coming up & we are down for another patrol after lunch but this will probably not be on as there is lots more snow where this came from. There were no air fights on this front yesterday at all & only one Hun was seen.

Well I have such a lot of letters to write today that I must stop now. Bestest love from

The Bunsoy

DIARY Wednesday 26th December

No patrols in morning – snowing hard. Patrol from 2-3, saw a few Albatri and dove on one from quite close but he got away.

Dinner at Mess, not revving very well. Perfectly mad show coming off tomorrow. Round the back of Lille! May it be dud!

65 Squadron.

27th December 1917

No news of any import to give you today. I was up on patrol yesterday from 2 – 3 but had no scrap – although an Albatross appearing, as is the habit of Albatrii, from nowhere in particular, saw us & dived away hell for leather! We followed but – what a hope – Old Man Fritz can out dive you every time!

We have a Cinema show in Camp now; I went last night – quite a good show too.

We were down for an early show this morning but awaking at 6.30 were vastly cheered to see a layer of clouds. However we got up – saying to ourselves "quite impossible for patrol". However the weather, in its stupid way chose to clear up at this moment & we set forth muttering imprecations at the grisly hour of 7.30 "and a sunny morning, sir!"

It was very thick up & there were no Huns at all (The Hun is a wise man & does not go up needlessly.) so to quote a song which is all the rage out here

> "For all the bally good we do
> We might as well fly Tanks."

Have wasted several gallons of Government Petrol & got really [?] chilly we got us home for brekker! We were down for another show from 12 – 1, a Squadron Show led by the C.O. & we all knew what that means, however the weather was really dud & it was washed out.

I went up for a joy ride this morning in the snow & cheered up the troops by diving on them! It was a wonderful sight flying over the Lines yesterday. All the world is snow covered & this more or less effaces the signs of war except for the black lines of the trenches where there are any. The view was marvellous! Well no more now.

DIARY Thursday 27th December

Up on 7.30 show, dud at first but cleared up. Very thick and no Huns at all seen, cold as ****. No 'tea party' on thank heavens! Dud properly in afternoon up for a dice fight with Matthews. Very thick – contour chase.

Tea, cinema and dinner in town Bon! Lovely moonlit night, very cold, two shows tomorrow not so bad.

65 Squadron.

28th December 1917

No letter from you today but I guess I'll get two tomorrow. The chief object of this letter is to wish you Dad many very happy returns of the day. I will send you a pipe if I can get a decent one, to add to your collection.

It's a lovely clear day today with frost & snow on the ground, we were on patrol this morning & had a scrap with a very sporting two-seater, I don't think we got him but I fired a lot of rounds into him & so did the others. This East wind is very bon for us aviators.

I went to tea in the town yesterday & to a Cinema & then had a very good dinner at the club. Higgins came back from leave yesterday & is feeling very fed up about it – I don't wonder! It's not quite so cold here today, pretty chilly but not so bad as it might be!

Bunsoy.

DIARY Friday 28th December

O.P. in morning attacked D.F.W. over the lines but he got away – very bad show. "Reuters" show in afternoon. East gale blowing and we did not go past Houthulst and only one archie up at me!

Jack went home with a dud engine.

65 Squadron.

29th December 1917

So sorry that I can't catch the post today but I was up on patrol. I was on patrol from 10 – 11 but about half way through my engine went dud & so I came back – anyway there were no Huns about so it didn't matter.

We were going out on a huge show together with No 70 at 2 o'clock but fortunately it was dud & so it was washed out! I know what these huge shows mean!! I find that I have done more "war flying" than anyone in the Squadron up till the present – 67 hours!

Poor old Higgins is going home tomorrow with a weak heart, it is rather bad luck but in some ways he is a lucky man-n-n!

The aerial Hun has been very quiet on this front lately but I doubt he is planning some devilment; he generally is when he is quiet! Yesterday there was a howling East wind – very bon for us. We went up on O.P. but did not see any Huns as I don't think any were up in the afternoon.

Well I am so sorry that you didn't hear from me on Xmas day – I have written every day.

Bestest love from the Bunsoy.

DIARY Saturday 29th December

O.P. in morning escorting R.E.8's. My engine dud – cutting out on both mags: and so came home at half time. Show in afternoon but it was v.dud and we didn't get past Ypres.

Bed early – Fed up. Dinner at Club.

65 Squadron.

30th December 1917

Thanks for yesterday's letter, today's hasn't arrived yet. I hope you get all mine eventually.

We were to go on patrol this morning from 9 – 10.30 but it is very dud at present with low clouds. We are down for an Off. Pat. at 1 o'clock in conjunction with No 19 S.P.A.D.'s They will fly above us to protect us from above while we mop up the low Huns. I don't think there will be a show as I think it will be dud, it has started thawing. No 19 did jolly well yesterday when on patrol – they met & attacked 9 Albatrii & got 7 of them! One in flames, 2 crashed & 4 out of control! Jolly hot work! I guess that Hun Squadron was feeling pretty sick with life losing 7 out of 9!

Well whatever the pessimists may say about the war at the present moment we have got the aerial Hun absolutely cold! The only times he comes over our lines are when he sends single two-seaters over at 19,000 ft. His scouts hardly ever come over whereas ours loaf about almost over his aerodromes! I am afraid he will pick up in the Spring though & simply deluge us with Albatrii. But somehow I don't think the deluging will be all on his side! However tell it not in Gath! I think the Hun peace terms are the most awful cheek I have ever heard. I am sure that if the men in the Trenches were given the choice of Peace on those terms or carrying on – fed up with the war as they are, they would all vote for carrying on!

We are just manufacturing a "suparb" fireplace in our anteroom. Wot ho!

Well dear folk I guess I'll knock off. I am ever so fit & happy.

Bestest love to you all from The Bunsoy.

DIARY Sunday 30th December
Down for R.E.8 escort but dud all day. Stayed in Gilmour's room in afternoon. To kirk in evening. Good service. Bed early – very tired. Thawing! Wally Higgins went home with bad heart.

65 Squadron.

31st December 1917

Thanks so much for your letter & the little Book. (The Vision Splendid by John Oxenham) That was a ripping little poem wasn't it? I guess it's just about right!

It was dud all day yesterday & there were no patrols, I just read & smoked most of the day. Today we were not down for any patrols but had to stand by to protect R.E.8s going up to take counter battery photographs. Heaven however has ordained that the clouds stay at 1000 ft. Ergo na poo pilots, Ergo no patrols! Bon!!!

Jolly cold here today it is freezing again after yesterday's thaw. I went up for a short flip this morning & did a little contour chasing. There is a small hill near here & a fascinating game can be played on it. You go to one side below the level of the top & climb up the hill just above the ground. When you make the top, you switch off your engine & slide down the other side.

Parlour Games for Aviators No 1

It is an excellent game & it bucks up the troops on the ground no end – who long to see you crash!!

Jenkins has been posted to another Squadron, isn't it rotten? Cocks is going to be "A" Flight O.C. instead of Higgins. This means that I won't get my leave for about 3 weeks, rotten!

Well luncheon calls & I am full hungry & so I guess I will stop. The last day of 1917 – ! Well it has been a jolly eventful year for me _ I hope 1918 sees the end of this beastly affair.

I went to Kirk last night. The Padre is a priceless old chap. He said the Prodigal Son was "no bon" & a "bad egg"!

Well cheerio folks & the best of luck in the New Year.

Bestest love from the Bunsoy.

DIARY Monday 31st December

Down for protecting R.E.8's but dud all day. Did Camera gun practice with Eaton in afternoon and got lost.

Moore and Patrick to dinner. Played auction till 12.30 and lost 13 francs what a good start for 1918! Orderly officer – slept in the office.

Service Overseas with 65 Squadron

1 January 1918 – 10 April 1918

65 Squadron.

New Year's Day 1918

New Years' day! A Happy New Year to all you folks & many many of 'em. Today for a change it is fine & this morning we went up protecting R.E.8s taking photos 4000 yds over [the lines]. There was a strong East wind & very few Huns about. We went over with them & then Gilmour came back & left the R.E.8s for some unknown reason. It was rather a rotten show – I don't like going over the lines myself but I do like doing a job properly. "Old Bill" has gone on leave today, I don't know for certain when I shall be going – in about 3 weeks I hope.

Last night Moore & Patrick from No 1 came over to dinner & we saw the New Year in playing Auction till 12.30, I lost 13 frs! which is a good beginning! "Unlucky at cards, lucky in love"!

Thanks for the verses by Auntie Mary; I rather like our "Artist Patriot" for Harry Lauder!

It is still freezing but honestly & truly this morning it was much warmer in the brilliant sunshine at 9000 ft than it was on the ground.

We have had these new Flying Suits issued; they are very nice & warm. McElroy rang up yesterday – he is on S.E.5s in No 40, further South than this. I am going to fly down to see him.

Well bestest love to all from The Bunsoy.

DIARY Tuesday 1st January

Dud in morning. On patrol from 3-4. No E.A. seen – went over the lines a good deal. Gilmour doesn't 'use his dome'! We went over from the N.W. with a run in the S.W. Beastly cold.

65 Squadron

2nd January 1918

Thanks so much for your letters & thanks most awfully Dad for the top-hole Cardigan – it is just lovely & will keep me as warm as toast!

Today the wind is in the West & it has been raining & is much warmer. I went down town yesterday afternoon & after dinner we had a Cinema show up here – quite a good one – Charlie Chaplin in great form! Today the clouds are fairly low & though we are standing by to escort R.E.8s taking photos I don't suppose we shall go up. I think there is a Reserve Patrol this afternoon but I don't know if it will go off.

This morning I went up for a flip & had a practice scrap with an R.E.8 from 53 Squadron quite close by – we fought for half an hour on end & it was most instructive & I got a lot of tips about fighting Hun two-seaters from it. I went round & saw the fellows in it after & they said they had enjoyed it. Well no more news now.

Bunsoy.

DIARY Wednesday 2nd January

Fairly dud all day. C.O. flew to Berck in morning no patrols at all. Shot on range.

Bed fairly early. Falling out with Gilmour steadily.

65 Squadron.

3rd January 1918

Thanks so much for your three letters from Mum Dad & Gran [?]. I am so sorry you feel this cold so much. As a matter of fact I don't feel the cold flying very much. It is jolly cold but my face is pretty well covered up except for a few small places & my body is quite warm in the Sidcup suit. My hands are the only parts that get cold & nothing on earth would keep them warm!

Today the wind is in the East again & there has been some

snow. We were down for escorting R.E.8s again this morning but it was too dud. I went up on Reserve Patrol from 1 – 2 & have just come down. I never saw such a sight as the air was! We went well over the Lines but the only Hun we saw was one two-seater at about 15,000 ft. The air was simply & literally black with our machines of all types; I guess we pretty well frightened the Hun out of the sky! It was some show!

I had the fellows I fought in the R.E.8 over to tea yesterday & we went down to a show in the town afterwards, but it was very dud & we came out at half time.

Many thanks for "Scrooge". I hope you are all quite "fit" now, no more colds or neuralgia.

"B" Flight has just come back from a week's Gunnery Course at a place on the coast & have had a very good time there apparently I guess "C" Flight will go soon. No more news now.

Bunsoy.

DIARY Thursday 3rd January

No patrols. Fought R.E.8 in morning – jolly good scrap. Went round to see him after. R.E.8 people in to tea. Trés bon! Went down to show in town – awfully dud and I came out at half time.

Bed at 12. Read and smoked till then. Very cold – frozen in bed. 'B' Flt came back from Break.

65 Squadron.

4th January 1918

Another simply priceless scrap this morning! Five of us in "C" Flt. were out on patrol. I was flying behind & trying to look after a new fellow – who was awful & lagged miles behind. So I had to fall back & keep with him. Then the first three escorted an R.E.8 away over the Lines. I went some of the way with them & then turned back because I wasn't going over with this fellow loafing alone behind. There were already 10 Albatrii in the sky which I had counted so I waited about. Presently I saw a large shemozzle going on about 2 miles over the Lines, so I shoved my nose down & went for it. I found our two Camels & 3 Spads having a merry scrap with "umpteen" Albatrii. I got on the tail of one & fired at it & it hove off, then another one dived across my front so I fired at it allowing deflection but missed it. Then in his obliging way the Hun turned his tail towards me & I fired about 100 rounds into him. He fell over on one side & went down. I couldn't see if he crashed but I have claimed him as "out of control", I don't know if I will be allowed to, I hope so! I saw a Spad moving on another Albatross then suddenly the Hun's left wing fell off & that was that!

Gilmour got two this morning & Eaton got one, possibly two! Not so bad for "C" Flt. 4 Huns. One of our fellows is missing & another Capt. Sydall was doing a practice dive & his bus folded up & he was killed – jolly rotten luck.

Well no more news. By the way as soon as we got down we were informed that "B" Flt couldn't raise enough machines & so we had to go up again – no more Huns tho'!

3½ hours today!

DIARY Friday 4th January

Up on Reserve patrol from 10-11:30. Huge scrap with Albatri near Roulers. Robb shot down? [2nd Lieutenant. R.E. Robb, G.L., reported missing] Gilmour got 2 crashed and 1 out of control. Eaton and I got one out of control a piece, not so bad for 3! Siddell [*sic*] killed in crash. 'C' Flt on patrol again from 1-2.30. No scrap – No E.A. seen.

To show with Moore after tea. Trés bon! Bed early, room smoked out! ****! Davis! [GMK's batman]. Heard from Joy – trés bon! The Huns lost 12 today. Damn good! Major and Jones to Rouen till the 7th.

65 Squadron

5th January 1918

Thanks so much for your letter of New Year's Day.

The Wing has allowed us 5 Huns in yesterday's scrap as there were only 3 of us that did any fighting – Gilmour Eaton & I (We always fly together now, I hope you will hear more of this trio!) it was pretty good! Gilmour was allowed 2 crashed & 1 out of control. Eaton & I were allowed one each out of control – my first proper Hun! "C" Flt is feeling very bucked with itself! In all 12 Huns were shot down on this Front yesterday. Très bon! My shots into the Hun were with best wishes from you Dad as you asked me to do!

I was jolly tired last night having done two shows. When I went to my room I found that my idiotic orderly had lit my oil stove & turned it full on with the result that when I went into my hut I couldn't see across the room for sooty smoke. Everything was simply smothered in soot – my blankets books toothbrush were all about six inches in it! I told my servant just what I thought of him this morning!

Today is dud & no patrols. I think I am going to fly over to No 32 to see them & fly back. Oh, huge success of my contour chasing. The other day coming back from patrol I came back just above the Lines & went below the level of a small hill near the aerodrome. Huge commotion on the 'drome – they thought I had crashed & sent the ambulance rushing out! They were quite disappointed when I reappeared above the hill – smiling! Anyway as you know contour chasing is invaluable for getting away from a Hun & it is the best fun in the world & quite safe if you are careful which I hope I am.

Well folks I am in great form & awfully bucked about my Hun! Please send me another small indelible pencil & cap.

Bunsoy.

DIARY Saturday 5th January

Low clouds and mist all day. No patrols. Stayed in bed till 11.15! Our Huns Confirmed allowed, good old 'C' Flt.

Standing by 'til 3 p.m. – rot! Flew over to No 32 at Dooglandt. Saw Pearson and the Major. Flew back just before dark.

Down to show in evening with Withington and others Bon. Much warmer.

65 Squadron.

6th January 1918

Thanks for your letter & for the cutting. The pilot referred to is Capt. Mc Cudden [later Major J. McCudden, VC]. He was Wing Fighting Instructor when I was at Croydon & used to fly a Sky Blue "Pup". He once lectured to me. At that time he was not so frantically popular as the Daily Mail makes out. I don't know what he's like now, he is flying S.E.5s.

Yesterday was dud all day & there were no patrols. Willington

& I flew over to No 32 & stayed there for about 30 minutes & came back just as it was getting dark. Then we went to a concert in the town, a most excellent show. I played "Auction" after dinner & wonder of wonders I actually won 3 frs 50 cts! Today we are going to do a Squadron Offensive Patrol from 2.30 till dusk. I hope "C" Flt gets some more Huns! I don't expect that there will be much Hun activity though as it is pretty misty up.

The C.O. is at present at Rouen & is staying till tomorrow. I asked him to look up May if he got the chance.

That ash tray is nearly ready & is very bon I think – it is made from the inspection plate near the tail skid of the Albatross shot down by Wigg on Dec 12th. I think Wigg is going on leave next, I don't know for certain when I shall be going – in about three weeks if all's well. I hope to get to church tonight.

Bestest love to all from The Bunsoy.

DIARY Sunday 6th January

Thick fog in morning. Up on A.O.P. in afternoon. Pretty thick still no E.A. seen.

To Church in evening with Withington. New padre preaching – very poor effort! Fell in tub on the way home! ****!!! Snow on the ground. Major still at Rouen.

65 Squadron.

7th January 1918

Thanks so much for your letter dated Jan 3rd; it only took 4 days to arrive which is quite good.

My ashtray will be finished tomorrow, I guess. I will try & get a decent pipe; if I can't Dad had better have the ash tray.

Enclosed is a poem called "Ten Little Albatrii". [Not available] I made it up yesterday afternoon whilst on patrol over the lines as I was so bored I didn't know what to do – rather a masterpiece, what! We saw no Huns. I was up on patrol from 2 – 3 this afternoon. The clouds were at about 7,000 & the visibility was poor. we ran into a snow storm about half time & flew about till it passed off. The air was pretty full of our machines & there was nary a Hun on the Lines – there were 4 well behind. The R.F.C. on this Front flies in pretty well any weather. You very seldom meet Albatrii when there are clouds at 9,000 because they know that since they can't sit up above your reach you can force them into a fight at that height which wouldn't suit them at all!

There is a thaw today & everything is beastly wet. Also there is a West wind blowing which is rotten as it blows you over the lines if you aren't careful.

Bestest love from The Bunsoy.

DIARY Monday 7th January

Thaw set in. No patrols all day.

Withington, Jones [2nd Lieutenant L.S.R. Jones] and I to dinner at No 32. Franticly cold. Went in Sidcup suit. Northwood away at Barck. Back at 12.30.

65 Squadron

8th January 1918

Many thanks for your last letter.

Not much news this time. Last night I went over to dinner with No 32 & had a very good time. We went in a tender & I wore my Flying Suit & a helmet. The Sidcup Suit "keeps you warm at 20,000 feet" granted but it utterly fails to keep you warm in an R.F.C. tender! I got back at 12.30 & was rejoiced to hear that I was down for patrol at 7.30 this morning (I don't think!) Anyway I crept out of bed & crawled into some clothes & emerged shivering only to find a cloudy sky. We waited to see if it would clear when 3 Camels from No 70 landed having been prevented from going back to their own place by snow. Presently it started here & has been snowing all day, it is jolly cold too! Patrols Na poo. The C.O. came back last night from Rouen & was quite bucked with "C" Flight's little show.

Gorringe in 70 was one of my pupils at Croydon. He came out just after I did & has done awfully well having got 10 Huns. Makes my ewe lamb look rather small doesn't it?

The ash tray is finished & is very bon; I will send it off tomorrow. I have done 87 hours flying out here & a total of 265 all told.

Well bestest love from The Bunsoy

DIARY Tuesday 8th January

Up for early show.   Gorringe from 70 landed and reported snow. Started to snow and carried on nearly all day! No Patrols; did nothing at all except read and smoke. C.O. came back from Rouen last night. Quite bucked with 'C' Flt. Bon, eh!

65 Squadron.

9th January 1918

Thanks so much for your two letters & the copies of "Flying" books – very good. I am afraid I didn't think much of Boyd Cable's story "Quick Work". The maniac of a pilot he describes as his hero would have been shot down at once! He did the very worst possible thing, diving away from a Hun! And as for shooting down a Hun with his top gun on top of a loop! – the thing's impossible & absurd! A loop is absolutely useless as a Fighting Stunt. A climbing turn & a steep spiral dive – (of my own invention!) are the only stunts I ever use in a scrap. I do wish people like Boyd Cable would not show their ignorance by trying to write about flying! The best article was "Impressions of Leave" which was priceless. The story "Eighteen" was unnecessarily lugubrious.

Well it was fine this morning & appallingly cold! There was snow on the ground & it was freezing. I was up on a two hours Reserve Patrol – there were very few Huns about & with the West Wind we did not cross the Lines. A lot of S.E.5s were about. Some clouds came over at about 6,000 ft. We were loafing along when suddenly a comic Albatross appeared from nowhere in particular – a habit they have! He saw us & climbed like mad for the mist. We all fired madly at him from long range but of course we didn't hit him & he hove off!

It is now snowing again with great gusto, cheery weather this! Wigg went on leave yesterday & Capt. Withington is going next & I think that with any luck I might be going after that i.e. on the 23rd. What ho! Last night it was simply freezing cold. I wore a waistcoat, a cardigan & bed socks & a hot bottle & I had 2 flying coats, a British Warm & a French coat over me & I was still cold!

Well Cheerio folks. Bestest love from The Bunsoy.

DIARY Wednesday 9th January

Snow very thick. On Patrol (Reserve) from 10.30-12. Clouds fairly low. Very few Huns. A lot of S.E.5's. Strong west wind. Fired at one Albatross which appeared and at once hove into a cloud.

To tea with No 1, snowing again. Down the town with Burbeck and Kelsey. Major out for Mess. Binge after.

                                                            65 Squadron.

10th January 1918

Thanks for your letters also for Gin's.

I have discovered that it is possible to obtain a few days leave outside your 14 days time home leave so I think I will run down to Rouen for a couple of days to see May.

This morning all the snow has gone awayee! It is beastly slushy & wet but quite warm. However this is rather spoilt by the fact that there is a 60 m.p.h. West wind blowing at 6000 [ft] which is na poo as it blows you over. I was up on patrol this morning, there were lots of clouds about with gaps in them, we got above them & loafed about – just about over the trenches but we did not go over. As usual never a Hun machine in the sky although the air was black with our buses, scouts & two-seaters. The ground Hun must be a bit sick of his Flying Corps but possibly he will improve in the Spring – in fact I have no possible doubt he will. I guess he is fostering his forces & we will probably be deluged with Albatrii then!! Anyway he hasn't a look in on this Front at present.

I didn't think much of Lloyd George's speech; it looked very like climbing down. Personally I have every desire to crush Germany & all its works. If we don't all this will have been for nothing!

I am going up on another patrol from 2.30 to 3.30. I had tea with No 1 yesterday & I think I am going to dinner with No 70 tonight.

Well no time for more folks.

Bestest love Bunsoy.

DIARY Thursday 10th January

Complete thaw set in. Everything wet and slushy. On patrol 10.30. Cloudy with hot air gaps. In a group of 9 split up into 3's. Strong west wind. No E.A. seen at all. Patrol again from 2.30. Fairly clear. No E.A. except one S.E. of Comines. Got archied. My engine is a collection of old iron!

Quite warm. Symons shot down Albatross at Armentières.

65 Squadron

11th January 1918

Thanks for your letter of today.

Great news! You will I guess be as delighted as I am to hear that I am coming home on leave this next Tuesday. What ho! That is to say Tuesday the 15th. I ought to get home on Tuesday night if all's well! As to my program of leave – well I would like to spend at least 4 days in Town as I have lots of people to see & some things to do also. I vote we all stay in Town for 4 days say from Wednesday till Saturday night or from Monday 21st till Friday, we can get rooms in a Hotel or stay with some relations or something. I shall wear mufti nearly all my leave I think – try to get my reefer coat from Hertford!

I was up on patrol at 8. a.m. this morning but it was very "dud" with low clouds & we saw nothing at all. No more patrols today!

Bestest love from
The Bunsoy.

DIARY Friday 11th January

Up on show at 8 a.m. Late getting off owing to a misunderstanding with Cocks' orders. Very thick – clouds at 3000 – impossible. Waste of good time and petrol! Jack well strafed by C.O. for being late. C.O. says we are not keen. I apologised to him for others but he did not take it very nicely. Over to No 1 for lecture but washed out.

To Cinema in camp after dinner. R.A.M.C. Col: in for dinner. Quite warm night. Bed early pretty tired.

65 Squadron.

12th January 1918

Just a wee line today. I am not on patrol today though I went up & down the Army Front seeing if I could see an odd Hun, but no luck! I am going down to see Mc Elroy in No 40 at once so will knock off.

Some Letter!
Bestest love from Bunsoy

DIARY Saturday 12th January

Dud for flying all day. We not on patrol at all. No patrols. Did a 55 mins: show on my own. Cloud at 3000 from Armentières to Houthulst and back. Shot up Hollebeke Chateau no E.A. seen at all. Down to Bruay with Eaton after lunch. Saw Mc Elroy then went to No 43. Saw Major Miles.

Back at 3.30. Played bridge and won 4f.50c! Bon, eh! Headachy all day. Bed early. Bombing show tomorrow – whotto!

DIARY Sunday 13th January

Orderly Office On patrol at 11.30. Clouds at 3000 with gaps. A few two-seaters high up – 4 Albatri sat on our tails but did not attack. Whole Squadron bombing dump at Lédignan [Ledegem] in afternoon. Very thick. Dropped one bomb from 8000 ft and then went home hell for split! Great show.

C.O. out for dinner. Bed early, headachy. Letter from Nickie Rowsell: Trés bon!

DIARY Monday 14th January

Not down for patrols. Weather fairly dud, did nothing in morning. Practised bomb dropping on aerodrome in afternoon. Got within 8 yds of the target. Fought R.E. 8 afternoon, got it slipped across me!

To tea at No 53 and then to show – the Panto in the town Bon. Played Auction after dinner – lost 7 francs! Gilmour got blotto – nearly fought him. Leave tomorrow What ɪɪO!!

DIARY Tuesday 15th January – First day of leave

Up at 7am. Tender to Arques. Train at 9.30 for Boulogne. Arrived at 1.30. Got on boat with great difficulty A.M.C.O. at Boulogne wants flogging to death! Pretty rough Crossing over but was not ill. Arrived Folkestone 5.30, Pulman up to town. To Grosvenor Hotel with another Sapper officer. To see 'Arlette' – very bon. No dinner. Supper in Hotel.

Bed bon, everything bon. Cheerie oh!

Oh Samuel! Oh Samuel! Beware the awful Cam-u-el!

DIARY Wednesday 16th January – Second day of leave
Down to Weymouth by the 9.30. Arrived 2.15. Saw Dad and Mum, Elsie, Gin, Gal, Leon, and the 3 kids. Priceless to be at home.
Bed early, raining hard all day.

DIARY Thursday 17th January – Third day of leave
Brekker in bed! Bon! Up at 11.30 – down town and bought some

things. Read and drew in the afternoon. To dance at Dr Lawrie's in evening, 8.30 till 1.45. Quite bon show. My dancing dud full of Australians. One V.C. there. Girls not very pretty – except Miss Desborough! Bon for troops. <u>Coming out</u> with me on Friday.

DIARY Friday 18th January – Fourth day of leave

Elsie and I to Portland with Robert to see Leon's ship. Back for lunch. Leon and I to the Jubilee Hall in evening. Very good show.

DIARY Saturday 19th January – Fifth day of leave

Down town with Dad in morning. To see "Bella Donna" at Pavillion in afternoon with Dad, Leon, Elsie and Gin – rather a tragedy. Eily arrived in evening Dad and Mum and I to meet her. Round to Gally's, Eily not very fit.

DIARY Sunday 20th January – Sixth day of leave

To early H.C. with Dad and Mum. To church with Dad, Mum and Gin in morning. Stormy day. To tea with Gally and Leon in afternoon. Did not go to Church in evening. Gin and Eily talking shop the whole time! Bed soon after prayers.

DIARY Monday 21stJanuary – Seventh day of leave

Down town in morning with Dad. To the Cinema in afternoon with Dad. Quite a good show, to "Jubilee Hall" in evening with Gin. Splendid conjuring show. House absolutely packed. Bed early. Town tomorrow.

DIARY Tuesday 22ndJanuary – Eighth day of leave

Up to town by the 9-3 train with Gin. Met by May and Uncle Jack. May felt faint but recovered. Lunch at Waterloo. To Cox's find I have £139 odd! Bon eh! Drew £25. No room at R.P. Left bag there. To see "General Post" with Gin. Très bon. Got room at Charing Cross Hotel. Changed for dinner. Met Nicky and May at R.P. all had dinner at Frascatis. Then Nicky and I to see "Cheep". Good. Saw Nicky to Waterloo: in taxi – <u>very</u> good! Met "Arthur". Nicky is simply sweet. Bon Eh!

DIARY Wednesday 23rd January – Ninth day of leave

To Gramophone Co. in morning. Got some records. Met Joy at the Troc; at 12.30, had Champagne lunch. To see "Aladdin" at Drury Lane in afternoon. Quite good. Then went for a joy ride in taxi! Exceedingly good! Had a great time in that taxi! Tea at 'Cottage Tea Rooms'. Saw

Joy off at Charing Cross then met Gin and May at Frascati's and had a great dinner. To see "The 13th Chair" in evening – Priceless most luridly thrilling.

DIARY Thursday 24th January – Tenth day of leave

To see Bob with Gin in morning then to Uncle Harry's. Then to see Pitt at 82, Eaton Square. Then got some Gramophone records. Lunch at Callards. Met May at Waterloo. Down to Weymouth by the 2.00 Train. Very full but a fairly comfy journey down. The whole family in to dinner and Leon and Robert; priceless re-union. Sang songs after – indigestion. Had great trip in town but very bon to be home again! Spent about £17.

DIARY Friday 25th January – Eleventh day of leave

To see Miss Desborough in morning with May. Elsie left. Had haircut, shave and shampoo. To Cinema with Irene in afternoon and tea at the Troc: very interesting too! Tried hard to find an excuse to tell her off but failed! Quite a bon girl.

To see "Ching Ling Soo" with whole family at 6 p.m. Very bon show. Read and wrote letters after dinner. Gally in to dine. Raining.

DIARY Saturday 26th January

Down town with Dad and Mum in morning. Gally and Leon in for tea and dinner. Dad read "Literary Lapses" after dinner – very bon! Bed early.

DIARY Sunday 27th January

To early H.C. in morning. To Church with family at 11. To call on Mrs Lawrie at 3.30 but she was out. Tea with the Wilkinsons after that, pretty appalling! Not to Church in evening. Read and had prayers.

DIARY Monday 28th January

To dentist in morning. Two teeth need stopping. Bought some things in town. Dad with headache all day. To the Jubilee Hall in evening with family except Dad, very good show.

Dad read "Literary Lapses" in evening. Bed early. Going back tomorrow ****!

DIARY Tuesday 29th January

Up to town with May by the 9-3. Met at Waterloo by Nickie, Arthur, King, Elsie and Elspeth. Lunch at Restaurant. King simply rich! Nickie and I to see "Zig Zag" – poor show but v.bon! Tea at Troc. Taxied to

Waterloo, kissed her in taxi, she was perfectly sweet.

Fixed up room at Grosvenor. Met May at Frascatis at 7.20 see 'Dear Brutus' Held Nickie's hand all the time. Responsive too! Air raid on and so walked back to the Grosvenor! Sat there till 12.30. No bombs near – Bed then. Kissed Nickie good night – she stayed in May's room. May is a perfect brick. I do love Nickie as a very sweet friend.

The Train 8.45 a.m.
En route to Folkestone

30th January 1918

Cheerio Troops!

Behold me at this grisly hour in the train en route for Folkestone – et après ça – la deluge!

I had a most topping leave dear folks & enjoyed every minute of it. Three months of "dud" weather & -- me voici encore.

The Bunsoy. v.cheerio!

DIARY Wednesday 30th January – Last day of leave

Up at 6.15. Brekker with May & Nickie. They saw me off by the 7.50. I kissed May and then Nickie who is the last person I kissed before I went out. Gave me a photo, baisers and mascot. Arrived at Folkestone 11.20. Boat at 1.45. Strolled around with Empson. Met Miss Lambart lunch at Grand – feeling fearfully fed up. Smooth crossing, met Major Duffin [*sic*] on boat. Got lift in his car to Bois-d'Haine. Rang up 65 and spent night in Y.M.C.A. at Omer.

65 Squadron

31st January 1918

Just a wee line to let you know I am quite fit & back at the Squadron. I had a lovely smooth crossing & met Major Duffus O.C. 25 on the boat. He gave me a lift in his car to his Squadron; I then went down to the base & stayed the night in the Y.M.C.A. hut there. At 10.30 the Squadron car came for me & brought me up here so I managed to avoid the "leave" train after all. The Squadron has done jolly well since I have been away – having got

7 Huns. They got 5 the day before yesterday. There is a thick fog here today – rotten! (liar)!!

Well dearest folks no more as I gave you all my news yesterday.

DIARY Thursday 31st January

Got C.O.s car at Omer at 10.30. Arrived 65 at 12.30, foggy. Patrol out but got lost. Shanks & Kennedy [2nd Lieutenant J.G. Kennedy] crashed. O.K.

Read in afternoon and played new records. Down town with Jack in evening. Bed at 10 – awfully cold. Room in an awful state. 65 got 7 Huns while I was away. Baker, [2nd Lieutenant E.J. Baker, G.L.] and Wylie [2nd Lieutenant A.E. Wylie, G.L.] missing. Reeves in No 1 killed. Dyer killed. Cowan [2nd Lieutenant R.H. Cowan] and Cameron [2nd Lieutenant J.D. Cameron] prisoners. Rotten to be back!

65 Squadron

1st February 1918

No news of any interest, the fog lasted all yesterday. A patrol had gone up at 8 & got caught in it & they all landed all over France – several crashed & two are in hospital slightly injured but all right. Everybody here is very fit, Cox & Eaton & the C.O. are on leave & Withington is acting C.O.

I was down for an O.P. today from 12.15 to 1.30 but there has been thick fog all day & no flying. Rotten weather isn't it? I am fed up – (l--r!!!) The C.O. comes back tomorrow or next day. I believe the Hun is pretty active in the air on this front & pretty stout too so I ought to have some fun shortly! Old Bill shot down a Hun in flames the other day & 6 other Huns were done in. We got 5 one day & lost nobody ourselves. Dyer has been reported as killed, isn't it awfully rotten? Cowan & Cameron who were missing on the day of our big tea party are prisoners. Capt. Reeves in No 1, a topping fellow, killed himself the other day in a Nieuport; he was doing violent stunts & his wings folded back. No more news.

DIARY Friday 1st February

Foggy all day. Down for patrol but no bon. Read in Mess all day. Wrote letters. Beastly cold.

2nd February 1918

I am afraid this will miss the post as I am just in from patrol. I was up on O.P. from 12.15 to 1.30 but the Huns were very quick & I only saw a formation of 6 Albatrii well his side of the Lines. They didn't worry us – Gilmour came home with a 'dud' engine & so I led the other fellows, we didn't get much "Archie".

The fog has pretty well cleared off now & it is a lovely day & quite warm, it was lovely flying. I went up for a joy ride to get my hand in as I felt a bit strange at first, so I did a few 'loops' & 'rolls' to get used to it. Everybody has been flying my poor 'bus' while I have been away but nobody likes it as it is very tail heavy. Bon eugh! Possibly that will keep them from flying it! I did nothing yesterday but read smoked & played the gramophone. The new mattress on my bed is a huge success & I was beautifully warm last night.

Well you poor dears will be by this time robbed of all your family again – still I guess I will be home again in April if all's well – not so long anyhow.

Cheerio – that's all my news for today.

DIARY Saturday 2nd February

Off Pat: in morning. I led after Jack had fallen out. Res: Pat: in afternoon. Got fed up with Ypres and so went up to the Coast at Nieuport!

Read in evening.

65 Squadron

3rd February 1918

Another thriller! Today 12 of us went out on O.P. we went well over the Lines & found about 13 or 14 Huns below us. These we followed & they all dived away from us as hard as they could. Then a lot of our fellows fell out with dud engines, leaving six of us, we then went over the Lines again nearly to the ---- Road . Then we saw some Albatrii below us & five above & some more knocking about. Jack & I dived on the ones below, the others stayed up above. I saw Jack get on the tail of an Albatross, the Hun then made for me nose on firing, so I pressed my thumb pieces & fired straight into him. His nose dropped & he fell over sideways & started to go down in a spin slowly at first & then faster & faster. I didn't see him crash but I have claimed him as "out of control". Jack & another fellow confirmed this. I think I slew him all right.

Then I turned away & suddenly heard pop-pop-pop-crack-crack very close behind me. I pulled my old bus into a right hand climbing turn when suddenly – - smack!! – something hit my elbow! Ha! thought I – I'm wounded! Exit me! So I changed my climbing turn into an "Immelman" & went down in a nearly vertical dive engine full out! Gee! I <u>was</u> going some! Presently I flattened out a bit & looking round saw that confounded Hun still on my tail firing like -----! They all went above me though. Then I saw a Camel dive on the Hun & he left off from following me! That was Jack who had seen me go down pursued by the Hun & had followed him; he shot him down "out of control" & pretty well saved my skin.

I came home & found that a bullet had passed right through the elbow of my Sidcot Suit without cutting my tunic, a near thing – what! I also found that another bullet had cut through a longeron in my fuselage & broken a spar in my left bottom plane & another had missed my petrol tank by about 2 inches. Why my old bus didn't fall to bits in that dive I don't know! The 'Everlasting Arms' again I guess. The total of that scrap was 4 Huns – Jack got two, one smoking & one out of control. Bill got one & I got the other. Bill had an end-on shot & got 5 bullets in his engine, he managed to crawl home with his engine firing on about 4 cylinders. We lost nobody – thank God. So once again only 3 of us did any scrapping against pretty good odds & 2 of the 3 were in "C" Flight – Vive "C" Flight! Bon enough! Awfully glad I have got another Hun.

Am very fit & happy. Thanks for your two letters – hope you are awfully fit. Must catch the post.

Bunsoy.

DIARY Sunday 3rd February

Not on early show. O.P. 10.15. Chased about 17 Huns East of Lille. Then dived on 7 Black & White Albatri S.W. of Roulers. Shot one down in a spin – got allowed him. Got shot to bits myself! Bullet through sleeve of my Sidcup suit – longeron and main spars shot. Jack [Gilmour] got a Hun.

To Kirk in evening. To dine with No 1. Kelsey leaves tomorrow. Letter from Nickie.

65 Squadron

4th February 1918

So sorry that I missed the post today but I was out to lunch.

My bus has been "written off" [Camel B2419] as it was pretty well shot up yesterday & it has done 160 hours. Today Jack put a couple of revolver bullets into the other longerons to make sure of it, "murder Most Foul" I call it – it is a good thing though as it <u>was</u> getting old & now I am getting a brand new one. I am awfully sorry to lose Pooh-Bah though – it has done me jolly well & had been in a good many merry scraps – in fact it was a good old pal of mine. R.I.P. anyway.

I shall take some time to get used to my new one; I expect I shall have the rigging altered to suit my own particular style of flying. I don't suppose it will loop as well as Pooh-Bah. I had looped her so often that I simply had to say "Loop" & she looped herself!

I was up on Reserve Patrol this morning but we only saw 7 Albatrii well East of the road & they didn't worry us so we had no scrap. I was not on the O.P. but there were no Huns about anyway. I went over to lunch at No 32 & saw Northwood. Flying back I did a simply priceless climbing turn off the ground.

A Handley Page Bomber landed here yesterday, you have no idea of the huge size of this bus, you could put a whole "Camel" on the planes on each side of the fuselage. They have two "Rolls" engines & can carry 16 112 lb bombs apiece, good line what! The passenger-carrying H.Ps can carry 14 persons. To see this monstrosity doing a climbing turn off the ground & then diving down & "zooming" the hangars was the finest thing you ever saw, it obscured half the aerodrome when it landed.

DIARY Monday 4th February

On Reserve Patrol in morning. Saw nothing to notice. Poor old Pooh Bah written off! Did nothing in afternoon. To dine with Williams [Lieutenant T.M. Williams] at Club in evening. Fairly 'happy' after! To lunch with 32 – saw Bulger.

65 Squadron

5th February 1918

This morning I was up on Reserve Patrol from 9 – 10.30. I patrolled most of the Lines at 14,500 ft & it was jolly cold! I dove on 5 Albatrii from a great height but they hove off East at once before I could reach them. I am just back from No 2 A.S.D. [Aircraft Supply Depot?] where I have been collecting a new "Camel" to replace mine; it is a very decent one with a good engine in it. I am having the rigging altered slightly.

We have been having lovely weather for the last few days with beaucoup sun & quite mild also beaucoup aviation! Today the C.O. is leading a large Off. Pat. but I am not in it. He [Major J.A. Cunningham] has been given the Croix de Guerre. Withington [Captain T.E. Withington, O.C. "B" Flight] went on leave today – lucky!

DIARY Tuesday 5th February

On Res: Pat: in morning. UP to 14500. Dived on 5 E.A. which hove off. To Serny to fetch new Camel. Very own bus. Huge tea party in afternoon apparently. Umpteen Huns. I not in on it – thank heavens! 3 Huns shot down.

To dine with Pat in No 1 – Mc Elroy there. We are going to shift from here to Pop: rotten. Letter from Nickie – exceeding bon too!

65 Squad.

6th February 1918

No patrols today as it was pretty dud. I tested my new "bus" which is very bon indeed, better than my old one.

I went down to the Base to see 3 Hun aeroplanes which had been brought down 'intact'. One was an A.E.G. twin-engine bomber, a rotten looking affair; a Rumpler two-seater & a comic little scout – a sort of cross between an Albatross & a Nieuport.

Then I flew back & had a very good practice scrap with a S.E. 5. I think I put it all over him as far as manoeuvring goes! We had a fellow missing from that scrap yesterday – however in the evening he strolled into the Mess with his head tied up! He had had both his petrol tanks shot through & a splinter of bullet in the back of his head. So he landed behind the Lines – he is quite all right now – good show what!

My bed is lovely now with that mattress, it just makes all the difference! I had dinner with No 1 last night & saw McElroy who had come up for dinner from No 40. He has got about 10 Huns.

DIARY Wednesday 6th February

Dud all morning and no patrols. Tested my airship and did some priceless loops. Cleared up after lunch. Flew to Omer with Jack and saw D.F.W., R.E.9 & S.8. Fought S.E.5 after – bon scrap – put it across him all right!

Down town with Major and Jack after tea.

65 Squadron

7th February 1918

I heard from May today, she is bound for 49 C.C.S. Some where South of this I fancy, I shall try to get down to see her if I can find out where she is.

It was dud all yesterday & no patrols – I am getting quite a decent rest with one thing & another. I was down for an O.P. today but it is raining hard at present & so it has been washed out.

It's awfully rotten that we have to shift from this aerodrome. We move on Tuesday. I fancy I shall be awfully sorry to leave No 1 as they are all such awfully good fellows. I think I shall share a hut with Jack Gilmour if I possibly can when we shift.

When poor old Pooh-Bah got shot up I was carrying a copy of the Squadron photo in a sort of dispatch bag fixed on the side of the fuselage in my cockpit & the bullet which hit my Sidcot suit passed slap through the photo. I will have it framed & sent home, it will make an interesting souvenir.

I think I am going to play in a scratch game of hockey this afternoon. Well no more now!

DIARY Thursday 7th February

Dud all day. No flying – Cocks returned – very chewed up with life in general! Did nothing, but read and smoke. Bed early.

65 Squadron

8th February 1918

Yesterday afternoon Balfour, Wigg the R.O. & I went up in a tender for a joy ride to have a look at the Trenches. We went up to a certain well-known ridge where we left the tender. We then walked up & saw the three huge mine craters – they are simply enormous, about 70 yds across & 20 ft deep. All along the roadway were the remains of old trenches & barbed wire. Then we came to an old Hun dugout with a pile of Hun hand grenades lying behind it. I would have collected one only I thought they might go off! There were dud shells & Stokes mortar bombs lying all round also old "Toffee Apples" – a round bomb with an iron slide for firing from a trench mortar. Then we walked along the ridge in front of our batteries which were firing at the Hun about 3000 yds away. The Hun replied with 5.9 Howitzers but all the shots fell short – I am glad to say!

The country up there – the scene of the famous battle of the Vimy Ridge, is an awful scene of desolation, all shell holes & blasted tree trunks. We saw a smashed up Tank lying in the open. The ground was dotted with smashed in "Pill Boxes" – great concrete block houses & concrete sniping posts. Then we walked down the – - – Road & picked up our tender & came back very tired!

Bad weather today & no flying.

DIARY Friday 8th February

Dud for patrols all day. Wind and low clouds. Read and smoked.

15 guests in for dinner! Cinema after. I read and stayed in Peacock's room. Bed early.

65 Squadron

9th February 1918

The dud weather continues & there are no patrols today, nor were there any yesterday, which is just as well as there is a strong West wind blowing! I hope to aviate down to see Dunkerley at No 2 this afternoon but don't know if I will be able to go, as the clouds are fairly low. I can't find out where No 49 C.C.S. is but will make further enquiries.

We are all getting ready for our move up North – it is a beastly nuisance having to move. Maitland came up to see me yesterday. He has just come out on "Camels" in No 80 Squadron. I told him some hair raising tales of 'Albatrii' & 'Archies' & 'tea parties'

A lot of fellows came in for dinner last night but I went to bed fairly early as I was rather tired.

Old Bill is in Hospital pro tem. with pyorrhoea & slight septic poisoning but is coming out shortly & is quite fit.

DIARY Saturday 9th February

Wind and low clouds. No patrols. Did nothing in morning. Flew down to see [?] and Caldwell at Auchel. Bumpy as ****! Landed at La Gorgue on the way back and saw Trollope. He came back for tea with us.

Played Auction in evening till 12.30. Lost 1 fr 50 c. Letter from Nickie.

65 Squadron

10th February 1918

The dud weather continues – howling West winds & low clouds & showers – no patrols today or yesterday, I am really getting a bit tired of dud weather.

Yesterday I braved the elements & flew down South & saw Dunkerley who is very fit & enjoying life pretty well. I also saw two or three other fellows I met at Tad. They are night bombing on F.E.s. I did a few choice stunts over their Aerodrome after taking off just to cheer them up! Then I went & landed at 43's aerodrome & saw Trollope who is new out – he killed a Hun two-seater the other day. he flew back with me & had tea here & then flew back. I enjoyed my little "Cook's Tour"!

We are moving on Tuesday [12th Feb.] & I am going to pack this afternoon, it is a vile nuisance having to shift, we are going to the same aerodrome as 70!

DIARY Sunday 10th February

Clouds and wind all day. To Church in a.m. in the Camp. Read and smoked all day. Messed around in afternoon. Went for a ride on No 1's horse – awful sickness!

To dinner at No 1. Rest played poker – back at 12. Wireless tomorrow.

65 Squadron

11th February 1918

Today we are down for Wireless Interruption – or strafing the Hun two-seaters doing Art. Obs. [Artillery Observation] but as there is still a howling West wind & low clouds; we won't have anything to do as there won't be any Huns up at all!

I went for a short canter round the aerodrome yesterday afternoon on a horse. I went in to a Service in the Camp yesterday morning; the Padre was very young & very nervous. I had a line from Jenkins today; he is in 46 Squadron & is having a pretty fair time of it – good fellow old Jenks.

I am going to play "rugger" this afternoon & so will stop. No news at all at present!

DIARY Monday 11th February

Clouds and wind all day. No Patrols. Rugger in afternoon v No 3 Aust: Drew 4-4. Good clean game. Read and Moore and Pat in to play poker. This weather is great.

65 Squadron

12th February 1918

I heard from May today – she is a good long way from here & it would be 'some' trip for me to fly down to see her but I will try to manage it if I can. Dud weather still continues, no flying yesterday or today.

I had a great game of Rugger yesterday, we played an Australian team & drew 5-5 after a v.close game.

We haven't shifted yet as we are waiting for the other Squadron to move, who are in turn replacing a Squadron which is going down South & can't move till the weather clears up.

I am going to have another game of Rugger this afternoon. I wonder if the Hun is preparing some form of devilment under cover of these clouds with no Obs. to worry him!

I am particularly fit now, I am glad to say & feel equal to any amount of Albatrii! Can't think of anything more to say so will draw stumps!

DIARY Tuesday 12th February

   High wind and low clouds. No patrols at all. Rugger v Australian team in afternoon. Won 7-6. Ripping game. Read and wrote letters in evening.

65 Squadron

13th February 1918

Today it is raining hard, this is the 8th day of dud weather. Amazing, isn't it? Consequently I have no news at all!

   I don't know when we shall be shifting, not till the weather breaks anyway. This Spring the "Camel" will be the only Rotary engined bus on this Front. We are getting 150 h.p. engines instead of the present 130 h.p., which ought to be pretty good – - – <u>when</u> we get them!

DIARY Wednesday 13th February

   Rain and low clouds all day. No Patrols at all. Read and played bridge most of day. Up for a 5 min flip in afternoon. Raining and thick as mud.

65 Squadron

14th February 1918

The wind has changed round to the East & fog & mist have replace low clouds & rain – it's all one though still dud.

   I went up for a short flip yesterday in the rain, just to get some air into my lungs but it was very thick & I soon came down again.

DIARY Thursday 14th February

   Thick mist all day. No flying. Soccer v Sergts. in afternoon. Lost 4-0. Very good game. Bridge in evening till 12.30!

65 Squadron

15th February 1918

Fog still continues & it is very chilly today. I went up for a short flip & couldn't get much above 1000 ft. & it was very cold. It is clearing up a bit since & so there may be a show but I doubt it.

   I played "soccer" yesterday & had a very good game. We played the Sergts. & lost 4-0. I was Orderly Officer yesterday.

Eaton came back from leave & that makes up our old three again – Gilmour, Eaton & I. I am very glad as I don't like flying beside someone I don't know. This afternoon there are going to be inter-flight soccer games, 6-a-side, 10 minutes each way – it ought to be rather thrilling!

DIARY Friday 15th February

Misty all day.   Short flip in morning.   Flt soccer matches in the afternoon. "C" Flt won and I won 10 fr. on it!

Read and played bridge in evening.   Lost 18 fr.   Beastly cold, no patrol.

65 Squadron

16th February 1918

I see Brian Baker is now D.S.O., M.C., Croix de Guerre. Pretty good work

Today is a lovely fine day with an East wind. La guerre recommence! We are standing by all day to strafe Hun two-seaters doing Art. Obs. & have been kept pretty busy. I was up on dawn patrol with Jack but saw no Huns near the Lines. Eaton however struck a single Albatross & fired at it; the Hun dived away East & dived straight into the ground & was slain. Jolly good work. A lot of Hun two-seaters have been over here today at 16,000 ft.

Huge excitement at about 12 noon! Archie started & we all went out of the Mess & lo, a single Albatross scout 'loafing' at about 3,000 ft. right over the aerodrome. He turned East & then "Archie" put him off & so he turned West again. Then a S.E.5 which was up at the time spotted him & dived on him. The Hun went down in a mighty dive, flattened out & landed in a field about a mile from the town, turning over on his back when landing – the pilot was unhurt & has been taken prisoner. I watched the whole thing through my glasses – it was a priceless show! A single Albatross over here at 3,000 ft.!!! I guess he was absolutely lost & had awful wind up, poor beggar – I don't blame him!

We are moving tomorrow at 8 a.m. Furious packing this afternoon! Awful Nuisance!

DIARY Saturday 16th February

Great war starts again.   On Dawn Pat: with Jack.   Cold as ****!   No

Huns to notice. Eaton crashed an Albatross! Bingo in club for dinner. Leaving tomorrow.

DIARY Sunday 17th February

In complete trance all day – with headache. O.P. from 9-15. Left Bailleul and landed at Proven. Res: Pat: in afternoon. Very reserve!

Settled down in hut with Jack. Balfour, Major. Dinner in Pop.

65 Squad.

18th February 1918

Thanks for your letters – awfully sorry I couldn't write home yesterday but I truly hadn't a minute. We got orders to move yesterday, & we had to get up early. Just so as to give us lots of time to settle down in our new place, the Wing gave us two Observation Patrols, one Off. Patrol & 6 new machines to collect from 2 A.S.D.!! Rather too much, wasn't it and yesterday was a perfect nightmare! I had a bit of a head [ache] as a kick off, too.

We left – - – on the O.P. & patrolled for 1½ hrs & landed here in our new aerodrome, which is a pretty deadly spot right on the main road running N.W. from – - – . The Mess however is very comfy & the huts very bon! I am sharing a Mess hut with Jack, Balfour & Major Howes. I couldn't stand Old Bill as a hut Mate any longer! No food when we arrived except Bully & Machaichie [sic?].

The fellows who were collecting the new buses hadn't come back & so "C" Flt had to do another patrol – a reserve patrol – this took 2 hours. I was in an absolute coma all the time with a rotten headache. A fresh soloist in a 'Rumpety' could have shot me down with a bow & arrow! However there were no Huns & in the O.P. we were all feeling too tired to want one! Then we had dinner down the town & then I fell into bed & to sleep – I was tired!

I am very fit this morning though, as I didn't get up till 10 o'clock.

DIARY Monday 18th February

O.P. led by C.O. in morn over to Roulers. No Huns at all. Got room started. Binge in Pop. with Matthews.

65 Squadron

19th February 1918

We are gradually settling down here. Yesterday "C" Flt only did an Off. Pat. – led by the C.O. We went right over to the – - – Road & loafed about over there but there were no Huns at all. I only saw one Hun & we were in Supreme Command of the air. Capt. Symons on early patrol ran across a Hun two-seater at 500 ft. He got beneath his tail & fired about 20 rounds & the Hun did a right-hand Immelman turn & dove slap into the ground & was slain.

That comic Albatross that landed over here the other day was the latest type of Hun bus, a D.E.5. The pilot said he had come over balloon strafing & had got lost & landed! He subsequently escaped from the P. of W. cage but was recaptured.

We have a v.bon fireplace in our new ante-room, a kind of brazier in an ingle with seats in the ingle nooks. We have an oil drum stove in our hut & are getting partitions fixed up & are pretty comfy.

Matthews went home on leave this morning – he & Jack & Balfour & I had dinner in town last night, a v.bon meal – there's a café called "Skundles".

Very cold today, blue sky with a fairly thick mist. We have had a good few crashes landing – the aerodrome is about the size of a postage stamp & about as even as a ploughed field!

DIARY Tuesday 19th February

Misty all day. R.P. in morning and O.P. in afternoon. No E.A.

65 Squadron

20th February 1918

Yesterday we went up on patrol but there was a thick haze & we came back. Today the wind has changed to S.W. & there is mist & rain & no flying – bon! I am just getting my new room fixed up & am going down town to buy some things.

Heard from May today. I don't know if I will be able to get down to see her but will try.

I am afraid my letters are very scrappy just now but I am rather in a muddle – they will improve when we settle down!

DIARY Wednesday 20th February

Dud and misty all day. Dawn patrol. No E.A. seen at all. Too thick for patrols in afternoon.

65 Squadron

21st February 1918

Sorry not to be able to post this in time today but I have been up on patrol. I did two O.Ps today but there was a howling W. wind & we didn't go far over – there were very few Huns anyway.

My hut is practically finished now, we have each got a corner for sleeping in & have left a wee sitting room round the stove in the middle of the hut, this we call the Ante room! I have my bed up against the wall & a couple of shelves 6' long along the partition, these were made by my riggers, it is awfully cosy & bon!

After patrol this afternoon I landed at the old 'drome & had tea with No 1. I was posted as missing here!

I have an acetylene burner in my room. There is a good gramophone shop in the town; I got some records there yesterday. You know the noise a ginger beer bottle makes when it is opened!!!

DIARY Thursday 21stFebruary

Thick mist and rain in afternoon. No flying at all. Down town in afternoon. Got some things – phone records. Got room nicely fixed up.

65 Squadron

22nd February 1918

Yesterday we did 2 Offensive Patrols of 1¾ hrs each. I was pretty tired at the finish! As there was a strong W. wind blowing, the latter O.P. was more P. then O.! Capt. Symons shot down an Albatross yesterday afternoon in company with a Belgian fellow away up North. That makes Symons' 6th; he ought to be in for the M.C. pretty shortly I think. The Wing O.C., Col. van Rynwel has gone on leave & Cunningham has taken over the Wing pro tem. Capt. Withington, who has just come back from leave, has got the Squadron while the C.O. is away. Jack goes on leave next.

Today there is a strong S.W. wind with low clouds & rain –

'dud' – bon entre! I guess I am going to stay indoors & read most of today as I have a bit of a cold. I have just been looking over my machine so my hands are a bit oily, so please excuse the grubbiness of this letter. The post hasn't come in yet but I will thank you for the letter I know I will receive.

A lot of the Scout Squadrons in this Wing are refitting & are in consequence off War Flying pro tem, with the result that we get an awful lot of work to do & are getting a bit fed up with it! Well there is no news at present as we haven't had much excitement lately.

DIARY Friday 22nd February

Two O.P.'s to Roulers on first one. Strong w wind. No E.A. seen anywhere near. Split up and fooled around. O.P. in aft in 3's. More P. than O. No E.A. seen and no archie near us.

Read and smoked (beaucoup) in evening. Bed at 11.00.

65 Squadron

23rd February 1918

That Hun that came down near us the other day wasn't hurt at all as the Albatross landed on its wheels & then just turned over on its back, a very common sight on some aerodromes – (not ours though!).

I know Hugo Dunkerley had an awful lot of moving lately, three times in one week, I fancy!

Yesterday was 'dud' all day with na poo aviation. Today the clouds are at 4000 [ft]. We started on a patrol but came back. I amused a lot of Tommies on a road just behind the Lines by doing about 6 loops straight off the reel! Well no more news pro tem!

DIARY Saturday 23rd February

Dud and no patrols all day. Read and smoked. Dinner in Pop. with Jack.

65 Squadron

24th February 1918

Today is overcast with clouds at 5000 ft. We are doing a Reserve Patrol this afternoon, I think & it is rather a bore as there won't be any Huns up & you just loaf about & do nothing & get "fed up"!

This morning I went to Church & H.C. [Holy Communion] in the Squadron – quite a nice service. Then after that "The Major" & I flew up to a Belgian aerodrome near the Coast to see a Frederickshaven Gotha which had been captured. It wasn't shot down but two of the struts bearing the left engine had split & the pilot got wind up & landed! It is a splendid looking machine – not so big as a Handley-Page. It has three Parabellum M.Gs & can fire more or less under its tail. It carries 4 men, 3 NCOs & 1 officer & it has two engines with pusher props.

DIARY Sunday 24th February

Too dud for O.P.'s. Did reserve patrol in afternoon. Went up to Belgian aerodrome to see the Gotha.

Church in morning. Read in evening.

No 65. France

25th February 1918

I hope you have by this time heard from me at my new place, I only missed writing one day, I think. The post goes out at all sorts of comic hours & you never know which post your letter will catch!

Today we were down for an O.P. only at 11 a.m. but it has been raining & blowing & so we didn't go up. It is a very blustery day with a howling N.E. wind & a layer of broken clouds. I fancy it will be fine tomorrow but I don't mind fighting with an East wind, the stronger the better!

Jack Gilmour goes on leave tomorrow at 7 a.m. – lucky beggar!

Yesterday I did a reserve patrol from 3 to 4.30 – <u>very</u> reserve – the clouds were at 5500 [ft] & we didn't cross the Lines. Three Fokker Triplanes, which have made a re-appearance on this front, attacked a R.E.8, but he got away all right. Then some lovely big mountainous clouds came up & I had a great game going into caverns & canyons in them, then I climbed up thro' the clouds into the dazzling sunshine – it was perfectly lovely up there, a brilliant blue sky, a gorgeous sun & a billowy white floor stretching as far as the eye could reach!

DIARY Monday 25th February

Raining in morning and strong wind. No flying. Down town in morning. Dinner in Pop. with Jack. Kissed Zoe! Bon Euh.

65 R.F.C. France

26th February 1918

Lovely clear morning with a N.W. wind blowing. We were out on an O.P. at 11 a.m. I was leading one of the rear lots of three. No Huns at first, then 9 Albatri came up & followed us around on their side of the Lines. I kept them well in view at first but presently I lost them – the next thing I saw was these 3 Blighters about 500 ft above me! Eaton had fallen out of our 3 with a dud engine & I was left with Brown [*sic* – 2nd Lieutenant D G Brown?], who is pretty fresh at the game & didn't know they were Huns even! I was sitting in my bus shivering & with wind up, waiting for old man Fritz to dive – but he didn't! Then he went East & apparently dived on one of our other lots of 3. I saw the Huns above them & saw them kind of half dive on them but I didn't realize there was really a scrap on or I should have gone over to join it. However we all came back all right & the Huns faded away. I wasn't feeling in the mood for a dog fight today. The Huns were yellow fellows with scarlet tails; I kept a jolly good eye on them as I wasn't being dived on unawares again!

Jack Gilmour went on leave today. This aerodrome is about 1 mile from the aerodrome to which we went when we first came out, before we went down to the one we shared with No 1. It is coming up "dud" now & promises "dud" for tomorrow! The reason we changed 'dromes was because the Squadron which was originally here is re-fitting with another type of "bus" which could not be landed on this aerodrome as it is too small, so we just changed places – see?

DIARY Tuesday 26th February

Jack went on leave 7.30. Fine day O.P. at 11 a.m. 9 Albs. came and sat above us but did not attack me. Attacked Symons.

Walked down town with Major Howe after tea. Read and wrote letters in evening.

65 R.F.C. France

27th February 1918

I am writing this afternoon in the "ante room" of our hut in front of a fine warm stove. Today was too dud for O.P. & so we did Reserve patrols instead. I wasn't on a show so I went out on a roving Commission but saw no Huns. I had rather an amusing time! There was a fairly thick layer of clouds all over but there was one gap in them over our lines, then a sort of bridge of clouds about a mile broad, then a gap over part of Hun land. I climbed through our gap & flew along the bridge of clouds & looked down through the other gap into Hun land to see if I could spot an odd two-seater which wanted shooting down! Being hidden by the clouds I could thus go across the Lines without any Archie at all!

Tomorrow I am on the Dawn patrol which consists in two machines flying along the Lines in "the wee sma hours" after dawn looking for the odd Hun two-seater strafing the Infantry in our Trenches. Rather an amusing job but it means getting up at 5.45! We are also standing by to strafe Hun Art. Obs. machines & bombing-parties of Gothas which may choose to stroll over the lines intent upon laying their eggs on our lines & billets.

Trollope [Captain J.L. Trollope] flew up here today & saw me; he was at Croydon you know & has got several Huns since he came out. His Squadron 43 is further South & there are apparently beaucoup Hun two-seaters down there. They are not very common up here, in fact the Hun hasn't got many buses up here at all just at present. I am on just the same Front as I was at the last place & we do exactly the same job, we have only changed our aerodrome, that's all! A Hun pilot was taken prisoner the other day & he said that the "Camel" & the S.P.A.D. were far better machines than the Albatross, which cheers me up a bit. I don't think the "Albatrii" like getting into a dog fight with "Camels" as they aren't half as good at manoeuvring as we are.

The post goes out at 9 a.m. each day so my letters are never sent off till the day after I write them. Afraid I can't manage any before 9 a.m. I am generally in bed till 9.30 when not on early patrol. Slacker!!

DIARY Wednesday 27th February

On Wireless. Dawn patrol with Eaton. Pretty dud. Shot up floor and got one bullet thr'o aileron. No calls thr'o all day. Dusk patrol. 5 albs: on the lines.

65 R.F.C. France

28th February 1918

After such a long yesterday, I find I haven't much to say today. I did the "odd" dawn patrol this morning with Eaton. No Huns at all, so I shot up the trenches till they started to machine gun me from the ground & put a bullet through one of my planes, then I padded the hoof & hove off. I did no patrols through the day as there were no Hun two-seaters doing Art. Obs. I also did a Dusk Patrol from 4.30 to 5.30. Apparently 5 Albatrii came & sat over the Lines at 12.00 p.m. but I didn't see them. It was a lovely evening & all the clouds which had been about all day had gone. There wasn't a "bump" in the air at all & so I came home just above the tree tops. All the district just behind the Lines was streaked with the trails of blue smoke coming from bivouac fires & blown out by the gentle wind – it was an awfully pretty sight. The only thing that spoilt it was that here & there Hun Archie shells had left a patch of black smoke exactly like a smudge on a piece of paper.

A Belgian pilot landed here this morning on a priceless French machine – the exact converse of a "Camel", i.e. it had a flat bottom plane & dihedral on the top plane. It did some good stunts when he took off – apparently it has got a splendid climb & is very manoeuvrable – I wish we had them!

Well it's dinner time & so I will knock off.

DIARY Thursday 28th February

Pretty dud. No Patrols. Down to No 1 in afternoon. Very cold. Read in evening. Belgian Hanriot over.

65 R.F.C. France

1st March 1918

No further news of any interest. A wild day today – a strong East wind with rain & low clouds & generally "dud"! We may be going to the seaside for a course of aerial gunnery but it isn't settled yet.

This morning I dug up part of my potato patch! All the Squadrons are growing potatoes & I believe that after June they are to be self supporting as regards vegetables! Hope I am home by that time!

Balfour is O.C. "C" Flight while Jack is on leave, a very good O.C. he. I am Deputy leader!

We had a gas alarm last night but nothing came of it. There was also a small minor show down on the Front. Quite successful I believe. No more news!

DIARY Friday 1st March

Strong East wind and no flying.
Read and smoked all day.

65 Squadron R.F.C.

2nd March 1918

Today has been much colder, a howling N.E. wind blowing, also snow & rain – very "dud"!

Hugo D. is at present on a night bombing Squadron on F.E.2Bs. Quite a good job I understand as "Archie" is the only thing that worries them.

Our new quarters are more comfy than the old ones I think. The C.O. sleeps at the Wing while he is acting O.C.

The weather promises "dud" for tomorrow, too. I did nothing at all today except read & smoke & play Bridge (with my usual luck!).

DIARY Saturday 2nd March

Howling E wind. No flying at all. One E.A. doing Alt. Obs: we left him to crash landing which he probably did!

Dinner in town with Withers [Captain T.E. Withington]. Very heavy barrage on at about 9.45 pm. Hun raids. See Daily Light for today.

65 Squadron R.F.C.

3rd March 1918

Thanks so much for today's letter – also heard from May, she is wondering why I haven't been over to see her!

I went to Service in the Camp this morning & had a very nice service & a fine sermon.

Still very "dud", the wind has dropped & there is a mist with a drizzling rain. I bought you rather a nice lace table centre at a shop in the Town, which used to be one of the lace shops in Ypres. I think the people were driven out; it is home-made – or supposed to be! I had been in Town walking in & back, I needed the exercise badly too as all I appear to do here at present is eat, smoke & read! I am very fit & happy & hope you are keeping free from headaches, Dad.

Well, I don't think there is any more news, so will knock off.

DIARY Sunday 3rd March

To Church in morning. Dud for flying. Down town with Eaton in afternoon. Got hair cut and bought [?] and hankies. Tea at Skindles. Northwood and others to dinner and 2 R.N.A.S from No 1 naval staying here. Slept poorly.

65 Squadron R.F.C. France

4th March 1918

Another "dud" day & the feelings of the Squadron have over-flowed & everyone has gone mad. This morning, a party of us digging potatoes turned into a bombing party & proceeded to hurl clods of earth at each other! This afternoon we organized a rat hunt with Verey Lights – we saw no rats but we got through several pounds worth of Verey Lights! A large formation of homing crows passed over us & so we "archied" them with Verey Lights, completely breaking up their formation & driving many of them off East! This afternoon we amused ourselves putting Verey Lights down the chimneys of the huts, with any luck the things go off in the stove & fill the hut with smoke. Unfortunately someone put one down our chimney!

It has now started raining & so operations have been cancelled. We were thinking of raiding 70 Squadron but as the last squadron that were here did it & "70" counter attacked & absolutely wrecked their Mess – we decided not to!

Five new pilots are arriving today, as the complement of the

Squadron is going to be 24 instead of 18 in future.

I had a short flip today to test my engine which has been returned & greatly improved.

Well I think that is all of interest for today so I will knock off.

DIARY Monday 4th March
Dud all day. Nothing doing

65 Squadron R.F.C.

5th March 1918

It was fairly clear today & I & 5 others went down to A.S.D. [Aircraft Supply Depot] to collect 6 Camels – as six new pilots arrived yesterday to make up the new complement. With this increased number of pilots it will mean that we can always have a full Squadron for patrols, whereas before there were always two pilots on leave. Williams goes on leave tomorrow & Capt. Symons on his second leave next week, I think.

I have been patching up my room today, putting up some Harrison Fisher pictures & some cloth on the walls, it looks quite bon! will send the names of the new "peelots" shortly as soon as I get to know them, they don't seem a bad bunch.

According to Intelligence, a new 180 h.p. Fokker Triplane is going to largely replace the Albatrii. I haven't met the gentleman as yet & so I don't know if this is an improvement for us or for the Huns! I don't think the Tripes are very strong & I have hopes that they will fall to bits in the air! Here's hoping!

The weather promises fairly fine tomorrow. I fancy we are on O.P.s again. I wonder if the Hun is back in force on this Front again. I haven't been to the lines for such a long time that I am forgetting where they are!

You see the most wonderful bird formations round here in the evenings, I should think quite 500 birds gather in one huge bunch & this expands & contracts so that in the distance it looks just like a kind of smoke or cloud, perfectly distinct & clear cut, no stragglers – a good example for the R.F.C.!

Well no more tonight dear folks. Bestest love from the "Bunsoy".

DIARY Tuesday 5th March

Dud all day. No Patrols except dusk patrol – 'C' Flt on that. No E.A. seen. E wind tomorrow.

65 Squadron R.F.C.

6th March 1918

Today was pretty fine with a strong East wind. We did an O.P. from 11 to 12.15 but there were no Huns anywhere near the Lines on this Front & so we had no scrap. We were up at 14000 ft & it was pretty cold. My engine has been returned & is awfully nice now, I am glad to say, it makes all the difference if your engine is running sweetly or not!

This afternoon, Eaton & I flew down South & saw Trollope in No 45. He said that there were beaucoup Huns down South. Apparently they have moved most of their Squadrons there, which looks as if one may expect the Push from that quarter.

Wasn't that a splendid message in last night's "Daily Light"? I don't see how the Hun Push can be a success in the face of it. "They that be for us be more than they that be against us."

No letter from home today but there was only one letter for the whole Squadron – so the rest must have gone astray somewhere I think. This afternoon a fellow in No 70 apparently took a violent dislike to our Squadron Office for, on "taking off" he charged it with his Camel & knocked a hole slap through the side! With the exception of a cut face the pilot wasn't hurt. I think perambulators are about the line for No 70.

Well I don't think there is much more news at present, so I will knock off. Hope you got the parcel I sent you all right – I registered it.

DIARY Wednesday 6th March

Finish all day. Cocks leading O.P. 9 Albatri sat over me but did not come down on me. Half came down on Symons – did nothing in afternoon.

65 Squadron R.F.C.

March 7th 1918

Just a wee wee one to thank you for your letter & to let you know I am still "going strong"! Very misty & no patrol today.

A fellow called Hancock [2nd Lieutenant J. M. Hancock] who was at college with me (Le Bas) arrived here two days ago. I went up this afternoon with him to show him the Lines but shortly after he had taken off, he did a right hand turn, stalled & spun. I watched him from above & he didn't pull out of his spin but spun straight into the ground from 500 ft. He was killed instantly, poor fellow, rotten luck, wasn't it. Quite his own fault poor chap – pulled the stick back to try & get the nose up & of course the bus spun faster than ever.

I am writing at 11.30 p.m. having spent all the evening from 5 p.m. putting pale blue cloth round the wall of my hut – it looks topping now. I am rather tired but I simply had to write home!

Bestest love dearest folks. Bunsoy.

DIARY Thursday 7th March

O.P. in morning. Symons leading. Very few Huns around. Went all down Seille and saw some Huns but did not attack. To No 1 & 19 & 43 with Eaton in afternoon.

Bed late. Papering room.

65 Squad. R.F.C.

8th March

Thanks so much for your letter of today & the lovely long one yesterday which I think I forgot to mention in last night's notes.

A fairly clear day today but with a slight haze & making it rather thick "upstairs". I was on an O.P. from 12 to 1.15. Fifteen machines went up but we split into 3s when we got to the Line as it was pretty thick. Presently 4 Huns appeared fairly well East of the Line & these loafed about at our level in an unconcerned way – in fact just asking us to come & shoot them down. We played about for some time & then Balfour, who was leading our three, made for them. I was quite sure that there was some hanky panky somewhere or these four would never have waited about, so I had a good look round & sure enough about 2000 ft above were 8 little Albatrii in a beautiful straight line all waiting for us to go & attack the 4 whereupon they would have come clattering down on us! In fact it was "Ye very ancient" Ha! Ha! a dud Hun asking to be shot down "Confidence Trick". However, Balfour, having

been bitten by that sort of thing before, did not attack the four &
as soon as he spied the eight above we hove off with all speed.
One learns wisdom in the gentle art of waging war after some
time out here!

I went to the Lines this evening & shot up the trenches – the
Hun was putting some gas shells over – they leave a huge stream
of gas when they burst. They machine gunned me from the floor
but nowhere near me.

DIARY Friday 8th March

O.P. from 12 – 1.15. The odd Hun about. Pretty dud and we split up.
The very ancient Ha Ha! Confidence trick tried upon us – 4 Huns below
& 8 just above – it did <u>not</u> come off! Shot up Hollebeke Chateau in
evening. Huns attacked at 6 o'clock on 22nd Corps Front – the
Poldernock Ridge. Result uncertain at present. Bridge in evening. Lost
6 fr.

65 Squadron R.F.C.

9th March 1918

Fine weather continues. I was on O.P. today & made the acquaintance of the Fokker Triplane. They are nasty fellows. Three of us
went at four of them. The other two dived away & the Hun dived
after them. I fired at the leading Hun & the whole four transferred their attention to me! Whereupon I went down in a spiral
dive at 160 m.p.h. with the Hun firing odd bursts at me, "and
that's the way I licked 'em", I only had three holes in my bus!

The Fokker Triplane is an improvement on the Albatross I think
& much more manoeuvrable. They are also pretty "stout
merchants" – much more so than the Albatrii pilots. I only saw
them in the distance as I didn't let them come very close. The
Squadron collected two of them today, 1 destroyed & one out of
control.

Well I don't think there is any more news so will stop for today.

DIARY Saturday 9th March

O.P. 10 – 11.16. Five Fokker Tripes dived on front lot. Went for four of them after but did not get them. I shot at one but all four came for me. I faded away! Res: Pat: from 4 – 5.30. 8 Albatri came over lines. Balfour did not attack – why? Cocks got a Tripe this morning and Bill [Lieutenant G. Bremridge] one in the afternoon. The wing got 10 destroyed and 15 o of c today. The Fokker tripe is a blaster!

Dinner in Pop: with Eaton. 2 O.P.'s tomorrow!!! Rumoured Hun push at Verdun.

65 Squadron R.F.C.

10th March 1918

No letter from home today but I guess I will get two tomorrow.

We were down for two O.Ps today but owing to a thick haze all day we didn't go on either, however we were 'standing by' to go up all morning, so I couldn't go to Kirk today – I was very sorry to miss it.

It was a lovely warm day & after lunch we lay down in the sun on the grass in a field nearby. Then somebody started bombarding us with clods of earth, so we had a pitched battle all round the huts & sandbag revetments & had rather an amusing time.

I got a lovely pair of socks from Eily today & wrote her to thank her. I have applied for leave to go to Paris from the 20th to the 24th; the C.O. has forwarded it & recommended it & thinks I ought to get it. I have written to May & asked her if she could manage to get leave for Paris at the same time, wouldn't that be ripping? I ought to have a pretty good time anyway & I think the four days' rest will do me good. I wish I could get four days at home but that I am afraid is impossible as we can't leave France on "Special Leave"!

There's no wind at present & every chance of tomorrow being like today! No 1 Squadron shot down 3 Hun Balloons this morning – good show, what!

Well dear folk, bestest love & God bless you.
Bunsoy.

DIARY Sunday 10th March

Thick fog – no O.P.'s or shows at all day. Lay on grass and ragged in afternoon. Very warm. Dinner in Pop. with Withers.

65 Squadron

11th March 1918

No letter from home today as yesterday – I hope everything is all right! I guess they must have got mislaid in the post! I wonder if you ever got that lace table centre I sent you. I hope that wasn't lost!

Really I think the Prophet who enumerated the "four things too difficult for him – yea which passed his understanding" forgot the fifth, i.e. "The Boche Flying Corps"! The day before yesterday when we were on O.P. the air was stiff with Huns – today we did two O.Ps, both led by the Major, who went miles over the Lines & nary a Hun to be seen on the whole Front! It was a lovely clear day with very little wind & a ground mist, the Hun is really the most incomprehensible beggar!

All Scout squadrons now carry one 20 lb bomb per machine which we deposit over the Lines. I don't think this is giving away information as I am quite sure the Hun has tumbled to it by now! It seems to make him awfully peevish & I am sure it worries him no end to have 15 bombs dropped on him every time a formation of Scouts crosses the Lines.

This afternoon we were to escort a R.E.8 & agreed to meet him over a Hun "Archie" Battery just over the Lines. We circled round the battered town containing the "Archie" for some time but 'divil' a shot did he fire. Then we all loosed off our bombs on the town. That simply enraged "Archie" for he chucked up a huge quantity of stuff. We circled round for about 20 minutes & "Archie" seemed to take that as a direct challenge to his ability for he grew simply rabid & hurled shells at us but he did pretty rotten shooting & only got about 4 anywhere near me! Strange to say, I was rather amused by it today & didn't have "wind up" at all.

I had a most comic dream last night. I dreamt I was in a kind of Zoo where they kept all sorts of comic pre-historic beasts, "iguanodons", "dinosaurs", etc. There was a pathway between two wire railings & I was walking up this when suddenly a whole bunch of these animals came howling down the path! I had awful "wind up" but I waved my arms & "boo'd" loudly & this seemed to frighten them for they hove off. Suddenly a fierce sabre-toothed tiger came howling along straight for me! I boo'd & gesticulated with great vigour but that seemed only to infuriate the beast. I was scared stiff & rushed to the railing & tried to climb through but found some silly ass had put up wire netting & I couldn't get through! So I turned round & as the tiger leapt at me, I kicked him in the stomach "à la Charlie Chaplin". This put him completely off his stroke & he faded away. Then I woke up!

DIARY Monday 11th March

Rather a shimozzle with C.O.! Going to lead all shows. Two O.P's – C.O. leading both! No Huns at all by the favour of heaven! Sat over Comines and got archied!

65 Squadron.

12th March 1918

No English Mail for the Squadron at all today & so no letter from home. I guess I will get them all tomorrow!

I was on O.P. today from 11 to 12. Beaucoup Huns about. I was in the top lot of six. There were about 20 Huns in 3 formations but they were not very brave & kept well East of the Lines. Our bottom lot of six attacked some of them with no apparent result – however this evening two Huns were reported as shot down at that time – this was reported by another Squadron, so we were allowed them. Bon Luck! No 70 Squadron got – or said they got – 7 today but No 70 are famous on this Front for claiming Huns whenever they shoot anywhere near them, a fact which is commonly known as "hotstuffing" Huns, so we don't believe they got anything like that number! I wasn't in the scrap as the "top lot" stayed up above them preventing "umpteen" other Huns, who were above us again, from coming down at all. The Huns today were all Albatrii & not "Fokker Tripes", who are much stouter fellows than the Albatrii pilots.

Fine weather still continues, it was lovely & warm all day today. I don't think I am on O.P. tomorrow, but don't know yet for certain. I had tea with No 1 today & dinner in town with Withington this evening.

Major Howes has gone away to hospital being rather run down & has been struck off the strength.

Well that's all the news for tonight.

DIARY Tuesday 12th March

C.O. led O.P in morning. The odd 20 Huns. C.O. and Withers got two. Reserve in afternoon Cocks and Balfour each got a two-seater. I attacked one which was being archied by the Huns. [Note: The Hun used black H.E. "archie" and we used white shrapnel. There was then no mistaking the Archie fire but one could naturally not normally attack a machine with 'black Archie' round it.]

65 Squadron.

13th March 1918

All the long expected letters have arrived – 5 in all. Thanks so much for them – also the cutting about Brian Baker [2nd Lieutenant B.E. Baker, 48 Squadron], I must write & congratulate him on his decorations.

Today I went to collect a new bus – it was pretty misty & I had rather a job finding my way back. The new bus has a topping engine & so I have kept it for myself.

I wasn't on the O.P. today but was on a Reserve Patrol in the afternoon with 2 new fellows – I spent most of the time collecting them when they lost themselves, which they did at regular intervals. I was over the Lines when I saw a machine coming from our side & being Archied by the Huns so I let it pass me. It then dived off East – I thought this rather funny & so I had a good look at it & I saw it had brown stripes on its top plane, obviously a Hun! So I dived after it & fired from long range but it faded away & I didn't get him. They are wily beggars Archieing their own two-seaters to put us off. The other two fellows didn't follow me down in the dive, when I asked them "why?" they said that they didn't know it was a Hun! So I said that when they saw a machine diving East as hard as it could with me diving after it spouting tracer bullets, they might almost assume it was a Hun.

Cocks & Balfour each got a two-seater today. Eaton went to a Base Hospital today with some trouble, I am awfully sorry he has gone. Balfour goes on 3 days' engine course tomorrow, leaving me O.C. "C" Flight till Jack returns. The Flight, as far as War Flying goes, consists of G. M. Knocker! The new fellows aren't good enough yet. Jack returns tomorrow night. Capt. Symons went on 2nd leave today.

DIARY Wednesday 13th March

Symons went on leave. I went down to Arques with him and then on to fetch a bus at [?]. Trés bon. Keeping it myself. Reserve in afternoon no E.A. seen to notice. C.O. not allowed to lead shows. Eaton to hospital 'C' Flt desolate!

65 Squadron R.F.C. France

14th March 1918

There was a fog on nearly all today & no patrols. I spent most of the morning lying on my back painting comic stripes on the bottom of the planes of the new 'bus' to camouflage it from the ground & incidentally camouflage myself! It cleared up later in the day & I took up two new pilots for a practice formation to show them the Lines, but it was pretty thick over there.

Jack Gilmour arrived back from leave this evening, adding one more to our diminutive Flight. The general won't allow the C.O. to lead shows any more, as Squadron Commanders aren't supposed to do so. Balfour went away for the 3 days' course this morning.

Well I don't think that there is any more news & as it is 11.15 pm, I am going to bed!

DIARY Thursday 14th March

Balfour went to E.C.S. I.O.C. Flight! Raining in morning, no shows all day – Bon!! Camouflaged new bus. Showed new pilots the lines in afternoon. Jack came back from leave. Capt. Jackson in for dinner.

65 Squadron R.F.C.

March 15th 1918

Thanks so much for your letter of today. I was on O.P. from 1 – 2 pm. but my engine was not firing well so I couldn't keep up with the rest of the formation, I therefore fired a green light & came home.

The nimble Hun came over here bombing at 6 am. this morning, but didn't go anywhere near us. I am down for an early Reserve Patrol from 8.30 till 10 tomorrow, I am leading two new fellows on it, we might run across an odd Hun two-seater with any luck. I took a new fellow up today & he frightened the life out of me by diving down after me to within about 15 yards of my left wing tip; I waved him furiously away but he seemed to think it was a huge joke & stayed on! So I had to do right-hand turns all the way home! That sort of thing scares me stiff!

My new engine is not a success at the present & I am having it fixed up as well as possible. There is an awful lot of dust & sand on this aerodrome & it is enough to ruin any rotary engine. No more so will stop.

DIARY Friday 15th March

O.P. from 1 till 2 my engine dud had to return early. Shot on revolver range. Fine day with clouds. Strong E. wind.

65 Squadron R.F.C.

16th March 1918

Thanks so much for your 3 letters – one from Dad. The fine weather is still with us.

I did an O.P. today from 1 – 2. I was with Jack & a new fellow & there were six of us up top. Four Huns appeared & one of them dived on a fellow in the other three. So I turned on him & fired beaucoup rounds into him. He went down all "wonky" & Jack fired at him as he went down. I think I got him all right but I couldn't claim him as I could get no confirmation & this Squadron has reputation for never "hotstuffing" Huns. Then another Hun appeared so I fired at him, he turned over & spun down but flattened out & dived away for home. The remainder all faded away & the air knew them no more! Just before they went one started shooting at me, so I didn't wait! Afterwards Withington & his two merry men dove on 8 Albatrii who all padded the hoof!

I was on Res. Pat. this morning early but saw no Huns. While I was up the Huns started shelling the aerodrome with 15 inch shells, one landed on the far edge & the others were wide, most annoying of him!

I saw the very latest type of Scout today, not yet used out here – it was a peach! But I can't say any more about it. (Enter Censor baffled!!)

Bestest love & God bless you all. The Bunsoy.

DIARY Saturday 16th March

Early Res. Pretty thick – I leading Sanderson and Greaseley [*sic* – 2nd Lieutenant J.R. Greasley]. No E.A. seen. O.P from 1-2. I with Jack and a new fellow. I shot a Hun off Whiteley's tail and he went down 'a over t'. I think I got him but did not claim him. Pfalz I think, good show. To M. Capell to see the 'Snipe'. The Goods!

Read and wrote letters after – walk before dinner. Shelling aerodrome this morning.

65 Squadron R.F.C.

17th March 1918

I was on O.P. today but had no scrap; there weren't many Huns near the Lines. The C.O. shot an Albatross down today while out on his own. The Hun dived straight into the ground from 7000 ft. No confirmation for my Hun yesterday but I think I got him all right though I haven't claimed him.

I went to church this morning in the Squadron just before the O.P. & had a very good service.

I went down to another aerodrome this afternoon to demonstrate the "Camel" to a lot of infantry officers on an Intelligence Course! I landed & they all came & asked all sorts of mad questions. They said "Did these two Lewis guns fire straight ahead?" I said "Yes, but we call them Vickers guns!" Then someone asked me how the planes were fixed on! I didn't know from Adam but I murmured something about "staples & pins". I then took off & did the "odd" stunt, I think they were rather impressed – & probably thought me rather a "dog"! The job of lecturing is new to me!

Beaucoup clouds came up this evening & it may be "dud" tomorrow. Here's hoping! I am getting a trifle fed up with fine weather! Well no more news dearest folks.

DIARY Sunday 17th March

To Church at 9.30 O.P. after from 10 – 11. No Huns about at all. We on alert. Lovely day, but a bit cloudy in evening.

Read and wrote beaucoup letters after. Started shelling a bit at night – slept rottenly. [The Hun started shelling the Proven road with 16" from

22 miles away, the other side of Houlthulst Forest.] To Marie Capell in afternoon to fly the Snipe but couldn't get it to start. Adventure in cloud on way back!

65 Squadron

18th March 1918

No letter from home today for a wonder, guess I'll get two tomorrow instead.

This morning I took two new fellows up for a practice formation. I then landed at another 'drome. Here I flew the very last word in scout machines – not yet out in fact. I can't say anything about it but I took the "bus" up to 20,000 ft & it only took 23½ minutes! That's some climbing, I tell you! Incidentally it established my height record, as I have never been higher than 16,000 ft before. There is no difference between 16,000 & 20,000 that you can notice.

I did an O.P. this afternoon from 2 – 3 at 15,000 ft & nearly froze to death but saw no Huns at all. Tomorrow I am on Dawn patrol – endeavouring to strafe the early Hun two-seaters.

I have been granted Paris Leave all right & hope to go the day after tomorrow. It ought to be rather fun but I don't quite know what I am going to do! Anyway, no O.Ps for four days which is always something!

The weather is still lovely & warm & clear, there are some clouds over tonight but they are too high for dud weather I am afraid. To our great delight, we now send two per week on leave instead of one & so that brings my "leave" much nearer, doesn't it – a good line – what!

May says she cannot get any Paris leave but she wants me to go down there to see her. I am afraid it is imposs. though as it would take a day to get there & another to get back. Am awfully sorry not to see her.

DIARY Monday 18th March

Took new pilots on formation to Marie Capell. Landed and took up the 220 hp B.R. [Bentley Radial Engine] Sop: Snipe and climbs like ****! 10,000 in 7 mins, 15,000 in 13 and I did 20,000 ft in 20½ mins! Doing 72 m.p.h. at that height. Quite warm bus, too stable and with too small a rudder tho. O.P. from 2 – 3, 15,000 ft and very cold. No E.A. seen at all. [Note: The original Snipe carried four guns. 2 Vickers through the prop and 2 Lewis sat at 45° on top plane for no deflection shots.]

Wrote letters after Mess. Wireless tomorrow.

65 Squadron.

19th March 1918

No English mail at all today & so no letter today.

We were on "wireless" today & as usual when we did have to do O.Ps it was very "dud"! I was on Dawn patrol today however as it was fine at that time. I got up at 5.30 am but it wasn't light enough to leave the ground till about 6.20. I took a new fellow with me & we patrolled up & down the Lines – "nary" a Hun to be seen. Shortly after we landed it started to rain & has been raining off & on all day.

I think I ought to have a pretty merry time in Paris. I leave for there by the 9.50 am tomorrow, it will be awfully nice anyway.

The Hun has of late been dropping 15" shells around here. He got two on the edges of the aerodrome but none near the camp. Glad I am going to Paris tomorrow! I think it is a sort of reprisal for our dropping bombs on our shows [sic]. One of our new fellow's dropt his bomb on our side of the Lines by mistake, but no damage was done fortunately.

Well goodbye, will write from Paris if I have any time.

DIARY Tuesday 19th March

WIRELESS – DUD WEATHER!

On Dawn patrol at 6.20 with Sanderson. No E.A. seen. Started raining after brekker rained all day. Being shelled most of the time! One on the Proven road most unpleasant! Won 7 fr: from Jack at Auction in morning. Ragged and revolver shoot in afternoon.

Dinner in Pop: Packed after dinner, Paris tomorrow! Wotto!

Guy went to Paris on the 20th. On the 21st the "Great Push" by the enemy began. Being a Flying Man he was not recalled but was permitted to complete his leave, which he greatly enjoyed. While in Paris the Monster Long Range Hun Gun began to shell the City & several times the "Alert" sounding caused Theatres,

Restaurants, etc., to be evacuated while the people crowded to the various underground shelters.

Mrs Janie Knocker, GMK's mother.

DIARY Wednesday 20th March

Up at 7.20 Paris via Calais. Left at 9.40 from Omer and arrived Paris at 8.30. Played 'cutthroat' with two M.G. fellows and lost 3 francs!

Pretty tired. Stayed at Continental v comfy bed.

DIARY Thursday 21stMarch

Up at 10.30. To see Mrs and Mr Seth at the Elysee Palace. Very good fellow. Lunch with him. To 'Les Invalides' in afternoon and then to the Casino with Stewart after dinner – very good show. Saw girl home in taxi after. Na poo! Talked and then to bed. To B. de Boulogne after tea for a stroll. Dinner at Ciro's.

DIARY Friday 22nd March

To Bois de Boulogne in morning – talked to an inhabitant! Lunch at hotel. The two M.G.'s ordered back. Rumoured v big Hun attack in South. To Bois in afternoon more Talks! To tea with Seth, Lett, Irene B. and Andrée. To dinner with them and Andrée's brother (an awful squirt!). Then air raid sounded and we were turfed out of restaurant. I saw Ir. Home. A great girl!

Bed.

DIARY Saturday 23rd March

Round to see Ir. in morning. Saw Mrs B. and got on v well! Took Ir. to lunch at Hotel and then we went to Sacré Coeur. Lovely view. Tea at the Tipperary 4 frs: for 2 cups of chocolate! The Huns shelled Paris at 10 mins intervals all morning!!!! [With 'Big Bertha'.] This is too much. Dinner at Hotel after taxiing to G. du Nord. Badly told off in taxi! To Folies Bergeres in evening with Ir. but an air raid cut it short. To an abri and then walked home. Ir. is sweet!

DIARY Sunday 24th March

To see Ir. at 11. Gave me a photo. Paris shelled again! To lunch with Ir. at the D'Orsay. Then for a taxi ride in the Bois. Tea at 3 Rue du Bel with Ir. I left at 6, rotten leaving her. For tuppence I'd marry her! To see Seth and had them to dinner with me. Left Paris at 11.40 p.m. train full. (*Acquaintance with Ir. renewed in December 1929 on return from Athens! and again in Paris in Spring 1940 – at war with the Hun again*) [Later addition to diary]

DIARY Monday 25th March

In train till 3.45 p.m. Slept about 5 mins all night! Arrived and had huge tea at Calais. Then down to Omer. Dinner there. Then to Sqn: in Tender. Sqn had been shelled out of Pop. Then to Droglandt then South, then to D. and finally to Clair Marais. Mighty battle down South. Hun has got Bapaume and is on way to Havre. Matthews [*sic* – 2nd Lieutenant C.B. Mathews] wounded in knee.

65 Squadron

26th March 1918

Back again from Paris after a great time there. I obtained leave from the R.T.O. to leave by the 11.40 pm train on Sunday night. The train was very full & I was in a carriage with 5 others. We stopped for an hour outside Paris as there was an "Alert". The big gun had been shelling the town all morning at intervals of 15 minutes, they say it was fired from a distance of 75 miles & the height of the trajectory was from 19 to 20 miles. Our train finally arrived at Calais at 3.45 pm on Monday, 15 hours trip – gee! it was awful! I slept never a wink! I met two other fellows on the train & we went & had tea in the town – 4 eggs apiece as we had had no meal since supper the night before! Then we came down to the base & had dinner there. I found that the Squadron had left our old aerodrome & is now on one further West. Since I have been on leave they have done nothing but move! Several of our fellows were having dinner in the town, so I met them & we all came out here together. I can't tell you where we are or why we have moved, so don't ask! We are pretty well upside down at present – but will soon settle down. Quite comfy here & I have a hut to myself.

Thanks so much for about 7 letters I found waiting for me, also the pictures, etc. I ought to get my Home Leave in about a fortnight I think, if all's well – wot ho!

Did a 2½ hrs Reserve Patrol at 10.30 am today, saw no Huns but got rather a hot time from "Archie"! Beastly cold! Well no more now.

Bestest love Bunsoy.

DIARY Tuesday 26th March

4 R.P.'s!! On R.P at 11. No E.A at all seen. From Houthulst to La Bassée. Archie like ...…! On R.P. from 6 till 7.30. No E.A., very cold. We are under orders to move again! Hun now in Albert! This is awful. Pray God we stop him. Felt dud. Bed early. Very cold.

65 Squadron

27th March 1918

Just a wee line today as I am in rather a hurry. Did two R.Ps yesterday with a total of 4½ hrs flying. Never saw a Hun all day, beastly cold up, though!

Last night we received orders to be ready to move today or tomorrow. I fancy we are going to try to kill as many Huns on the ground as we can possibly manage. That's about all I can tell you at present.

This morning I arose at 6 am & went to fetch a new "Camel" with 160 h.p. Clerget engine, a jolly good "bus" too, we all have them.

Pretty dud today with low cloud. We are all just waiting to move. I guess May will have had to retire, as the Hun is at present in occupation of her place!

A pretty good shot on the part of a sentry on a 'drome down South. A Hun two-seater dived on him firing his gun – this made the sentry feel rather fed up so he ups with his gun & fired one shot at the Hun & brought him down!

Don't be alarmed if you don't hear for a wee while, as things may be a bit muddled!

Bunsoy.

DIARY Wednesday 27th March

Up at 6. To Marquise to fetch new 160 Camel. High wind and low clouds all day. No flying all day. We are going down South tomorrow. Packed in afternoon.

To dinner at farm with Jack and William [Lieutenant T.M. Williams?] in evening. Sang songs, played piano after. Quite good fun. Letter from Nickie.

DIARY Thursday 28th March

Up at 7 a.m. Brekker in farm left at 10 a.m. Lost way and Jack and [?] landed again. Found Withers and went down with him. Landed at a field at Conteville full of machines. Slept on a bank in my Sidcup till 5! The odd spot of bully and biscuit to eat! Very hungry! Started to rain – no hangars. 'buses all pegged down in rain. Crashed round in a tender looking for billets. Na poo! Slept in a barn in some hay. Quite comfy but a bit cold. Saw McElroy in 24 Sqn, 2 M.C. and 21 Huns. Raining and blowing hard. What a War! Here the Hun is checked.

65 Squadron

29th March 1918

Good Friday. In the Field (very much so).

Thanks so much for your three letters received today. So sorry I couldn't write yesterday but I had no time or anywhere to post it.

On Wednesday we all packed up ready to move & I spent the night at a farm house nearby. On Thursday morning the Squadron moved, we got off at about 9.30 a.m. but as I hadn't a map I had to land again to find out the way. I finally arrived with six other fellows at about 12.

We landed in a large field where there were some other machines, then as nobody knew anything about us (or cared for that matter!) we all sat down on the ground in our Sidcup [Sidcot] suits & went to sleep. There was no food except a tin of bully beef one man had & a few biscuits & a bottle of bad white wine! We stayed there till 5 pm. & slept. It then began to rain which improved matters no end! Machines had been landing all day & about 4 Squadrons had arrived. Then a tender came & we chased about in search of billets – with complete lack of success. Finally we got to a farm near here & had a bit of supper with another Squadron quartered there. There were no billets & so I went into a big barn with a lot of straw & chaff in it & made a kind of bed with masses of straw & lay down. After a bit I got to sleep all right. There were no blankets but it was a pretty warm night & I was quite cosy in my Sidcup. I woke up feeling pretty cold tho' & so I burrowed under the chaff & soon got warm & slept till morning.

This morning it was blowing hard. The mechanics arrived & set up the hangars for our air ships, which by the way had been out all night – & tents for us. This afternoon I went out & had a look at our present line but I can't give you any particulars of that at present. I don't know if this letter will reach you as things are a bit deranged at present – but we'll hope for the best.

Well am going to bed now as I am on an early show the morn.

Best of love dear folks from The Bunsoy.

DIARY Friday 29th March

Loafed about in morning. Hangars put up and tents. Blowing hard. Up to see the 'Lines' in afternoon. Our Line to one trench between the Somme and the 'Splitarse' road held by 500 Balloonites and G.H.Q batmen! Simply stacks of machines about. Pretty thin job – this low strafing. No leave and no mail! Poor! Fine day but high wind. Jack in my tent.

65 Squadron

30th March 1918

No mail at all today, in fact I don't think we get any mails down here.

Had rather a priceless flip today! I left the ground at 7.15 am. with another fellow who, however, crashed taking off & so I went on alone. I reached our line & flew along it at about 50 ft. Then I went East (per instructions) to look for the Hun line. I soon found it, or at least it found me for they started machine gunning from the ground, so I climbed up to about 2,000 ft & crossed the Lines. About a mile over I saw an Albatross in a field with a man beside it, so I dived on it & shot my guns, the man disappeared. Then I dived down to within 400 ft & dropped a bomb. I saw it go off but it missed the Albatross. I then dived twice more & dropped two more bombs but although I got very near it, I didn't hit it. Meanwhile as they had been "Archieing" me pretty well & also machine gunning me from the ground & I had felt a couple of shots hit my engine cowling, I hove off for a bit. Presently I saw a Hun Officer on a horse in a field so I dived at him – the horse pranced about & the officer promptly fell off! However he got up again & when I dived & fired at him again he hove off with all speed. Then I looked round & saw 4 Hun soldiers walking across a field so I dived at them & shot at them & zoomed up. When I came round again I saw all four lying in grotesque attitudes on the ground. I went very low & could see their steel helmets, grey uniforms & packs as they lay there. I think I killed all four of them. By this time as my time was up & I had been machine gunned pretty badly from the ground & 7 Albatrii had appeared, I went home.

Halfway back my engine started to vibrate like anything & I thought the whole bag of tricks was going to fall to bits – then it conked altogether & so I landed in a field quite near here. I found that I had six bullet holes in the cowling of my engine & that one bullet had made a hole as big as my fist in one cylinder & when I turned the prop round half the "innards" of the engine fell out! No wonder it conked out! Altogether I had a great time.

This low strafing which the Squadron is on at present certainly is frightfully exciting & mostly amusing – I laughed like anything when that Hun fell off his horse!

I went to collect a machine when I came back but it started raining so I didn't get it. I find that my adjectival tent leaks & has leaked all over my bed! What a war this is!

I am very fit, more so than ever in this wild existence. One of our fellows was wounded in the wrist today [2nd Lieutenant D. G. Brown?] & another shot down a Hun. A third met a Hun Division on the road & bombed it killing a great many & dispersing the rest!

Well bestest love dearest folks from The Bunsoy.

DIARY Saturday 30th March

Up at 7 on pat: at 7.15. Towne [2nd Lieutenant L.N.F. Towne] crashed taking off and I went on alone. Crossed lines and dropped 3 bombs on an Albatross on the ground but missed it. Shot at Officer on horse who fell off, four Huns walking across a field who all collapsed. Shot up badly from ground. Engine conked near Auxi le Chateau on way home. 5 holes in cowling and a hole as big as your fist in one cylinder! No wonder! [?] to collect machine but started raining and left it. Saw Dennison at A.S.O.

Raining in evening. Tent leaks. Bed under the leak! This is an awful war! Towne missing and Browne [2nd Lieutenant D.G. Brown?] wounded in wrist.

65 Squadron

31st March 1918 – Easter Sunday

Just a wee line today – please excuse this paper (buff slips) but it is all I have handy. Not much news at present.

I was on a show this morning forming an escort for some of our "buses" bombing & shooting up a road – but though we saw a few Huns we didn't have a scrap. This afternoon I was out annoying the Hun on the ground – I saw a lot of men in a chalk pit & I thought they were our men so I went down to look at them from about 20 ft. Suddenly a perfect tornado of machine gun & rifle fire was directed at me! They were Huns! So I buzzed off & came & shot them up & dropped three bombs on them but I am afraid I missed them. This is real open warfare now! You see batteries out in the fields firing also cavalry prancing about. Then I went over & shot at some fellows in a wood & they machine gunned me for about 2 minutes on end but I so skilfully dived, twisted & turned about that they never hit my bus once! I guess we have got the Hun pretty well held up down here for the present!

Coming back I got caught in a rain storm & had to land at another aerodrome but got off again when it stopped. I meant to go to the 7.30 Service but as I didn't get back till 7.15 & felt pretty tired I didn't manage it. I was very sorry as I should have liked to have gone.

We got no mail here at all which is pretty rotten but still there is a war on & this is the first bit of roughing it I have had – & it certainly agrees with one as I feel very fit & sleep pretty well.

Well that's all for the present. Don't worry if you don't hear for some days as the mail is very erratic, I am writing every day tho' as before.

Bestest love from The Bunsoy.

DIARY Sunday 31stMarch

In bed till 9.30 for a change! Very high wind. Up on patrol in morning to protect Withers [Withington] dropping bombs on the S.A. road. A few Huns around but did not have a scrap at all. On patrol at 4.15 in afternoon. Shot at Huns in Chalk pit and got shot at like ****! Tried bombing but missed them. Huns concentrating in front of Moreuil. Got caught in rain storm on way home and landed at Vert Fallon. Took off after it had cleared up. Bed early. Rained in night and dripped on to me! Took cover under my waterproof sheet!

65 Squadron

1st April 1918

No mail for this Squadron as yet but I think we may get some today – I hope so.

I was up from 8.30 till 10.30 this morning. I didn't see very many Hun troops but I saw a few on the road & these I shot at.

Things are going pretty well just at present, I think, but I can't tell you any definite news at all. It is a fine sunny day with patches of clouds & a fair wind. Last night it rained hard & my hut leaked frightfully onto my face with great apparent gusto! However I covered myself with my waterproof sheet, which rather cramped the style of the drips for they pattered down onto the sheet while I lay underneath & laughed at them!

It is very uncertain weather just now & may rain at any time. I hope you are all very fit & happy at home. There seem to be a good few pretty ridiculous restrictions about having all theatres etc. shut at 9.30. They try to make the war as unbearable as poss. at home – it's bad enough without that Heaven knows!

The mechanics are working frightfully hard at present as there are beaucoup crashes – & buses to repair & very little time to do it in. No workshop or anything & all work has to be done in the open or in a sort of extempore hangar.

McElroy is in No 24 Squadron on the same aerodrome as this flying a S.E.5. He has got 21 Huns & an M.C. & a bar. Makes me look a bit small!!

Well no more news so will knock off.

DIARY Monday 1stApril

On show at 8.30 with Spreadbury [Lieutenant H.J. Spreadbury]. No ground movement seen and only shot up once. Fairly fine all day. On show in evening with Jack. Climbed up to 13,000 but saw no Huns. Dropped bombs on barn but missed it.

Home at 8 very dark but managed to find the way. Bed early.

65 Squadron

2nd April 1918

Was up on patrol last night with Jack [Captain J. Gilmour]. We went up pretty high & looked for Huns but saw none. Then I came down to the floor & floated round near the Lines.

There is one very insolent barn with a corrugated iron roof which I tried to bomb but missed it. I must try again as a bomb would make a lovely splash going through the roof.

I was on patrol again at 10.30 this morning & managed to identify the front line – no easy job as there are no trenches – only shell holes & rifle pits. There was no transport or anything on the roads behind the lines to shoot up or bomb. However there were 4 Hun two-seaters just above the lines, I was going to attack them but couldn't as I hadn't dropped my bombs, then some of our buses appeared & the Huns hove off. One of our fellows Hugh, got a Hun this morning & saw him crash. It is very bumpy here today & you can't go down really low at all. I guess we have got the Hun pretty well held up here now – I hope we keep it up!

I wish this show would quieten down a bit for while it is on there is no leave & no mail – what a culmination of ills. "Remalle de mals" as Gin would say! Matthews [sic] was wounded in the knee some time ago & is now home – tell Gin.

Last night it rained & my wretched hut again proved its inability to repulse the attack & so I had to take cover beneath my waterproof sheet – which be it said is not waterproof.

Your letters of Good Friday have just come – the first I have had down here. Thanks so much for them dears.

Bunsoy.

DIARY Tuesday 2nd April

On show at 10.30 with Jack. Identified the front line in front of Maricourt Wood and also Hun rifle pits behind it. Shot at once with rifles. On show at 5pm with Jack. Bombed barn. Four Hun two-seaters in morning but couldn't attack as had bombs on. Saw no Huns in evening at all but four came over Amiens apparently shot at balloon from long range at Aix. Rain at night. Tent leaked.

65 Squadron

3rd April 1918

Just time for a wee line today. I was up this morning on a show. A whole Squadron Off. Patrol. The clouds were pretty low. We met No 84 Sqdn. on the line also doing an O.P. – they are S.E.5s. Then the lot of us ran into about 20 Albatri & had a splendid scrap. The S.E.s got 6 but we got none. Still it was a great show. I ought to have got one as he came straight at me & I fired like 6 but he didn't go down. I only had one gun as the other had jammed. I also fired at two bright orange Albatri. They went down but came out again. It was a wonder there were no collisions as the air was stiff with aeroplanes, half in the clouds!

I have rather a sore throat just now but not very bad. Thanks for your three letters of the 25th, 27th & 28th. I expect you will have heard from me by now.

Well no time for more now.

Bestest love dearest folks from The Bunsoy

DIARY Wednesday 3rd April

Clouds low 10! O.P. in morning got split up in clouds. Beaucoup of 84's, S.E.'s on line also beaucoups Huns! Shot at 2 orange coloured fellows. Then shot at Hun who came straight at me. Two more dived on me but were driven off by the S.E.'s! Apparently we got 2 Huns destroyed but no one knows who got them. Rain in afternoon and no show. Feeling pretty dud with head and throat. Faben out with Gilmour but je m'en fiche de cas.

Dinner with McElroy at 24. Felt v dud with bad throat and head.

65 Squadron

4th April 1918

Just a line to let you know that I am quite fit again & that my cold & throat have gone.

Really 'dud' today with rain & low clouds but I did a couple of shows in spite of it! I got lost on the second one & came back early. I am afraid that as I can't give you any news at all I shall have to stop. Thanks awfully for your letter of the 28th received today. Hope my mail has arrived home by this time. Heard from May today – she is having quite a quiet time & a pretty good one too!

DIARY Thursday 4th April

Raining and low clouds in morning. O.P. washed out. Hun attacked at Warfusée at 12.30. I went out to find out the line and strafe the Hun. We are back to the Aerodrome at Billers – Bret: found out our line and bombed and shot up Huns on a road. V.thick. Landed at Bertangles. Silly ass A.M. broke my tail skid. Back at 3.45. Had tea and went out again. Ran into rain storm at Amiens.

Got lost and landed at Sur Camps. Perfect fool A.M.'s who couldn't swing a prop! Took off and wandered back by luck. Too dud for a show. Raining most of time.

Heard from Nickie. This war is getting the limit! Feeling much better.

65 Squadron

5th April 1918

No news today I am afraid. The weather is very "dud" with clouds at 200 ft. & amazing to relate we haven't been sent on any shows. We quite expected to though as just at present there is no such thing as "too dud to fly"! However we are all pretty thankful for the rest!

I had a pretty miserable night last night, I wasn't feeling too fit as my throat was hurting a bit & it rained hard all night & simply poured through our adjectival tent, down upon us in bed! I had my waterproof sheet over me but it was beastly uncomfy!

We are contemplating another move tomorrow I think but I am not sure about it yet. I think I am going into a fairly big town near here for dinner tonight to have a merry time & get away from the war for a bit. There is some prospect of leave starting again fairly shortly but nothing is settled yet. The mail hasn't come in yet but I am sure to hear from home by it. I hope some of my mail has reached you by this time. I have written every day since I came out nearly. My throat is much better today I am glad to say & I have taken some medicine for it.

Well as I have no news that I can give you, I will now stop. Do hope you are all fit & well.

DIARY Friday 5th April

Low clouds all day.

DIARY Saturday 6th April – WOUNDED IN LEG, BON!

Fairly dud early. Flew down to Bertangles at about 10.30 a.m. one show with 3 of No 84 at 1 p.m. Up high – chased 20 Huns East. I attacked a 2 seater but he hove off and I didn't get him. Down low after. Jewkes [2nd Lieutenant J.L. Jewkes] wounded at Aerodrome at Villers – Bret. Evacuated. Got tent fixed up after lunch. On show at 6.30, with Spread [Lieutenant H.J. Spreadbury]; I identified line at Thezy. Then went over to Warfusée and went thro' hell from M.E's! Crossing trenches at 2000 got hit in right calf by one bullet from a rifle! Some shooting! Landed o.k. in great style. Went to No 46 C.C.S. [Casualty Clearing Station] and got in by a fluke as they weren't receiving and praise be to God, met May!! Tophole! Got wound, a lovely cushy one, dressed and went to sleep.

DIARY Sunday 7th April

Inoculated for a.t. Carted off on a stretcher in an ambulance with May to Abbeville to No 2 Hpl. Wound dressed. Feel v fit! Will I get home! In bed all day.

DIARY Monday 8th April

In bed all day. Read and smoked. Talked rot to the T.wire most of the time. About time I went home, the Day sister hates me! Raining on and off. Heavy shelling heard in early morning. Leg rather sore. Evacuation for some fellows in evening.

Copy of rather alarming telegram received on April 11th before arrival of letter April 9th 1918

Air Ministry to Colonel Knocker
  Post Office Telegraphs
  Apr 10 1918

S. 6.20 London V. Redtd fm Dover
  To Knocker, 12 Belvedere Esplanade, Weymouth
  P.2.Cas. AAA regret to inform you that 2nd Lieut G. M. Knocker Royal Air Service is reported wounded sixth April. particulars follow when received.
  Secy Air Minis.

In about an hour's time we were greatly relieved by receiving a second wire from Guy himself in London.

Guy to his Parents
  Post Office Telegraphs
  Golders Green. 11.10 11 Apr 1918.

To Knocker, Queens Hill, Hertford
  Slightly wounded in leg. Very fit. At present in R F G Central Hospital, Hampstead.
  Guy

By an extraordinary coincidence Guy was taken to No 46 C.C.S. where May had arrived as "Theatre Sister" the day before, so she was able to dress his wound & give him an injection for tetanus & next day she took him down to the base hospital at Abbeville in an Ambulance where he stayed 4 days & was then given a ticket for "Blighty" to his great satisfaction. On his arriving at No 46 they said they were full up & could admit no more cases but, as it was raining hard & Guy was on a stretcher, they finally decided to take him in & he was laid on the floor of one of the wards. So he narrowly escaped missing his sister after all.
  Mrs Janie Knocker, GMK's mother.

Extract from May's letter written on evening of 6th April 1918

No 46 C.C.S. France

6th April 1918

The most wonderful thing has happened. Guy was brought here wounded, just fancy – to 46 C.C.S. where I only arrived yesterday. The C.O. came to me & said "Another case, Sister, name of Knocker, funny isn't it?" I said, never dreaming of Guy, "Oh, I suppose it must be one of my numerous relations, is he a Major?" "No, 2nd Lieut – ginger haired" & I simply flew! He was as much surprised & delighted as I was, as he had no idea I was anywhere near him.

  Well, I dressed his wound & gave him his anti-tetanus injection & next morning I took him down to the Base in an ambulance. Dreadfully sorry I could only have the care of him for so short a time. His wound is a perfectly safe one & you will soon have him home – he is sure to get a good spell of sick leave. How glad you will all be to get him back safely wounded.

It really was the most extraordinary coincidence that of all the Casualty Clearing Stations in France, he should have been brought to mine & further the C.O. had said that no more cases could be admitted as we were full up, but as it was pouring with rain when Guy arrived he stretched a point & took him in. Had he been taken to another C.C.S. I might never even have known that he had been refused admittance to ours.

No 2 Station Hospital

9th April 1918

Dearest Dad & Mum,

Just a wee line to let you know that I am quite fit & hope to get home very shortly. I expected to be sent home yesterday but there was no evacuation then, so I hope to go today or tomorrow. My wound is very slight. I got a rifle bullet right through the calf of my right leg just as I was crossing the line on my way home at 7.30 p.m. on Friday last (the 6th). It didn't hit the bone or nerve & just went right through the muscle – a lovely Blighty one in fact – which I had been waiting for 5½ months! I will wire you as soon as I get to a hospital in London. Wasn't it just lovely seeing May at the C.C.S. I went to. I will wait till I see you to give you all the news. Don't worry about me as I am really quite all right & very bucked with life in general.

Bestest love to you all from the Bunsoy

DIARY Tuesday 9th April
In bed all day. Dr says I will get home today. Feeling v.fit. Raining on and very dud. Going tonight.

Guy was sent home on 10th April and did not go out again.
                    Mrs Janie Knocker, GMK's mother.

DIARY Wednesday 10th April
Evacuated at 2.0 am! Down to station, train left Abbeville at 3.30. Arr. Boulogne at 11. Carried on to the boat. In a cot, v comfy – more so than

train which was awful. Boat left at 2.15. Smooth – thank heaven! Arrived Dover at 5. Train left at 8! Arrived London in rain at 12.15! Going to R.F.C. Central Hampstead. Twist going to Russian Hosp. 23 & Forsyth with me. To Hpl at 2! Pretty dud place! Gee! But its great to be back in Blighty. Now for Nickie!!! Hun advance between Armentières and La Bassée!

May Knocker to her Parents

46 C.C.S.

17th April 1918

My darling Mum,

Tonight I got the first letter you have sent direct here & I was just wearying to know if you had heard about Guy, and now you have seen him as well, that is just splendid. How relieved you & Dad will be to get him safely at home, it must have been a tremendous weight off your minds. You needn't worry in the least about me, I am <u>perfectly</u> safe here & in a few days we are moving to a more conveniently placed hospital as this little house is too small to be much good. The night Guy came we were not receiving as we take it in turns with another C.C.S. & take in 100 or so for 24 hours. That is why he might have been sent to the other one. But it was very wet & being an officer they referred to the M.O. fortunately for us both! Did he tell you all the fun we had over his arrival & how I was chaffed & how he refused to let me wash him! I did wish I could have kept him a little longer! I am so glad to hear his leg is doing so well, sometimes those muscle wounds take some time to heal especially if a piece of clothing gets inside. He got home very quickly, did not he, & sent you the wire we arranged, but it was a great pity you got the other one first. I hoped my letter would arrive before anything. I hope you did not get a great shock. Tell the boy I thought his C.O. charming.

No more news at present I think.

Ever so much love to you & Dad & Ginger

Your loving girl

May

From the Reminiscences of May Knocker

That leave (January 1918) was a most joyful one. I discovered that my younger brother, who was now flying in France, was also home for a few days. We did a round of theatres in London and dined at the Cosmopolitan restaurant known as Frascati's. Then we went to Weymouth where the whole family was assembled for the first time in years. One night while at a theatre in London the sirens screeched a warning of an air raid. There was a light rustle and whisper of comment among the audience but the show continued as though nothing had happened. No one I saw left the theatre. At the conclusion of the performance all was again quiet outside. Although I had been through several in France, this was my only air raid experience at home out of the many which occurred in England. As we walked through Hyde Park after-wards in the dark we saw one small light only shining in one of the many windows of Buckingham Palace. The 'Lamps of London' burned but dimly during those anxious nights of air raids and alarms.

My brother returned to France January 30, and I followed him a few days later.

I then proceeded to No 46 Casualty Clearing Station at Pecquigny. Pecquigny is 12 kilometres west of Amiens, which at this time was threatened by the enemy. However, the excitement in store for me had nothing to do with gunfire or gas attacks.

At casualty clearing stations, patients arrived direct from the front line dressing stations and field ambulances, and after wounds were redressed they were passed on to base hospitals. These casualty clearing stations were small units. It was customary for one unit to receive patients for so many hours at a time and then for another in the same locality to do likewise, an arrangement which permitted each to empty its beds.

The second night while no patients were being received and we were chatting up in the office and the rain was coming down in torrents, one of the doctors suddenly entered and casually remarked: "I have just admitted a case." "But we are not receiving", said I. "No", he replied, "but as he is an officer, the sergeant sent for me and I could not send the poor beggar away in this pouring rain. Name of Knocker, too."

Now Knocker was my name and my brother, a boy of 18, was already flying in France somewhere, I had no idea where except that he had been stationed in the Ypres salient and had lately returned to duty from leave in Paris. He was constantly in my thoughts since he was in the Air Force and we had already had some terrible cases of injury to flying men. But strange to say, for the minute, I did not think of him but of some cousins of the same name, several of whom were serving in various regiments.

I turned to Captain Gompertz, the officer who had made the announcement and asked: "Is he a major by any chance?" "Oh no, "replied the captain, "a second lieutenant with ginger hair." Now I was sure there was only one of that name and description in the British army, so with a gasp I leaped up and tore down the stairs, the captain calling after me reassuringly: "Only slightly wounded in the leg."

I entered the officers' ward which was the salon of the little dismantled chateau, and at the far end by the mantelpiece on which was standing a small basin of water was my beloved Brother Boy, very dirty, washing his face and hands. "Guy", I called. "May", he ejaculated, turning in amazement. "How on earth did you get here?"

Neither of us was able to grasp the extraordinary coincidence of the meeting. It took place in that chaotic interval which followed the furious onslaught of the Germans in March. The attack had taken the British by surprise and driven them back in confusion. The advance hospitals were hurriedly withdrawn and reorganised some miles to the rear, and it was in one of these that this dramatic meeting took place. It was as if the hand of fate had stretched out to a huge chessboard on which one set of figures lay overturned, and picking up two insignificant pawns at random had placed them opposite one another. Unexplainable, indeed, save to those who firmly believe, "There is a Divinity which shapes our ends."

All the other officer patients were by this time sitting up and taking notice. The hospital staff chaffed me unmercifully and wanted to know how often I had brothers arriving unexpectedly. Sister Webb who was in charge of the ward allowed me to take peeps at him all night long, and in the morning the orderly came in and said: "Like some bacon and eggs for breakfast, Sir?" "You bet I would", said brother Guy.

It turned out that while flying back from patrol duty that night, and just as he neared the British lines, a rifle bullet aimed at the plane pierced the floor of the cockpit and passed through the fleshy part of his right leg. He said he went back to his commanding officer much ashamed to have to report being wounded because this young officer was almost at his wits end as so many casualties had occurred in his squadron, and in the Air Force at that time, that they were compelled to recruit it from the boys who were beginners.

After breakfast my brother enquired if he should not be given a dose of anti-tetanus serum. This was administered to everyone who received even a scratch, and the number of lockjaw cases was thereby reduced to a minimum. It was usually given at the time of the first dressing. In the excitement about his arrival, and believing him to have had the serum, no one had inquired about it and he remarked that he thought us a 'nice bunch' at that hospital. After receiving treatment and greatly rested by his excellent sleep he and a chest case were taken by ambulance to Abbeville and I accompanied them with the colonel's permission. From there he returned to England.

Back Home

11 April 1918 – 30 June 1918

DIARY Thursday 11th April – IN HOSPITAL WOUNDED – HOME

At R.F.C. Central. Pretty dud spot! M.O. a perfect fool! Food appalling! Wired Mum and Nickie. Nickie came and stayed all afternoon and held my hand, trés bon! Mum came after. Lovely to see her again!

DIARY Friday 12th April

In bed all day. Dad and Mum came in afternoon, Great. Nickie and Northwood called after. Read and smoked all day. Played bridge. Huns have got Messines, Plugstreet & Steenvoorde – this is awful!

DIARY Saturday 13th April

In bed all day. Elsie in afternoon. Read and smoked all day.

DIARY Sunday 14th April

In bed all day. Elsie and Mr and Mrs Sapte in afternoon, leg better. We retake Neuve Eglise. Northwood in evening.

DIARY Monday 15th April

Ten letters in morning! Heard from Twist and Symons. Nickie in afternoon bon heur! Long talk. Concert in evening. Not so bad. Neuve Eglise retaken.

DIARY Tuesday 16th April

In bed all day. Bob Craig and Janie Clark in afternoon. Bob gave me 'Traffics and Discoveries'. Leg much better. Bailleul has fallen. <u>Damn and Blast it!</u>

I wish I was out to shoot up the accursed Swine in that town.

DIARY Wednesday 17th April

Fall of Wythschaete and Meteren. Back to our old line on the ridge. In bed all day. Gin and Kathleen and Cousin Aggie in afternoon. Read and smoked all day.

DIARY Thursday 18th April

In bed all day. Nickie came in afternoon. Trés bon. Also Mrs Sapte and Aunt Minnie, they left at 4. Nickie stayed till 4.30. Going to get up tomorrow.

DIARY Friday 19th April

Up for first time for lunch. Mummie came in afternoon and Cousin Maggie. Played Auction in evening and won 2 fr.

DIARY Saturday 20th April

Up after brekker. Eily called at 2pm. We went out and had tea and to the Pavilion Cinema. Went to Cox's. Have £50 in bank, drew £5. Raining hard.

Played Auction after supper and won 6/-. News better. Line held pro tem.

DIARY Sunday 21stApril

Up after brekker, met Eily at 12. Lunch at the Craigs, then to see Molly for tea, then back. Read after dinner. Heard that poor old Moore has been killed by a shell and that Pat is missing. Awfully sick – all my best pals go West. Maybe I'll meet them in Valhalla some day. Bo has a rash, ward in quarantine.

DIARY Monday 22nd April

Quarantine washed out. Met Eily and Mum and Hugo at Euston. Had lunch and saw Eily off. Then went and got wound stripe and sticks and gloves at [?]. Mum and Hugo went to Coliseum. Met Nickie at R.P.H. and joined them. Good show. Ethel Levy and Phyllis Monkman. Saw Mum off by the 6 train. Then to New Gallery with Nickie, good.

Dinner at Frascatis – better and then taxi ride to Victoria – best of all taxi rides, beaucoup intimée! Then home by tube, so to bed.

DIARY Tuesday 23rd April

Cavalry Captain Baron von Richtofen of the Imperial Flying Corps has met his match and has been shot down and killed – good work. Rest the Soul of a brave man and a fine pilot. Went to see Fladgate. Raining, back at 6. Zeebrugge show. The finest in the war. "We gave the dragons tail a damned good twist."

DIARY Wednesday 24th April

Met Jack at 12. Went to see 'Yes Uncle' in afternoon. Quite good but didn't enjoy it v much as my nerves are a bit wonky. Tea at the Criterion. Saw Jack off and then back to hospital. Letter from Nickie.

DIARY Thursday 25th April

Met Cox at R.P.H. at 12 and had lunch with him. Got M.C. Poor old Balfour killed. Cox sole survivor of original 65. Went down to see Nickie at Norwood in afternoon. Topping afternoon! On sofa all time! Wotto! Nickie saw me off at Station. Had a priceless talk, cleared the air successfully. Home at 6.30. Had a letter from [?]!!! Priceless!! alls well! Priceless duck person from Ir. Feeling trés buckie! Poor old Bo going away I think to Fever Hopl with Scarlet. Mathews at London Hopl, White Chapel.

DIARY Friday 26th April

Met Dad at the Club at 1 p.m. Had topping lunch and then went to see a 'Box of Tricks' – very good. Went round to see Dr. T. after but I missed him, saw Miss Spink. Back to hospital at 6. To see Kennedy with Tubbs after dinner. Delightful evening. Air raid at night – frightened out of my life!

DIARY Saturday 27th April

Met Jack and Nickie at the Ai: Lunch at Callards – trés merry! To see "When Knights were Bold" simply golden! Saw Nickie off and then dinner at Troc: with Jack. No drinks tho' on a/c of blue band – rotten. To Cinema with ? after! Back at 10.

DIARY Sunday 28th April

Down to Bishops Stortford with Eggy after lunch. Saw W.M. I very good time. Back to town by the 6.30 train. Trés bon dinner at the Troc: – cigars!

Home late at 10.30! Slept rottenly and leg sore.

DIARY Monday 29th April

Ticked off by Major in morning for being late. Met King at 12.30. Lunch at Troc: I stood it!! Am pretty short of cash really! To see Mathews in afternoon, looking v fit but still in bed! Back at 6 and then to see Kennedy with Tubbs after dinner. Greatly soothed! Bed and slept v well.

DIARY Tuesday 30th April

Met Kathleen at 12.30. Lunch at Frascatis and then to see "Peg of my Heart" after, v good. Kathleen is without doubt a peach of a girl and awfully pretty too! There is something in this! Back in time for once. To see Kennedy after v soothing.

DIARY Wednesday 1st May

Down to Croydon for lunch. Saw Taylor and went up in an Avro with him. Then took up a Pup and did 5 loops. O.K. Trés bon to be up again! Tea with Nickie after, v bon too! Saw Northwood at Croydon, v.cold day.

DIARY Thursday 2nd May

Met Jack and Vi at R.D.s and had lunch at the Troc: then to see "Brig Boy's", good show but I was a bit muzzy and couldn't understand it! Then to 65 dinner with Cox, Withers, Wigg and Turner, v merry.

Back late but squared the man!

DIARY Friday 3rd May

Lunch with Padre Wilson and others at the Pic: Then down to Putney and to Katies for tea. Jack goes tomorrow.

DIARY Saturday 4th May

Down to Home for lunch. Saw them all and had v good time. Lovely day and v warm. Back at 9pm. Gland in my leg sore.

DIARY Sunday 5th May

Saw Dr about Glands, o.k. Down to Putney for lunch and tea. Saw Uncle H and then to Orrs.

Back at 6.15. Went to Church in evening, not a very good sermon tho!

DIARY Monday 6th May

Met Cocks at R.P.H. and had lunch at Frascatis, good lunch. Cox goes back on Wednesday. To Cinema after he had gone and then back home at 6.

For a stroll on Heath, with Whitehead after dinner. Lovely evening.

DIARY Tuesday 7th May

Lunch out with MC went to Cox's, balance of £46. To Cinema with girl in afternoon, quite good fun. Back at 6.15. Read and smoked and talked in evening. Raining <u>nearly</u> all day, v.rotten.

DIARY Wednesday 8th May

Went and bought bike 2 1/4 Levis two stroke £20. Lunch with Whitehead at Les Gobelins, sat in his digs in afternoon, played gramo-phone. Dinner at Frascatis – v.good too!

Back at 10. Read and smoked, Whitehead a great man!

DIARY Thursday 9th May

Met Gin and Mum at Whitely and had lunch. Sat in park with Mum in afternoon. Lovely day.

Sat on Heath with Whitehead after dinner!

DIARY Friday 10th May

Got some of Whitehead's petrol. Down to Croydon after lunch and went up for about an hour in a Camel. Trés bon!

Back at 6.30. O.M.O. out – so went out for a walk after dinner with Sister's leave, strafed by M.O.!

DIARY Saturday 11th May

Got a petrol licence with difficulty. Got bike then took taxi out of the City. Rode bike down to Hertford – Some grid! Goes like 6! Conked on hill tho'.

Tea at home, taught King to ride after tea! Ran out of petrol, back at 9. Stiff as -----! Board on Monday.

DIARY Sunday 12th May

Lunch with Eggy at Trock: then to see Mathews in hospl: saw Gorringe. Then back early.

DIARY Monday 13th May

Board in morning. Then to Cecil – rushed round for long time and got told off by a mangy Capt about my collar – lip!! Finally got 4 weeks sick leave and then Croydon if poss: got petrol licence. Came down home by the 4.30. Changed into mufti and taught King the Mo: bike.

DIARY Tuesday 14th May

Biked to college in afternoon. Dinner with J.A.J. Saw Mathew and Turner and Tennant and others. Back at 9. Lovely day. Leg dressed by Gin.

King and Elsie left in morning.

DIARY Wednesday 15th May

Down town with Dad. Mess about on bike all day and read and smoked in garden. Leg rather sore.

DIARY Thursday 16th May

To see Dr Odell in morning. No biking at all! Rotten! Messed about all day, couldn't go to Coll: in evening. Lovely warm day.

DIARY Friday 17th May

Played in garden in morning. Uncle H. and Aunt Minnie came in evening.

To dentist in afternoon, two teeth stopped, didn't hurt much. Got leg dressed in evening. Iodine hurt like stink. Sang songs.

DIARY Saturday 18th May

Leg a bit better. Up to College to meet Tubbs but didn't turn up. Tea with George Critchley – great! Saw Tennant – scoring college match on all out for 57. Pretty poor. Nelson Captain!!!

Back after tea. To Baker's to watch Gin playing tennis, Gin beaten!!!

DIARY Sunday 19th May

To Kirk and H.C. in morning, poor Sermon. Tennant to tea in afternoon v u 2. Brian flew over. Kirk in p.m. I did not go as leg pretty sore. Read poems in afternoon, felt rotten at night. Air raid at night, 6 Huns down. Bon.

DIARY Monday 20th May

To see house in [?] on bike no bon! Bike fell to bits and shed exhaust pipe! Brian Baker came over on a Bristol and landed. To see him at the Bakers and then to see Harrison's model railway. To Dr after lunch – leg poor, no tennis for fortnight and no biking!

DIARY Tuesday 21st May

V quiet all day, rested leg. Read and sketched most of time.

DIARY Wednesday 22nd May

Sketched and read all day. Leg rather sore – did not dash about much.

DIARY Thursday 23rd May

Uncle and Aunt left and Evelyn came in evening. Did nothing much all day.

DIARY Friday 24th May

Down town by 9.49. To Taylors and Cox's and Shoe shop.
Down to Byfleet by 2.15. Got Canoe, stayed on river till dusk.

DIARY Saturday 25th May

Paddled about all day. Coolish all day and not too hot. Ragged with kids. To kiddies show in afternoon – v good.

DIARY Sunday 26th May

I stayed from Kirk as my leg was sore. Punted and paddled about all morning. Tea at West Hall. Back in Punt. King punting. Mum to Kirk in evening.

DIARY Monday 27th May

Back from Byfleet. Punting in morning. To H & C in town and then to Hospital, collected all my things and got leg done. Home by 5.17.

DIARY Tuesday 28th May

Did nothing much all day. Got bike fixed up.
Great Hun attack at Rheims. Huns advancing.

DIARY Wednesday 29th May

Wire from Symons. Not coming. The little rotter.
Down town. To Cinema with Winnie Baker in evening _____!

DIARY Thursday 30th May

Read in morning, down town with Gin. Tennis in evening with the Farly girl. I played – poorly, leg o.k. Huns in Soissons.

DIARY Friday 31st May

Down town in morning. Ginger to Rec office. Got bike back – 5/-! Played Winnie Baker singles at tennis in afternoon v.hot. To dine at College in afternoon with Kennedy, v.nice. Sat in garden. To Chapel and then to Study. Called [?]! Biked home and took Winnie on carrier!

DIARY Saturday 1st June

Motor biked in morning. To tennis at Bakers in evening. Winnie and I won 2/3 sets. Then Gin and I to see the Apache Concert, very good indeed. But gee! Some heat! Miss Strubell apparently excellent! Wotto!
Huns got to the Marne! This is bad.

DIARY Sunday 2nd June

To Kirk and H.C. in morning: good sermon but v.funny and we in front seat! A man Lawson from Chingford came in a 'Camel' I went to Links with him and swung his prop.
Back to Ch: – half an hour late! Read in evening.

DIARY Monday 3rd June

Mowed lawn all morning with Dad. Then biked down town. Then biked round and round the lawn! Ginger then tried and came off crash! Too golden for words! Walked down with Gin to Soldiers Home after Supper and after short stroll came back and finished "The Red Planet", perfectly great.

DIARY Tuesday 4th June

Uncle Jack came down for lunch. To dentist in afternoon. Read and smoked all day. Saw Uncle J off. Read in evening.

DIARY Wednesday 5th June

Planted lettuces in morning. Messed about on bike in afternoon. Went down the hill after dinner and bike conked. Pushed it up the hill!

Read in evening. Headache and sore throat. Mummies birthday, God bless her.

DIARY Thursday 6th June

Up to town with Dad by 9.49 train. Went to Taylors and Cox's. Find I have £60. Got hat and went to the Air Board and after a lot of lip from a rotten Capt: was told to report at Croydon. Then to see "Chu Chin Chow" – wonderful spectacle but play poor. Home by the 10 train.

DIARY Friday 7th June

Heard from C.O. and F.E.C. in morning. Jack [Captain J. Gilmour] has got 2 bars to his M.C., Leitch [Captain A.A. Leitch], Peacock and Williams got the M.C. 65 has got 53 Huns since April 1st – Damn good! To dentist in morning teeth stopped and cleaned. Down town with Mum and Dad after tea. Florie left in morning and Mary after giving the most ghastly lip in evening and was hoofed out of the house on the spot! Read and stuck in pictures after tea.

Winnie Baker in after dinner and asked us to tennis tomorrow. Shall take [?] without doubt! Slight French success in evening.

DIARY Saturday 8th June

Planted tomatoes and dug bed with Dad in morning. Mrs Garratt and Mrs Landorf Smith in to tea. To tennis at the Bakers in evening. Played rottenly and lost every set! The Vicar consistently cheated and the lawn was awful! Played bowls with Dad after dinner.

DIARY Sunday 9th June

To Kirk in morning. Fair Sermon. To tea at Garratts in afternoon, raining. Saville Garratt there. To Kirk after that v.good sermon but not an "Excuse me"! "War march of the priests" as voluntary after service. Read and looked at Joe's Bible after Kirk. Bed early v.tired.

DIARY Monday 10th June

Packed all morning. Down town twice. Got shoes and bag and a few books and things. Coldish day. Finished packing in afternoon. To tennis with Winnie Baker after tea. Played poorly, lost 2 and won 1. Ground bad and wind fierce. Ginger to Soldiers home in evening. Played bowls with Dad after dinner.

DIARY Tuesday 11th June

Eheu! Alas!

Up to Town with Mum got my new tunic. To see the "Maid of the Mountains" in afternoon. Very good show. Tea at the Troc: Down to Joyce Green by the 6.20. Posted to No 63 T.S. Withers as C.O., Vann [?] and Shanks here. Did a little flipping very tired.

DIARY Wednesday 12th June

Flipped about in morning and did a little dual after tea. Feeling fine flying again. Some Aerodrome! In a hut with Nicholson. *In 'A' Flt with Capt. Lee as O.C. Pretty hard work here.

* See his Book p 212 "No Parachute" (Jarrolds 1968) P.

DIARY Thursday 13th June

Instructed in morning. To Biggin Hill with Nick in afternoon to see Brian. Saw new Scout and Handley. Back contour chasing. Nick is some pilot! Instructed after but none of buses would go! Wisrlet fell off in evening! Bad omen!

DIARY Friday 14th June

Early flying at 6.a.m – Instructed in morning and then Withers and I flew off in Avro to Ware. Ran into rain, landed o.k. Got taxi up to Home. Had lunch and then at 6 Withers and Dad and I went to Ware. I was going to swing prop for Withers. Withers got in and I sucked in when the bally thing suddenly started and prop hit me on head – cut a 6" gash! Carted to hospital and bled like a pig. Skull not bust – thank God! Taken to theatre and seven stitches. Feel pretty rotten.

DIARY Saturday 15th June

Some headache all day! Not allowed to move or read or anything. All family to see me. Head stopped bleeding.

DIARY Sunday 16th June

Better. Read a bit and smoked a bit. Head still bad. Bed all day.

DIARY Monday 17th June

Bed all day. Better, v.nice here at County Hospital – v.nice nurses. Got a lot of letters.

DIARY Tuesday 18th June

Better. Read and wrote and smoked all day.

DIARY Wednesday 19th June

        ditto;   ditto;

Stitches taken out. Head all healed up. Just collodion dressing out, now bandage, as bald as a coot!

DIARY Thursday 20th June

Bed all day – Better.

DIARY Friday 21st June

Bed all day o.k. Getting up tomorrow.

DIARY Saturday 22nd June

Up for lunch and came home with Mum in a cab. Feeling v.groggy but all right otherwise. Back to hospl: at night.

DIARY Sunday 23rd June

Up for lunch and home. In to Hants in afternoon. Ronnie Strubell there! Wotto! Back to sleep at hospital.

DIARY Monday 24th June

Up for lunch. Home. Gardened in afternoon. Dud day and v.cold. Walked down town. Slept at Hospital.

DIARY Tuesday 25th June

Home for lunch. Up to college in afternoon. Inspection by Sir William Robertson, v.good show. Saw Lowe and others got a lift down town in Daniel's car. Saw Winnie Baker. Slept at Hospital.

DIARY Wednesday 26th June

Discharged from Hospital. No word from Air Board. Matron to tea in afternoon. Swept paths etc and read and smoked. Chilly day rather. Mum bad gout in foot.

DIARY Thursday 27th June

Down to Hospital in morning. 3 letters, 1 from Air Board but no news of M.B. – they are rotten people! In garden fete at Hants in afternoon. Ronnie there. Awful. Felt like a wet rag! Bought things I didn't want! Mum still bad.

DIARY Friday 28th June

Went down town in morning and carried home all Mum's things. Dad bought 'em. That fish!! Read in afternoon and then clipped all the border for Dad. Pretty tiring work. Gally and the kids came in evening.

Bed at 12. Finished book "The Pendulum" – rather poor. Pretty tired.

DIARY Saturday 29th June

Heard from Air Board in morning. "Are you on leave?!!?" So I went up and saw Mr Blooming Findlay. Got to report at 63 T.S. and wait there for a Board. Phoned up Withers, told him what I thought of the Air Board, was Air Board phone! Findlay heard me, simply coughed blood and foamed at the mouth! Awful. That's put the Air Board's back up!! Lunch at Callard's and then down to Jack. Tea at Young's. Watched tennis – what tennis!

Then home by the 6.30 train – almost missed it. Headache in evening, rather tired.

DIARY Sunday 30th June

To Kirk in morning with Dad. Gin to College. Mum in bed. Ronnie Strubell in for tea in afternoon. Very nice too, awful pretty girl but I couldn't say a word!

Talked to Mum in evening.

Back Home

1 July 1918 – 30 September 1918

DIARY Monday 1st July

Up town by 10.50. Met Jack and Fergus and lunched at Troc: Then to see "Tails up" – jolly good show. Splendid tea at Troc: and then down to J.C. by 6.30 train. Rather a head in evening. Made an awful noise in Mess after till 1am. I foamed at the mouth and raged and gnashed but to no purpose. Sleep na poo till 1.30!

DIARY Tuesday 2nd July

Got up late. Read and loafed around 'drome all day, v hot. Did nothing in particular.

DIARY Wednesday 3rd July

Flew down to Wye in morning with Holland. Forced landed having lost prop. in a field. The prop started on "switch off" nearly hit it! Saw the DOC: at Wye. Up to town with H. in staff car in evening and went to see "The Boy" on a borrowed £1.10s! Dash good show. Back by 10.50. Stood up most of way – v full! Up in Withers car. Chilly night.

DIARY Thursday 4th July

Loafed around in morning. For a flip with Baron before lunch. Prop started on one bus, knocked out an A.M. Was going to Bexhill but couldn't start engine. To a dance at Vickers in evening 'dashed' good show. Met Miss Baker and 'clicked' sat out most of time – held her hand. Going to tea on Sunday. Back at 2 a.m.

DIARY Friday 5th July

Fooled about in morning. To Gravesend at 3-5. Met by Barbara and John. Trip in pony cart! Barbara v pretty but no v bon! Up to town with John after tea.

Dinner at Frascatis – Turbot with our old friend the Waiter. A1 meal.

To see Tabs' after – dashed poor show. Down by 10.55. Bed at 1am. Gee I am tired!

DIARY Saturday 6th July

Tired with rather a head in morning. V.cloudy day. Down to meet Barbara and Nickie in afternoon but they neither of them dropped up – dashed rude of 'em. Head worse in afternoon pains all over. Sports in afternoon quite good but I was too dud to notice them much. Bed directly after dinner: saw Doc, no temp, but feeling poor. Soaked up 5 quinines and slept fairly well.

DIARY Sunday 7th July

A bit better, 3 more quinines up at 12. Still feel sore and headachy but simply must go out this aft.!!! Withers heard from JC, poor little Eaton has gone West. Most awfully sick about it – one of the v best lads that was ever seen. R.I.P. guess I'll skate with him in Valhalla, anon.

DIARY Monday 8th July

Up at 11.30. Did nothing much. Feeling pretty poor. Too much quinine.
To bed after had bath at 3. Stayed in bed till 6.30, then up. Feeling better.

DIARY Tuesday 9th July

Up after brekker. Down to aerodrome. Feeling better – nearly o.k. Met Prudence at Station at 5.40. Up to town. To dinner at Frascatis, then to see "Tails up" – damn good show. Then down by 10.50 and saw her home. v good day, v nice too!

DIARY Wednesday 10th July

Just loafed about aerodrome in morning and did nothing. Up to town with Baron by 6.40. Cloudy day and inclined to rain. To see 'Fair and Warmer' – goodish show. Then to R.P.H. till 11.30 – then bed at Charing Cross Hotel.

DIARY Thursday 11th July

To Arkwright Road for Board at 9. Sat there till 11.15. Then examined after much trouble managed to wangle 14 days leave and a free warrant to Troon! Dashed good show! Down to Sqn: and packed up and grovel a free return from Troon. Up by 5.40 and caught 7.50 train down home. Raining most of day. Gal and Leon here – v tired – bed.

DIARY Friday 12th July

Down town in morning with Mum, Gal and Leon. Sent off a few wires etc, walked up. Slept in afternoon. Mrs Young into tea and brought Gladys here. Nice wee kid. Sore throat all day and pretty bad in evening. Compress round throat at night.

DIARY Saturday 13th July

Down town with Mum in morning. Did some shopping. Back for lunch. Winnie Baker in to tea. Played bowls after tea. Pretty hot day. Throat better but a bit sore in evening. Slept in afternoon. Read in evening. Got up bike from garage.

DIARY Sunday 14th July

To Kirk in morning. Loafed around in afternoon. Kirk with Mum in evening.

DIARY Monday 15th July

Gally left. Dad and Mum and I up to town in morning. To see "Going Up" in afternoon, v good but I had a sore throat. Saw D & M home. Dinner at King's Cross after sitting in R.R.H.

Up by 10.15 train. Awful trip – packed train. Didn't sleep and v sore throat. 6 in carriage.

DIARY Tuesday 16th July

Arrived Edinburgh 8 am. Raining hard. Brekker at N.B. Hotel. Got book at Elliotts. Taxi to Dodds. Cleared up in afternoon. Tea at Cairn's then to Molly's then to Burnhead after dinn. Climbed tree and went all round house. Met Maddy. Sore throat.

DIARY Wednesday 17th July

To see Mol. in morning. Left at 4.45. Taxi to town at 2.30. Met Maddy and had tea at Mackie's Très bon. To Troon by 4.45. Arrived for dinner. Bed at 10.30. Sore throat awfully bad. Slept rottenly.

DIARY Thursday 18th July

Sore throat better in morning. Did nothing much except loaf about house and played gramophone. Asprin at night.

DIARY Friday 19th July

Throat rotten. Brekker in bed. To tennis party at Blair's in afternoon. Did not play, don't like Mrs Blair! Raining later. Took Jubes for throat. Poor night. Letter from Ivy. Topping.

DIARY Saturday 20th July

Throat better. Brekker in bed. Played tennis in afternoon. Pretty badly but v good time. Big crowd in but not anything to notice. Played gram: in evening. Molly is a good girl.

Wrote letters. Molly put things in my bed.

DIARY Sunday 21st July

To Kirk with Auntie in morning. Loafed about all day. Grand day. Took 12 photos. The Boyds in for tea. Simply ragged Molly's head off at night.

In bed late.

DIARY Monday 22nd July

Saw Molly and the Georges off. Jack to Glasgow. Raining all day. To bridge with Aunt to tea in afternoon simply awful! Aunt talked all time. Lost 1/-. Played bridge after dinner and won 1/4d.

Leaving at 9 tomorrow. Rotten!

DIARY Tuesday 23rd July

Left by the 9am train. Fairly good trip down after changing at Kilmarnock. Seat in dining car. Funny little man got in at Leeds and would pay for my tea!! Arrived London at 8.30. Caught 9.16 from Lpl St. Nightmare trip! Brox at 10.30 and got home at about 11.15 v tired! May here – how topping.

DIARY Wednesday 24th July

Rather a head all day. Down town in morning. Gally came in afternoon with Mrs Young; Binnery. All 'family' here except Elsie. Played bowls with Dad and Mum after dinner. Then taught girls to play "Auction" till 11pm. Bed v.tired.

DIARY Thursday 25th July

May and Eily and Mum and I down town in morning. May and Eily left at 2.30 – went for a stroll with Dad. Gin and I to End of Term cagger at College in evening v good show sat next to I. Then joined in rage and went to hear "carrying" in Colvin. Taxied home.

DIARY Friday 26th July

To town with Mum by 10.40. Met by Eily and Dorothie then met May. Lunch at Corner House – v full. Things went a bit wrong and rather a quibble – Also rain – To see "Tails Up" again – trés bon! Saw Mum and

May off in taxi. To G. & S. Coy with watch and then down to J.G. by 6.20.

Poor old Baron killed also fellow from my room – Gunther.

Lost 7/- at bridge!!

DIARY Saturday 27th July

Down to shed in morning: saw Lee. No flying at all for me! Washed out at 12 and then up to town after lunch with Campbell. Rainy day. To see Hun busses at Islington. Dinner at Frascatis before that sat in R.P.H. Home by 9.30 after long discussion on higher ethics with C! Mo: biked home in dark.

Brown killed and Taylor burnt in collision. This is some Squadron!!

DIARY Sunday 28th July

Up dual with Lee in morning. Fairly fine all day. Washed out in afternoon – down to Dartford on bike Ch: with Baker biked home. Took a Camel up after dinner and flat spun trying to loop it! In a trance! Bed fairly early.

DIARY Monday 29th July

Up at 7.30, v thick, took up Camel didn't feel very happy! Loafed round after brekker. Took up Campbell in Avro before lunch and then washed out. To see Barbara at Northfleet. To Cinema with B. & Phyllis not so bad. Home for dinner, played billiards with McGuire after dinner.

DIARY Tuesday 30th July

Did nothing in particular all day. Flipped twice v.hot & stuffy day. Dance in evening. Jolly good show. 9 – 2.30. Danced a lot and quite well on the whole. Flew to Dover at lunch and brought back awful Camel. Saw Cummings [2nd Lieutenant J.C. Burnay-Cummings?].

DIARY Wednesday 31st July

Took up man in morning. Washed out after lunch.   To Fete at Gravesend. Saw Barbara and went to Cinema and then meal at Kings Head! Up town after. Slept at Charing Cross Hotel – v tired.

DIARY Thursday 1st August

To Board at 9 a.m. Finis at 11.30.   Lunch at Elysée with Shone and then down home in afternoon. Dorothie there and May and Eily. Played croquet. Bed at 11.

Got to leave at 7.40 tomorrow.

DIARY Friday 2nd August

Arrived at 11 a.m. Pretty late! took up Sgt Drew. Williams drowned in Camel in Creek. Went to forced landing.

One or two flips in day. Rain in afternoon. Yank nurses in to mess!! Bed at 11.

DIARY Saturday 3rd August

Rain till 10.30. Then flew hard all day and afternoon. Showery. Took up Camel and dual Camel and instructed on Avros. To Australian hospital for small dance at night. V v.dull. v.rude girls those M.T. drivers are!

Bed at 12.30. 3 hrs flying in day. v tired.

DIARY Sunday 4th August

Flew in morning. Gin and Bunty came down at 4pm not having had my wire. Tea at Sqn. Did a few stunts in Camel for them. Then they left and I instructed rest of time. Not to Kirk. No time.

DIARY Monday 5th August

Early flying. Dud after 7. Rain at intervals in day. Instructed a bit till 12.30. To tennis at Keyes with McGuire – what tennis and then played frantic games. Raining hard. Bridge in evening. Lost 1/- played with Fenton – shan't again.

DIARY Tuesday 6th August

Fairly fine all day with Showers. Down to Biggin Hill with Sgt Drew in morning. Saw Brian and Jack for lunch. Instructed in evening and got Moxom off on Camel avec beaucoup difficulté!! Did about 3 hrs. Read after Mess. Bed at 10.30.

DIARY Wednesday 7th August

Showery all day. Instructed in morning. Flew down to Brooklands with Nick in afternoon saw "Snipe" "Salamander" "Snail" and "Scooter". Then came back for tea. Got off Sgt Drew Solo. Crashed undercarriage landing! His is the edge!

DIARY Thursday 8th August

Early flying. Got off Drew again. Instructed till 12 and then I flew Sleigh to Chingford, landed caught 1.20 train at Ponder's Enf and to home, Sleigh flew back. Saw May. Tea and Supper at house. Caught 8.37 up. Great way of getting home. Down by 10.30, v tired. British push on the Somme v.good show.

DIARY Friday 9th August

Instructed in morning. Not much to do. Fine day. Washed out at 6 and went to town with Withers. Dinner at Frascatis – v good dinner and then to see half of "The Lilac Domino" – quite good. Down by 10.55. V.full train. Capture of Warfusée and Caix, and Severin. <u>Dash</u> good show.

DIARY Saturday 10th August

Davis landed into Leaton. Instructed in Morse. Sgt Drew crashed at some spot miles off. Down to Isle of Grain with Nick. Ragged 'em like sin! Saw "Guiffon" then to tea with Taylor – in real Croydon form. Back at 5. Got King off solo and did dual Camel with Grant. Got Morley off solo but he crashed taxiing! Ye Gods! Ives and May – both spinning hard – played billiards after dinner.

DIARY Sunday 11th August

To Kirk at 9. Flew in morning. To Wye in evening. Came over at 15000 and back at 1,000 in the dark. Heavily [?] on landing. Saw Diamond the Major at Wye. A very good chap.

DIARY Monday 12th August

Dud till 7. Early flying then. Withers down in afternoon. Flew till 12.30. Up to town and met Withers at 7.30. Saw Tenant in R. & H. To dinner and "Tails Up" with Withers and Shone. Slept at Withers flat great rag! Down by 7.30 in morning.

DIARY Tuesday 13th August

Flying a good deal all day. Did nothing in afternoon. Moxom landed at Tilbury. Tuck and I sought him at 9.15 but failed. Bed late v.hot.

DIARY Wednesday 14th August

<u>My "buffday"</u>

I attain the great age of 19! Flew in morning and Moxom then Nick and I landed at Halls Park and got out and pushed off home. Gally there. Came back at 8.57 and down here by 10.50. Rotten indigestion all day. King crashed after finding Moxom.

DIARY Thursday 15th August

Early flying at 7.15. Flew in morning. Wash out at 12.30. Up to town – saw Joy. Tea and Cinema. Trés bon! Dinner at Frascatis, indigestion bad. Down by 7.30. Dance in evening till 2 am – Miss Mansell good fun. Ives and Nick spinning hard!

DIARY Friday 16th August

Flew hard all day. Did 3½ hrs – 1hr 40 landings with Morley no bon! v.hot day. Bathed in afternoon – v.nice. Played bridge in evening and won 1/-. Awful indigestion at night. Slept rottenly.

DIARY Saturday 17th August

Faber came, took away "Snipe". Flew all day. Lee washed out and I carried on. Indigestion better. Did nothing much.

DIARY Sunday 18th August

No Church in morning. Flew all day. Pretty hot day. Nothing in partic. happened.

DIARY Monday 19th August

Early flying. Did 1 hr 40. Washed out at 12.30. Met Dad at Station and lunched at Club. Man had a fit in middle! awful! There got cig. holder. To Cinema in afternoon, Dad left by the 6. I to meet Shone but he didn't drop up. Met Major Hague, a lad and he stood me dinner and a show – B.B's. Don't like him much. Down with Nick and some Yank nurses by 10.55.

DIARY Tuesday 20th August

Flew in morning and afternoon. Did two hours. Started at 3.45 and washed out at 6.30. To dance at American Hospital in evening. Very great rag indeed. Big Ball and "bookoo bon" memories!! Met Miss Cavo an' ah! Stopped at 10.30. Great show.

DIARY Wednesday 21st August

Pretty hot day. Did a good deal of aviation. Harvey quite good. Very few foul ups most of mine sick. Read in afternoon. Dropped note to Miss Cavo. at American. Then to forced landing with Nick in morning. Nick to dinner at Dettering with Tubbs. Flew back in moonlight at 9.15. Lovely up. Got into searchlights and field lights. Nick and I did night landings. Trés posch!

DIARY Thursday 22nd August

Early flying at 6 a.m. did 1 hour 5 mins with Harvey, v.hot day. Went around in shorts and shirt. Did no flying in afternoon. Met Miss Cavo. at the Station at 5.5. Up town. Dinner at Frascatis – iced Anjou! Then to see the "Bing Boys" on Broadway. Trés bien! Down by 10.55. Estelle is a great girl, v.good fun. Spanish to boot!! [?]!!

DIARY Friday 23rd August

Flying in morning did 1 3/4 hrs dual. Down to Croydon in Pup in afternoon. Tea with Nickie Rowsell in Y.M.C.A. Quite a different place now. Flew till dark on return.

DIARY Saturday 24th August

Inoculated in morning. Flew in afternoon. Sgt Drew forced landed at Cobham. I flew Lee over river and landed in field. To Bexley to see House, no bon at all. Back, played Bridge, lost 2/- to Douglas. Good game but bad hands.

DIARY Sunday 25th August

Collected Lee in morning then went to Cobham with him after Drew, v bumpy and no good fields around at all. To concert at America in afternoon, not too bad at all.

Miss Cavo and two others came round here to tea after. Good fun. Did 15 mins flying and then rained. Talked to nurses in 'accif' till 8. Read in evening.

DIARY Monday 26th August

Flew early and did 2 hrs 5 before brekker. Flew after and arranged about new flight. Washout at 12.30. Bridge in afternoon lost 5/- to Mac! Up town with Duggie at 5-6. Met Thews, Drummond, Peacock and Withers at Carlyle Club. Dinner at Savoy, v.good, sat and listened to band after. Great time. Then to dance at hall, v.poor £1's worth. Jenkins is a prisoner, thank God. 65 has done v.well. Slept at Charing Cross Hotel.

DIARY Tuesday 27th August

Flew in morning but didn't do much. Low clouds and rain at intervals. Got office fixed up. Two Camels only left!

DIARY Wednesday 28th August

Flew all day. Nothing much doing. Leading formation of Camels – wind up 'orrid'. Recapture of Bapaume, splendid. Eric Coates has been killed – found shot in head 3 months after.

DIARY Thursday 29th August

Early flying. Washed out at 12.30. Up town and met Quinn at 3.20, 40 mins late – rotter – confound Potter. Tea at Callards, then to Cinema. Saw Quinn off by tube. Down by 6.20. Enormous dancc in evening! All America here, Estella Cavo trés bon! Danced almost every dance till 1.

The girls left. We danced together till 3 and so to bed. Damn good show. Winchester killed at Eastbourne – rolled his wings off, R.I.P.

DIARY Friday 30th August

Flew in morning at 12. Pretty dead after yesterday but feel v v.fit. Instructed in evening. Played auction, won 6 /- off Adams. Billiards after dinner. Bailleul captured by U.S. Topping, Hooray!!!

DIARY Saturday 31st August

Flew in morning a bit – nothing much! Rang up Miss Cavo and arranged show. Flew in afternoon till 4.30. Then washed out and took Potter's car to Station with the White Rabbit. Awful lip from Potter. Met Miss Cavo at Station up town with Quinn and Newell. Met Jack at R.P.H. To dinner at Frascatis. To see "Naughty Wife" – jolly good show. Down by 10.55. Raining. Top hole evening. Got on trés bon! On outskirts of Peronne.

DIARY Sunday 1st September

Duggie with v.bad throat. Up for flying in morning, v.high wind all day. Flew down to Dettering with King in morning. Had the odd spot with Northwood and Tubbs. Jack for lunch. Flew in afternoon. Morley forced landed but I couldn't get it off owing to wind. New Camel arrived. I did in a King Post taxiing out Camel. Flying washed out at 6. Duggie to hospl: my room shut up cold day – very. Kemmel retaken by us.

DIARY Monday 2nd September

Flew a bit in morning, then took up Jack for a flip and looped him twice. He took it very well, liked it. Lunch at Charing Cross, down home by 3.30. Arrived at 5. Girl in for tea, not too bad at all.

Read and played croquet in evening.

DIARY Tuesday 3rd September

Up by the 9.45 down here by 11.45. Flew in afternoon and had formation. Down to Riley's crash at Ditchling, handed on Camel and saw him in hospital. Then flew off to Shoreham to get filled up but got dark and so I spent night at Shoreham. Passed away shortly! V.good fellows there.

DIARY Wednesday 4th September

Left Shoreham at 9.30. Flew 110 Le Rhone in morning and did a little formation. Washed out at 12. Up town by 2.30 sat in R.P.H. till 5. Saw Varley discharged from Army with paralysed arm. Tea at Callards and then down to Putney. Music song after dinner, slept in Jacks room.

DIARY Thursday 5th September

Raining early and cloudy all day. Played piano at Putney in morning. Down by 11.45. Flew in afternoon, led formation to Maidstone and back. Lots of Camels now. Thunderstorm washed out at 6.30 for night. Lost 6/- to Adams at Auction.

Cold in evening and rough throat.

DIARY Friday 6th September

Flying in morning. Rain and low clouds in afternoon, was going to fly home but too dud. Wired Joy. Up town by 6.44. Joy didn't drop up. Caught 8.30 down home. Slept at home. Cold coming.

DIARY Saturday 7th September

Brekker in bed. Left by 9.49. Down here for lunch. Pretty dud in afternoon. Flew a bit. Played auction and went down 5/6 – to Adams! Rotter!

DIARY Sunday 8th September

Dud for early flying, to Kirk in morning. Bad cold. Flew once - formation.

Down home by 3-5 train, sat in house all day, cold awful! Trebene, hot bath, aspirin, and hot Whiskey. That fixed it all right!

DIARY Monday 9th September

Brekker in bed. Cold better, caught 9.49 up. Down by 11.45. Howling wind. Only flew once. To American hospl, for concert but got there too late. Small dance instead, great fun. Learnt a lot from Miss Lewbell. Raining hard.

DIARY Tuesday 10th September

High wind. No early flying. Up once in [?] to Biggin Hill, nearly "crashed" landing. Up town by the 1.44 with Nick. Went to Cox's £49.16.9. To exhibition of Huns. Tea at Troc. Dinner at Putney. Jack's last night at home. Katie and Charley there and Orrs. Pretty cheery evening, talked to John till 1.30.

DIARY Wednesday 11th September

Saw Jack off at Waterloo. God speed him and send him all the luck in the world. My v best pal and the best lad in the world.

Heres to our next meeting. Uncle and Auntie awfully brave. Down by 11.47. Did 1½ hrs flying formation. Down to Detling and climb to 11,000. Pretty high wind. Tried loop roles with poor success! Read in evening.

DIARY Thursday 12th September

Did 2½ hrs flying in morning. Did formation to Chingford and Shod. Then fought Suttons farmer. Then he formated with me and scared me stiff! Came home did v.good loop rolls.

Met Joy at R.P.H. in afternoon. Tea at Troc: and then to Cinema – saw Raffles Dance at Sqn: in evening. Good fun. Learnt a lot of dancing. American attack at St Michael – dash poor.

DIARY Friday 13th September

Brekker in bed! Went on leave in morning, met Gin and Mum. Lunch at Troc: £4.4/-! Then to see "Soldier Boy" – jolly good show. Down by 6 train. Dad with a frantic cold! My legacy. Little Eaton is a prisoner. Thank God hooray! Americans doing splendidly.

DIARY Saturday 14th September

Raining hard nearly all day. Down town with Mum in morning and then sat and read and smoked in front of fire. Dad in bed nearly all day. Up in evening. Played piano in evening.

DIARY Sunday 15th September

Fine day. To Kirk in morning. Stayed to HC. Vicar v.poor. Saw Milford after. Dad up after brekker, better. Bowls with Dad after tea. Phoned for extension of leave and got it granted till Tuesday. Bon. Stayed at home with Dad in evening, not to Kirk with Dad and Mum. Long talk with Mum in afternoon, bless her.

DIARY Monday 16th September

Fine warm day. Down town with Gin in morning. Then came home and took house to bits. Took up carpets and rods and rolled carpets and packed pictures. Crashed in W.C. and nearly broke my back. Down town after tea and ordered cab. Sang and played after dinner.

DIARY Tuesday 17th September

Up by 9.47. Arrived for lunch. New Major here, seems rather a hot air Wallah! V high wind. Did a little flying and fired at Chingford. Rain at intervals.

Great dance in evening. On till 2.30. Danced a lot and enjoyed it awfully much. I am mad on dancing. Bed at 3.30. May it be dud tomorrow.

DIARY Wednesday 18th September

Alas no! A cloudless day. Up at 6.15, awful!! Feel v tired. Flew a bit and led formation. Flew after brekker. Led formation to Chingford. Engine cut out, piston broken. Landed at aerodrome at Chingford. Came back in a 1½. Flew in afternoon but engine dud.

To 'America' with Houseley after a dinner at the Cont. Good time. Bed 11 v.tired.

DIARY Thursday 19th September

UP at 9.40. Missed brekker. Had bath, v cold day. Flew to Orsett [?]. Gowans crashed. Only one Camel left!! Hardly flew at all, v high wind and rain at intervals. Collected Gowans at 7. Read after dinner. Feel at peace with the world!

DIARY Friday 20th September

Flew in morning. V high wind. Washed out in afternoon.

To town with Houseley after tea. To see a 'girl' of his but she was out. Dinner at Frascatis. "[?]" at Bing Boys. Down by 10.55. Pretty cold.

DIARY Saturday 21st September

Up late. Down to drome at 12. Flew a bit. High wind. Flew bit in afternoon. Painted Camel red and white, trés bon effort!

Bed at 11 slept rottenly. Down to Detling after lunch good show!

DIARY Sunday 22nd September

On at 9. Flew to Chingford with Gowan where he landed and crashed after lunch. Formation in morning on new Camel.

Home by 4.30 from here. Arr: 7.49. House upside down. Read and talked and smoked. Last visit to Homeland. Bed, slept rippingly.

DIARY Monday 23rd September

Up by 9.49. Flew in afternoon. Formations etc. Flew over to Dunton. Got Sgt Henderson off. Landed in ploughed field and couldn't get off.

Rushed about in rain and finally g<u>ot</u> flown back from Orsett.

To binge at Aussie in evening. Quite good fun on the whole. Danced a bit v.cold.

DIARY Tuesday 24th September

Did 3½ hrs flying. Up early. Everything went wrong in afternoon. Very bad up and wild generally.

Dinner at Bull with Houseley. Tried to find P. Baker but failed. Loafed about Dartford after dinner trying to find car. Bed 11. Dashed cold.

DIARY Wednesday 25th September

Did 2½ hrs flying, misty day. Flew to Hainault farm after tea, v.bumpy. Talked philosophy to Houseley after dinner and then bed. Cold.

DIARY Thursday 26th September

Flying hard in morning. Down to Detling for lunch with Houseley. High wind. Back in afternoon. Houseley feeling rotten and I with a cold. Fire in room.

Talked and went to bed early, v cold day. To Aussie Hpl after tea. Saw Robbie.

DIARY Friday 27th September

High wind. Flying at 11. Formation or [?]. Flying in afternoon. Washed out at 6pm. To see "Bat" at Orsett.

Read in evening in front of fire. Duggie back from leave.

DIARY Saturday 28th September

Early flying at 7.30. V high wind. Didn't do much. Flew off 1574 for Sgt Henderson from field across Creek. V.little room. Got flying start and got off in 15th. Up to town after lunch. Down to Putney. Walk (route walk) with Uncle, Gin and Mum before tea. Up town with Gin and Vi. Dinner at Frascatis – not a great success. To see "Roxana" jolly fine show. Back by tube, awfully full. Jolly cold and tired. Saw Baker in morning. Poor old Forsyth killed.

DIARY Sunday 29th September

Down by 11 train. Raining. Sgt Henderson spun 1574 into Ground this morning. Choked – same as yesterday – tried to turn. Killed at once.

Wonderful news. All Houthulst Forest and Sladen captured. General advance all along line and the Bulgars suing for peace. To Am. hpl in afternoon. Tea at Bull. To Kirk in evening.

DIARY Monday 30th September

Raining all morning – no flying. Cleared after lunch. Flew over to Brooklands and landed. Spent night with Elsie.

Rather a rotten cough. Saw the Tarrant Aeroplanes.

Back Home

1 October 1918 – 31 December 1918

DIARY Tuesday 1st October

Left Brooklands at 12.45. Flew back for lunch. Dashed cold. I am taking over 'A' Flt for Grimwood. Dam' and blast. I hate Avros. Did a little flying. To Auzzie for binge, jolly good fun.

Miss Holroyd is v.bon. Left at 12.30.

DIARY Wednesday 2nd October

Up at 6!! Nearly dead. Flew all morning, did 3 hrs. Formated on Camels.

Kathleen wired she couldn't come. Up town with Duggie. Tea at Troc. Bought gloves – £3-3/-. Putney for dinner and bed. Saw Mum and Gill. Mr Wilkins in after dinner.

DIARY Thursday 3rd October

Down by 6.49. We are going to Redcar on Saturday. Curse it. I am flying two-seater Camel. Curse it again!! To Aussie after lunch with Houseley. Down to Sqn for conflab after. Round to shack with Houseley after dinner. Topping time. Talked about everything under the sun till 11. Duggie turned up at 10.30. Long talk with Holroyd. I am sorry for her she is a good sort.

DIARY Friday 4th October

Moped about all day and discussed move. Up town by 10.30 train. Went to Cox's. Have about £40 odd. Down to Putney for lunch. Up town with Mum in afternoon.

[Remaining part of page unable to be read]

DIARY Saturday 5th October

Rain in morning. Set forth on two-seater with Adams. Grew v.thick and [?]. Landed the noxious beast with difficulty and had another brekker. Rain again. Flew back to J.G. where Adams crashed! I landed by brute all right. Rain all day   prospect of starting finally – abandoned. Stick with Houseley after firmly determined not to go to Shack. Met Miss Wardle and finished up finally at Shack for supper.

Talked till 9 and then to bed.

DIARY Sunday 6th October

Rain till 9 and then cleared up. Set forth at head of my Camels who at once lost formation. Bumpy as sin! Boyd, Harvey and Gidding left after Hunt. Landed at Grantham – spittle gate. Houseley crashed, Mayes and I o.k. Mac: turned up later with a Sgt Burridge who crashed! Graham and Rogers arrive later. That's all! Awful place this. Dinner in town and then bed right early. Apparently both my Camels are crashed and six or so Avros!

DIARY Monday 7th October

Raining all day to beat the band. Simply loafed about and got fed up. Pat up at the 'Angel'. Spent day phoning all round the Country and playing Auction where I lost 4/- in half an hour!

To music hall after dinner. Jolly good show on the whole. Bed after that. Talked to Houseley in bed.

DIARY Tuesday 8th October

Up at 6. Fine day and not wet. Took off at 7.5 and pushed off. No bumps at all. Got over York by 8.15. Very cold up. Finally arrived at Redcar at 8.50 nearly frozen to death and having landed at Marski first. I was first to arrive Mac and C.O. arrive later. Maye crashed on way up and others either got lost or didn't start. Good old Rednose! Wonderful flying here.

Wired Gally and met her at Middlesbro' at 6.15. Still a pretty little devil as ever but rather sweet. Got on pretty fairly! Back at 9.10. Cold evening.

DIARY Wednesday 9th October

Rain and then rain all day long. Played billiards in morning. Loafed around all day. To M'boro' with Adams after tea. Met Gally and we went to see "Nothing but the Truth" – jolly good show. Had a v.posh evening altogether. Back by 11.20 after a long wait in a club.

Bed v.tired.

DIARY Thursday 10th October

Loud and fruity gale all day. V.little aviation. Played billiards and loafed around tarmac all day. Went to bed fairly early and slept well. Duggie arrive with some others.

DIARY Friday 11th October

Lovely day. Flying hard. Amused myself by sand hopping – absolute paradise. Did several formations – one v.good one with Houseley. Lecture by Major at 6. Talked till 6.40 when I hooked it and ran like sin to the Station and hopped into train as it was moving off – nearly dead.

Dinner with Gally and then for a stroll, v nice time. Trés bon kid. Back by 9.10. Squadron is in a spin – no A.M.'s or pickups or any bloomin' thing!

DIARY Saturday 12th October

Early flying at 6.30. Warmish day but squally. Did a formation or so but rained on and off. All the buses got soaked and I got v.fed up and cross.

Washed out at 4pm. Talked in room till mess. Then listened to Capt Blake till 11.30 and so to bed. Pretty chilly at night. Gally rang up. Dance washout.

DIARY Sunday 13th October

To Kirk in morning v.good service. Finish day. Did some Aviation – formations etc.

Wrote to Gally. To bed at 9.30. Pretty tired. Fire in room. Hun accepts the 14 points. Hope we don't give him an armistice.

DIARY Monday 14th October

Misty and dud all day. Not much flying. The Major to Confab York. To Middlesboro' with Duggie by 6.48. Met Gally for dinner. Tried to get into shows but all full up. Sat in Grand and then saw her home.

Chapter of accidents:

1.　　　　　Couldn't find my eye mask.
2.　　　　　Broke identity bracelet.
3.　　　　　Gally pinched silk hanky and knife.
4.　　　　　Lost fountain pen – hence this pencil!

Pretty chewed up. Various rumours abroad.

DIARY Tuesday 15th October – FALL OF ROULERS

Lovely fine day. Formated a bit. Went over to [?] to try and fly mono or tripe. Washed out [?] [?] pinheads. Came back and did a lot of dashed silly low stunting. The demon entered into me. However D.V. I shall not do any more stunts below 1000ft. 63 are going to France as a service Squadron I think. Jolly good news. What ho for the merry men!

<u>Roulers has fallen.</u> Praise the Lord of battles hooray. Wonderful news.

DIARY Wednesday 16th October

Fine day. Flew a good deal. Formations etc.

Concert in evening. Fair show but too long. Gally couldn't come. Bed 11.30.

DIARY Thursday 17th October

Finish all day. Raced Houseley on Camels. Didn't fly v much.

Toggs, Mac and Shanks abso: blotto at dinner! Had a binge after and got rather tight myself. The news came thro' that Lille and Ostend had fallen! Cheerie ho! That finished me off! Naval No 3, other efforts. Bed at 11.30.

DIARY Friday 18th October

Still a bit blotto in morning! This wore off after brekker. Up for early flying at 6.30. Flipped a bit and felt better.

Dud all day, with rain. Mooned about and bed early.

DIARY Saturday 19th October

Dud all day. Rain on and off. Did a bit of flying and one formation.

Tried to get on to Gally but failed as she was out. Stayed at home and read in evening v.fed up. Zeebrugge has fallen.

DIARY Sunday 20th October

To Kirk in morning. Flew after for a bit. Rain on and off all day low clouds. Footled about. Kirk in evening with Pilcher and Houseley. The only three there – rather a fiasco.

Bed early.

DIARY Monday 21st October

Fine in morning. Formation with Burns – couldn't lose the man! Rain after lunch and clouds at 50ft – no good. Washed out flying.

To M'boro' to see Gally in evening. Dinner and then sat in Grand. Had a ripping time, but made an awful fauxpas!

Bed at 11.30.

DIARY Tuesday 22nd October

Early flying at 7. Formation with Burns. Had row with Graham and Ives at brekker. They try to run my flight. They can go and eat coke. Fairly fine. Sent up Burns on Rednose to do 15000 at 12 noon. Not yet returned – a snip crash. Gas chamber at G. Filthy C.O. foaming around the tarmac talking brick dust about 10 pilots.

Only one good Camel. Rest in A.R.S. Flew Bristol Scout and looped it – Bon. Just heard Burns been picked up by Trawler in the North Sea and Rednose has sunk. Oh heck is right: isn't it pitiful.

DIARY Wednesday 23rd October

Flying all day. Fairly fine. Formated with Sgt Higgins. Duddish later. Met Gally after dinner, sat in Grand Hotel and talked. Topping time – she was so bon but I insulted her rather I fear. Back at 9.10. Slept well. Taking course here bon.

DIARY Thursday 24th October

Early flying. Not much doing. Flying in day. Formations etc. Rather short of Avions just now. Sankey forced landed after tea and I had to go out in the pitch dark to run up his engine – wouldn't start, rather a fool errand. Up with Hansard, f. landing.

Slept rottenly.

DIARY Friday 25th October

Flew back Sankey's avion after brekker – Flying in day, not much tho. Mostly foulups doing tests. None of our gunbuses are ready! To M'bro' in evening to see "13th Chair" with Gally. Quite good but when the lights went out – oh tush! Can't get Gally at all. I don't like the signs and wonders! Back by 9.10 but Gally didn't come to see me off – rotten! Slept rottenly – and reading and smoking till 2.

DIARY Saturday 26th October

Irving crashed 6.30. The other Camel used for tests 15000 etc all day. The other one in and out of A.R.S. for repairs all day. No great work done – luffly day. Fullars over on Albatros which I photo'd. Sgt Burridge then crashed 4197 – the pinhead. Leaving us one Camel. Duggie and Tors and I to dinner at the Bull. Walked back. Slept well.

DIARY Sunday 27th October

Lovely day. Kirk in morning watched Philips loop and roll. Lost 2/6 to Sankey! V .bored. Lead a formation on the two-seater but was scared down. No buses = no pilots – there you are. Read in evening. Wrote 5 letters.

DIARY Monday 28th October

New bus out of Flight. Quite good bus but engine throws oil. No formations. Sent up Phillips to stunt. Then had them cleaning avions. Woolhouse did his 15000, came down to 7,000 on his back! Bus in an awful state, wires in knots. Rang up Gally but in bed with flu. Lecture by C.O. – who talked awful tripe for an hour. I am getting fed up with this anyhow. Bed late – slept well.

DIARY Tuesday 29th October

One bus only. I flew a bit. Wind rising in afternoon.

Wrote many letters. Concert in evening – not a bad show – rather too long. Rough house in mess after. Bed at 12 slept v.well.

DIARY Wednesday 30 October

V.high wind all day. One bus out of A.R.S. – a rotten bus with a dud engine. Sent up Sankey. No formation. Wind rose to a gale after lunch and I washed out flying. Turned an Avro over.

Walked down town with Houseley and Mac. Tea at Lonsdales and then to show. Quite good. Supper at Lonsdales after that with Maggie and [brother in law?]. Sang songs and then walked back singing. Letter from Mum saying King had shot himself on Monday afternoon. May he rest in peace and may God comfort poor Elsie.

Collapse of Turkey. Splendid news.

DIARY Thursday 31st October

Feeling v.fed up altogether – C.O. nearly drove me mad talking about his pilots! Working v.hard all day and flying like sin. Managed to get out 8 pilots. None of them can fly worth a damn but still the C.O. hotaired on the tarmac all day and got in the way so I told him off!

To dinner with Gally in Middlesboro! I got rather blotto: as I was so fed up. Ives and Duggie there carried off Gally. Back by 9.10. Woke up at 4.a.m. Heart over revving!

DIARY Friday 1st November

Went on leave by 9.30 with Graham. Fairly comfy trip but v.long. Got a seat all right. Down Byfleet by the 5.55. Found Elsie simply wonderful she is a brave women. "Nothing moves a man so much as to see a women brave". R.L.S. Mum and Dad there.

Bed at 10.30 – rather tired slept v.well.

DIARY Saturday 2nd November

Feeling v.fit. To King's funeral at noon. R.I.P. he did his bit and I think all is for the best. Lunch at West Hall with Dad. Home for tea. Reading "Our Admirable Betty". Quite good. Bed early. Elsie is splendid.

DIARY Sunday 3rd November

Raining hard. To Kirk and H.C. with Elsie. Good service. Dad not v.fit and he and Mum stayed home. Lunch at W. Hall. Kathleen not there – talked to Cousin Fred.

Austria has collapsed, is out of the War. Germany is alone – Wonderful news. Trieste taken, only 2½ mile from Ghent.

Peace by Xmas – wotto! Did not go to Kirk in evening. Read and talked. Am going to apply to go to France.

DIARY Monday 4th November

Packed in morning. Elsie gave me £2. Left by 12.58. Bought pen and knife in town. Balance of £45:16:5 at Cox's. Saw Northwood. Tea at Callards. Taxied to Kings Cross. Tea again there! Booked seat at 4. Left town by 5.30, v full train. Comfy seat. Walked up in pouring rain and howling wind with bag – awful!

DIARY Tuesday 5th November

Rather tired! Flew once or twice – high wind and washed out aviation in afternoon.

To dancing class in evening with Gally – dinner at Red Lion – awful – Gally too dud for words. Jolly good fun at dance – learnt a whole lot. Tender back.

DIARY Wednesday 6th November

Luffly day! Early flying – enjoyed it v.much lovely up. Tested a few buses. Wired Eily to meet me 5.45. Flew to Tad. at 3.30. Arrived York at 4.15 and couldn't find Tad. in mist. Going to turn back when I found it. Landed o.k. Taxied to Leeds. No Eily. Finally found her just as she was going having waited from 4.45! Dinner at Queens with Bakie and Eily. Slept at Bakies. V.nice girl.

DIARY Thursday 7th November

Up for 8 train, v foggy and train late. Arrived Tad. at 10. Too dud to start. Left at 12 and found York by luck. Home at 1000. V.thick everywhere. Not much aviation. Rumour of Germany having signed peace at night. Something of a celebration! Washed out later!!! Time to get out yet.

DIARY Friday 8th November

Up at 9. Fine day. Bokoo aviation. Mit formations etc, all day. Americans take Sedan. Further 'hush hush' rumours going. V.cold, went up with Blake and find I can't fly at all!!

Dance washed out in evening. To pictures instead. Wrote to Holroyd.

DIARY Saturday 9th November

High wind all day, v little aviation. Duggie away. Massive dance at Saltburn in evening till 3.a.m. The best fun in the world! Priceless. For a 13 mile walk with Mac: all day – to Guisboro' and back. Lunch there. Feel v.fit indeed. Further advance as far as Hauberge.

DIARY Sunday 10th November

High wind and no flying v.tired! Not to Kirk in morning. Loafed about indoors all day. Abdication of Kaiser! All in a spin like!

To Kirk in evening – only one there. To bed early – tired.

DIARY Monday 11th November

Armistice signed!!!!!   Peace – Hoo bally ray wotto!!!! Capture of Mons. Formated in morning and then came down and heard the joyous news! Everyone went mad! Low flying all up Tees and beach. Flew under bridge at M'boro' twice. Damn good show.

Foamed about in afternoon. Huge great dance in evening till 4.30 a.m.!! That's the spirit. Fireworks and bonfire and fizz supper! Miss Jeffs is topping.

DIARY Tuesday 12th November

Up at 10.30. V.little flying. A couple of joyrides. Too dud in afternoon and so washed out. The C.O. asked why!

Welch Dance in evening. Supper at Lonsdales with Miss Jeffs in evening. Got a mascot v.nice too. Then dance till 3.15! Pretty tired but great fun! Walked home with the girl. Bed at 4. V.cold.

DIARY Wednesday 13th November

Holiday all day. Up at 11. Brekker in bed. V.cold. One set of tennis in afternoon but too cold and court too soft for any fun. Washed out after that. Tea with Bartlett at Lonsdales – 3 eggs v.good tea. Tendered back. Jolly cold. Rather a head and a bit chilly. Thought I was getting the flu. Bed at 9.30. Slept badly till 11 and then well till 9.

DIARY Thursday 14th November

Fine day. Not much aviation though – that 'peace' feeling still about! Washed out at 4. Pretty tired all day. Bed late – v.cold. Dinner with Rogers and his wife.

DIARY Friday 15th November

Misty all day v.little aviation. Rang up Miss Jeffs. Down to tea with her at 7.30 and then on to the Welch Dance – v.good time indeed! Not many there. Saw her home after. Some kid! Lovely night.

DIARY Saturday 16th November

Fine all day. No early flying – C.O. v.fed up with us all! Did a formation after brekker. Low strafed Jeffs house! Golf in afternoon with Miss Jeffs, Mac and Miss Burns. I was playing execrably!! Lost 4 down! Tea with Miss Jeffs and then party after supper. 7 girls and 4 men. Played blow feather and piano and danced. Left at 12. Topping evening and good fun. Effected nothing however!!

DIARY Sunday 17th November

Misty all morning. Church Parade at 9.30 for all. Good service. Too dud for flying. Barker in for lunch. Cleared a bit after. Took him up for a flip and looped and stalled turned and contour chased. Said he enjoyed it but looked v.green! To tea at farm with him after that. Miss Jeffs and Miss Walker in. Played piano and gramophone and card tricks. Walked home with Miss Jeffs, couldn't say a word but got to the "Annie" stage! Look. I am far gone. "Good night Annie" – that's the spirit! Long talk to Duggie.

DIARY Monday 18th November

Mistier than porridge in morning. No flying. I for live flips. Cleared up after a bit. Gibb and Alex did forced landings. Gave a lecture on formation and generally hot aired about all round. Fair days work. V cold indeed. Down town after ten – bought photo frame and ring for Mascot. Bed early v tired. Lost 3/6 at bridge – I am a luckless man!

DIARY Tuesday 19th November

Fine cold day but with a thick mist. Not much aviation for me. V thick later in afternoon. Took up SE5 and did 6 loops and some rolls. Nice bus but not as good as a Camel. Rang up Annie and Smith and I took her and Mary Callum to dancing class at the Gem. Not too bad and I danced a lot with Annie. Saw 'em home singing and dancing. Cocoa at Callums house.

Bed, v cold.

DIARY Wednesday 20th November

Lovely day but v thick on ground. Did an hours formation at 12000 ft with Alexander, nearly killed me in a dive! Cold. Alexander landed into 2 Avros and bent all 3 machines! Up for a mad flip after lunch.

Smith and I took Annie and May to supper at the Lonsdales – v good meal and then to Cinema after. Long theological discussion! Snooker at Mays after v bon time.

DIARY Thursday 21st November

Cold day. Forced landing on Avro in morning. Lost my prop and sat in a field for 3/4 hour! Up on a Camel after lunch for a short while – all the cartridge cases fell into the officer! Awfully dangerous. Kicked up the _____ of a row when I came down.

Tennis with Houseley in afternoon. Beastly cold and we quit soon. Read and smoked after dinner.

DIARY Friday 22nd November

Cold day and a fair amount of flying. Managed to get dance tickets. Called for Annie and went to Welch Dance – awful good fun. Col. Page's buffday – fizz. Back at 3. Danced a whole lot with Annie.

DIARY Saturday 23rd November

Thick mist v little aviation. Rolled tennis court in morning. Annie and Madge came up at 3 and had a great game with Houseley and I. We lost 6-4, 6-4.

Tea in Guest Room and then down to Supper with May Callum. I developed a sore throat and felt v dud. Good time.

DIARY Sunday 24th November

In bed till 11.30. Down for Annie at 2.20. For a five mile walk across fields v muddy but jolly good fun. Back to tea and Supper with her – Tom and May in. Learnt how to gold divine! Back at 11. V good fun.

DIARY Monday 25th November

No flying – raining on and off. Played badminton with C.O. in afternoon. Rather sore throat. Boxed with Bill and Houseley and then did some Gym. Smithy and I had Annie and May up for dinner in Guest

Room. Smithy v tight but splendid fun and good meal. Gramophone. Saw them home – <u>very</u> nearly kissed Annie – very nearly. She is a sweet kid. Bed at 12.

DIARY Tuesday 26th November

Fine day. Some morning. Flew to Marske and took up Bristol Monoplane – Gorgeous bus – simply lovely. Looped and rolled wonderfully. Then took up Sop Triplane – v nice – loops nicely. Parade in afternoon. Did not fly. Played billiards with Houseley.

To dancing class with Annie in evening. Priceless – danced every dance with her. Saw her home and then abso: tore <u>everything</u> by asking to kiss her – badly told off. I am sorry about it. Fearfully fed up. Pray hard she sees me tomorrow.

DIARY Wednesday 27th November

To Byfleet by 9.30 train – good trip – v cold.

DIARY Thursday 28th November

Up town by 11.30. Bought a few things – Lunch with Gin and to see the "Box o' Tricks". Down by 6 train.

DIARY Friday 29th November

Loafed about all day. Brooklands in afternoon with Dad. Dinner at Swifts – v dud.

DIARY Saturday 30th November

Town with Dad and Bob. Lunch at club with Uncle H. To see B.B's on B – good fun. Dinner at Elysée with Avison. Fair. Saw me off and kissed her!

DIARY Sunday 1st December

To Church H.C. in morning. Up by 7.30 train up to Kings Cross. Caught 10.30 train – chock full. Avison saw me off v sweet of her. Awful trip. Half an hour sleep.

DIARY Monday 2nd December

Arrived at 7am, v tired. Flew twice. Bed at 8.30.

DIARY Tuesday 3rd December

Slept till 8.30, v tired still. Up with Blake, flipped once or twice. Rang up Annie – To dancing class in evening. Too tired to do anything at all. Bed late.

DIARY Wednesday 4th December

Better! Flew a good deal. Up with Blake.

Tea with Annie at Lonsdales – made my peace – hooray. Played gramophone at her place after. To men's dance – awful blooming show. Had pocket book with £5 pinched from my pocket simply wild.

DIARY Thursday 5th December

No sign of my perishing pocket book. Now hear that flight O.C.'s pay is washed out – I am out of luck. Not much aviation. Fooled about in afternoon. To Gym class in evening. Great fun. Learnt Jujitsu. Throat still sore. Am going to fly back Hun machines – grand.

DIARY Friday 6th December

Flew hard all day. Took up Snipe. Hockey in afternoon v the men. Jolly good game – we won 4.2. I played quite well. v stiff! To Welch dance in evening. Took Annie and danced quite well and a lot with her. Back at 12. V tired. Sat in Callums and had Oxo. Issued ultimatum!

DIARY Saturday 7th December

Joyous flip on DH9 in morning. Played tennis in afternoon with Major, Scott and Collison. Great fun. V sore! Won 3f at auction! To billiards at Callums in evening, great fun. Annie not there but still Smithy and I there. May is a good kid.

DIARY Sunday 8th December

To Kirk in morning – v good service. Walk along sands with Annie in afternoon. Great. To May's in evening. Rough housed and pillow fought. Play gramophone and sung. Very merry evening. Nothing doing tho.

Bed at 11.30. Throat again.

DIARY Monday 9th December

Flipped around in morning. Cold. Formation in afternoon, rotten! Got up flying speed after tea.

To dance in evening. Good fun – v hot tho! Danced a lot with Annie. Drew heavy bomber with affinity _____! Knew I should! Talked to Annie – I sat out. What ails me? I can't say a darned word!! The old old story I fear! Saw her home and held her hand! Lust! Bed at 3 – v tired – oh so tired – and thirsty – ye gods – guts thirst!

DIARY Tuesday 10th December

Flying in morning. Luffly day. To dancing class in evening with Annie. Great fun – danced a lot with her. Saw her home – nuffin' doin!

DIARY Wednesday 11th December

Feeling a bit tired! Flew in morning. Fooled about. Nothing of interest. Hockey v Welch in afternoon. Great game 2-2. I played fairly well.

DIARY Thursday 12th December

Flying all day. Gorgeous day. Fixed up dance hall in afternoon. Binge in Mess. Home late. Concert in evening not bad.

DIARY Friday 13th December

Flying in morning. High wind and v bumpy but good fun. Huge dance in evening. Wondrous show. Danced even numbers with Annie. Topping. Took her to my room, saw her and May home in cab. Wotto, walked back – Bed at 4.30.

DIARY Saturday 14th December

Up at 10.15, v fit. Flew a bit in morning. Landed at Callums with Smithy in afternoon. I saw Annie to hockey field after – looking like nuffing on earf! Smithy _____ but tush! Norraword!!

Tea at Callum's and then flew back. Annie and May to Supper and then to Concert. Topping fun and enjoyed it hugely! Worro! Walked back – lovely night.

DIARY Sunday 15th December

Raining. To Kirk in town with Smithy. Walked back with May. Down to tea at Annie's in afternoon. Lovely time. Sat and played gramophone – arms around her! Tush! Then sang songs and had a long and v candid talk with Annie. Saw [?] _____ Back at 11.30. Feeling too tired for words.

DIARY Monday 16th December

Fairly fine day. Flew in morning and a bit in afternoon. Phoned Annie, had dinner in Middlesboro. Then to see "The Live Wire" – jolly good show. Then sat in Grand till 11.15. Had a topping talk with her. She is a sweet girl. Caught train at 12. Walked home. By God's Grace Annie will keep me white. V happy.

DIARY Tuesday 17th December

Flying in morning. Flew Bristol Fighter at Marske – my 16th type, v nice bus and loops rippingly. Hockey v N.E.A.F.I.S. in afternoon, we lost – I played rottenly. Dinner at Red Lion with Annie, May and Smithy.

Quite fun but I too tired out! To dancing class in afternoon. Not much fun – danced a lot with Annie. Tired. Walked home, asked a question.

DIARY Wednesday 18th December

Flew a bit. One formation. Up 3 times on pup. Called for Annie, and May at 8pm in tender. To Saltburn dance. The best fun ever. Danced even No's with Annie. Ripping – stopped at 2.30. No cab. Raked it up. Got v comfy and warm when cabby refused to go on after a time! Got lift in train to Marske crossing. Then walked – fearfully cold but still! Arm around her. Said goodbye and God speed. Received my answer, just too happy for words. I would do anything for her. Bed 4.30.

DIARY Thursday 19th December

Up at 8. Down for 9.33 train, met by Annie. Train 35 mins late! Up to Middlesboro with Annie. Awful nice of her. V cold, but feel fit. Caught train at Darlington. Packed, sat on floor till York. Then seat v uncomfy and cold as sin! Am going to take up Col. McGregor. Wrote Annie. Train arr: 1 hour late. Met by Dad and taxi. Caught 7.58 train, cold, tired and hungry! Arr: 8.

Bed at 10. Jolly cold.

DIARY Friday 20th December

V cold day. Up for brekker. Up to village with Mum in morning. Read after lunch. Then to Bramptons for tea. Cold. Am reading "Rough Road" v good. Feel v fit but tired.

DIARY Saturday 21st December

Up to town by 10.15. Bought a record for Annie. Paid £46 Cox's drew £10, £16 left. In bed to 10 – awfully full. Down by 1.45 no lunch to notice. To dance practice at W Hall. None of us could dance! Chilly after lunch. Wrote Annie.

DIARY Sunday 22nd December

To Kirk in morning. Raining. Stayed in house in afternoon and read and wrote letters. Read aircraft book and the "Rough Road".

DIARY Monday 23rd December

Pains within – felt rotten! Stayed in all day. Dud weather. Read and fooled about "Scrooge" in evening. Bad. Billinghurst in.

DIARY Tuesday 24th December

V cold. Quite o.k. To Woking in morning with Dad with £2.10. Came back with 4d! Letter from Annie – just ripping, oh she is the goods. Fixed up Xmas tree. Walked with Dad. "Scrooge" in evening.

DIARY Wednesday 25th December

A merry Christmas to everyone (including Annie!) Feeling v fit. To Kirk in morning v cold, presents at lunch. Lovely scarf from Mum, cigars from Dad, six silk hankies, socks and calendars. Present giving to kids after. Tea at W Hall. Sang songs with Gin after dinner. Walked home with Frederick and then Gin. Bed at 11.

DIARY Thursday 26th December

Fine frosty day – rather cold but lovely. All for a long walk in morning. Took some snaps. Read in afternoon, Dad chilly in evening. Retired to bed. I had pains and felt rather ill. Worse after supper. Bed early, felt awful _____! Was 'orrid sick!! Slept fairly.

DIARY Friday 27th December

Much better! Up for brekker. Letter from Annie – bon. Raining, wrote to Annie. Out for a stroll. Dad in bed all day. To Bevingtons for supper. Eily arrived. To dance at village hall after supper. Great fun. Enid a lovely dancer – Miss Comerford v nice. Danced all but 2. Stopped at 1.15. Bed at 2. Slept well. Still a bit wonky within!

DIARY Saturday 28th December

Taxied back from Bevingtons. Dad up for lunch. To W Hall in morning. To see Major Landon for tea. Talked after supper and read. Eily to W Hall in taxi on a/c of rain. Long talk with Mum after supper. I am a selfish beast. Too much ego in my cosmos. Must change in New Year. Letter from Annie and Duggie.

DIARY Sunday 29th December – DADS BIRTHDAY GOD BLESS HIM

To Kirk with Mum and Eily in morning. Stayed to H.C. – only 3 there but v nice. Read in afternoon and played with kiddies. Packed after tea. Saw Eily to West Hall after supper and said goodbye all round. Awful posh those girls up there talk! Walked back. Bed. Last day of leave – rotten. God bless Dad on his 61st birthday and may he see many another.

DIARY Monday 30th December

Up by 10.15, missed Gin at Waterloo. Taxied to Kings Cross and had lunch. Met Bartlett. Gin turned up at 1. Train v full. Arrived Redcar at 10pm – just in time for a dance – heck! Annie all booked up! Had four with her. Bed at 3.30. Glad to be back.

DIARY Tuesday 31st December

Flew once in morning. High wind. I was C.O. Did nowt in afternoon. Supper at Annies and then to Welch Dance. The best ever in the world! Topping supper, bags of fizz – all full out. Auld Lang Syne and Cheers. Had 13 dances with Annie had a topping time. Sat out. Saw her home and kissed her at 4.30 am. Well jolly old 1918 began with a war and bullets and ends with Peace and a kiss. "and you find at the end of a perfect day the soul of a friend you've made". A HAPPY NEW YEAR AND GOD BLESS US ALL.

Postscript

by Dr John Thackray

Guy obtained his permanent commission with the R.A.F. as a flying officer on 2 August 1918. He served in India from 1920 to 1922, taking part in the Mahsud campaign, Waziristan, with 28 Squadron, in 1921. He served as a flying instructor at RAF Cranwell from 1923 to 1927, and in 201 Flying Boat Squadron, 1928-1929. Guy was at Air Staff Headquarters, Far East Command for 1930-1934, being promoted to Squadron Leader in 1935. He was Chief Flying Instructor, Oxford University Air Squadron for 1934-1937, and became a Wing Commander in 1938. He was Officer Commanding 144(B) Squadron in 1938 and again in 1940-1942. Guy served in the Middle East in 1942-1945, being promoted Group Captain in 1942. He retired in 1946 and began a new career as an archaeologist with the Ministry of Public Buildings and Works. He became an Inspector of Ancient Monuments and conducted a number of digs – notably Anglo-Saxon work at Thetford, Norfolk.

Guy married Cynthia Burgoyne Lamb in 1923 and had two daughters, June Mainwaring (b.1925) and Susan Elizabeth Mainwaring (b.1928).

He lived in retirement in Ashton Keynes, Wiltshire, and died in September 1971.

Appendix 1

Article by GMK for Ex-Army Quarterly – July 1964

AN AIRMAN REMEMBERS

Vignettes from the Sketch-book of an undistinguished Sopwith
Camel pilot in the winter of 1917-18

BY GROUP-CAPTAIN G. M. KNOCKER

"Old men forget; yet all shall be forgot,
But he'll remember with advantages."

These pictures, drawn from memory, may perhaps induce a
feeling of nostalgia in others of my generation and may be of
some antiquarian interest to the warriors of another war and
perhaps even to those who came after.

THE YPRES SALIENT FROM THE AIR

Between the ruins of Armentières in the south and Passchendaele
in the north lay a strip some 15 miles long and 10 miles broad of
sheer and utter desolation. The water-filled shell-holes appeared
to touch each other, like the holes in some monstrous honeycomb
or like the hoofprints in a muddy farm gateway in a wet winter.
Woods, fields, roads, villages and even trenches were blotted out.
Only the blurs of what had once been Ploegsteert Wood and the
Forest of Houthoulst showed up dark against the muddy mosaic
and the Jew's harp of the Étang de Zillebeke shone with a metallic
brightness when the light caught it. Sitting up aloft in the cold,
clean air, it was hard to believe that thousands of men were
actually living in that abomination. In a morning after a fall of

snow, you could always tell where there had been a "strafe" the night before, because the shells had blackened and sullied the pure white of the ground. Sometimes in the evening, the jagged ruins of Ypres would flush with a warm, yellow light and, away to the east, Menin and Roulers with their German fighter aerodromes, showed up like menacing shadows. Kite balloons hung motionless along the Yser Canal and always, almost always, the wind blew from the west... into Hunland. Such was the Salient and yet those who served there on the ground or in the air had a sort of wry affection for it and would later have a kind of pride at having fought there.

CONFIDENCE TRICK

"There's a Hun two-seater low over Passchendaele and a dozen Albatroses to the east and higher up. Can I get the two-seater without being jumped?" Down I go, full of optimism, but of course the Hun dives away east at once... and then all around come the well-known whip-lash cracking and the streams of tracer as the Albatrii come clattering down. I can see their black and white chequered wings and hooped fuselages and recognize them as Von Bulow's "Circus"... "Into a tight turn now and stay there... ah! there's a Hun straightening out ahead... let him have it!" Pop-pop-pop-plopple-lop-plop-plop go the two Vickers... "here comes another head-on... (no Hun will face a head-on shot; they always give way first... and that's what this one does, the blighter!)"... Crack-crack-crack and a bullet nicks the elbow of my Sidcot suit as I climb away in a turn. The Albatros overshoots and as he dives past I can see the pilot in his cockpit. He is wearing a light-coloured flying helmet like mine... "queer that there are actually people in those aeroplanes...." After that I go a little mad and try to collide with another Hun but mercifully miss him (no parachutes in those days). Then nose down and into a spiral dive ("never *spin* away"), with the wires screaming and the whole bus tense and rigid.... "I hope to God the wings stay on...!" Down I go to 20 feet above the shell-holes and back west as fast as the old Camel will belt. The Huns follow me down to 500 feet, but no lower. A shell bursts on the ground below me and scares the daylight out of me. And so back home, to shoot a line about it... but I wish I'd been a better shot....

MUTUAL PROTECTION

"'B' and 'C' Flights will carry out independent patrols at 10,000 feet, giving each other mutual protection."

Two flights of six aircraft, each flying in a tight formation of two threes, patrol up and down the Line. You are the inside man of the rear three of "B" Flight. There are broken cumulus clouds at patrol height and all seems quiet and peaceful until "B" Flight enters one of the clouds and to your dismay you see "C" Flight coming through the same cloud in the opposite direction. You clap your elbows to your sides, as if that would make your Camel slimmer, and hold your breath until you slide through the cloud and out into the sunshine again. And then you see bits of wing and wreckage floating down and you know that the man next to you has collided with the outside man of the other formation. Not very funny (no parachutes in those days).

DOG FIGHT

Twelve Camels and as many Albatroses are milling round each other at 12,000 feet. After a few circles there seem to be twenty-four Huns and no Camels. Streams of white tracer and the red of Buckingham incendiaries cross and recross each other, and now an aeroplane breaks away from the mêlée with black smoke pouring from it. A Camel comes diving past you with both guns firing and the enemy on your tail pulls away. Another comes into the ring of your Aldis sight and you press both firing levers. Your guns rattle away and the Hun goes down in a vertical dive, but you can't tell if you've got him for someone else comes round onto your tail and the crazy dance starts again.... And then suddenly you are alone in the sky. You turn west and make for the Lines, looking for the rest of the formation, leaving a trail of "Archie" bursts to mark your errant passage.

ARTILLERY OBSERVATION

It was not nice to see an R.E.8, flying at 8,000 feet and ranging an 8-inch howitzer battery get in the line of flight of one of its own battery's shells. It took a long time to flutter down, with one of its top planes flapping, like the broken wing of a duck... down, down down and then splash into a shell hole (no parachutes in those days).

PERSONALITIES

We went out as a new squadron and suffered from the fact that very few of us had been out as pilots before, with the result that we had heavy casualties for the first six months without a corresponding dividend in enemy aircraft shot down. Nearly all of us were seconded from various regiments and corps and we had little idea of fighter, or as they were then called, scout tactics. Some of us were very young and nobody had sufficiently dinned into our heads (at least not into mine) that time spent watching the mechanics overhauling one's aircraft was time well spent or that a scout pilot, fly he never so well, who could not shoot straight was quite useless. The Balls, Bishops and McCuddens would spend hours lining up their guns and sights and doing practice attacks. As a result they would shoot down a Hun with half a dozen shots. I used to loose off 400 without the slightest apparent result and it never occurred to me that the fault was not bad luck but bad shooting. We learnt better later on and the squadron had the distinction of being credited with the destruction of 15 enemy aircraft in one day.

There is no doubt that Trenchard's policy of the relentless offensive was the right one, although on the occasions, when the Hun would not come up and play with us and the trail left by our coats, as we patrolled over the enemy lines, was marked only by black "Archie" bursts, we may have felt inclined to doubt it! Camel squadrons were usually compelled to fight at an initial tactical disadvantage. The enemy aircraft had the height and speed of a Camel, which with a 130 – 140 h.p. Clerget rotary engine, had a performance only slightly higher than a Tiger Moth. I can only remember two or three occasions when we actually dived on German fighters, so that it was they who could decide whether to engage or not. I must say they usually obliged! Once the battle was joined of course we could make rings round the Albatroses, which could however always break off at will by diving away. We could not catch them if they did.

Our C.O. was a bluff gunner major. He spoke to us all before we flew out and he said, "We are not going to France for the good of our healths. There are bound to be casualties, but I don't want them to be mentioned in the Mess: and call me 'Major' and not

'Sir'." He was very brave and used to lead many of the offensive patrols himself and as a result collected a lot of Huns.

Two of our pilots had been observers, one having gained an M.C., but poor S. did not have much luck this time for the very first round "Archie" threw up, the first time we crossed the Lines got a direct hit on him (no parachutes in those days). The other ex-observer, who was also later killed and oddly enough also by a shell, had been with Alan Bott in 70 Squadron of "An Airman's Outings" fame. He was a droll Londoner, whose favourite form of abuse, reserved for his special friends, was "Do you want a thick ear and a mouthful of blood?" Another B. was a great character, known as "Old Bill" from his mossy appearance. Before we went out he used to delight in beating up a certain house in the neighbourhood, inhabited by a lady whom he called "my windy aunt." The Recording Officer was the C.O.'s brother, a captain in the Liverpool Scottish and the guide, counsellor and friend of all us young ones. Our Equipment Officer was a mournful soul with a very long nose. We used to say that he wore a sock on it at night in cold weather. A replacement Flight Commander was a very gallant officer, who had been flying Martinsydes on a previous tour. He collected a dozen or so Huns with us and survived the war, but died in tragic circumstances afterwards. He was a great leader.

We used to paint names on our aircraft. One I remember was "Tid'apa," which made more sense to me after I had been to Singapore, where its pilot had lived, than it did then. Another had his wife's name painted on his Camel. To each his fancy... .

A Camel was a tricky little aircraft to fly, which spun very easily and fast, but it was much loved by those who mastered it. One lad had the distinction of flicking from one spin to another four times before he finally finished up in a wood from which he miraculously emerged unhurt, only to be killed in that collision in the clouds. Another bunted over onto his back while firing at a ground target. He righted it just in time. I myself had a close call when ground strafing. We used to strap in very loosely when on offensive patrol, so that we could look behind our tails frequently. The belts of those days were broad, lap-type affairs with a quick release, and not the shoulder harness worn nowadays. I had omitted to tighten my belt when flying low and on pushing my stick forward to dive at a ground target I got a "bump" under my tail which flicked the aircraft into a vertical dive, with the result that I was nearly shot out and found myself hanging over the gun. I just managed to reach the stick and pull it back to right the aeroplane. When it is realized that the replacement pilots used to arrive at the squadron with a total of only 25 hours solo flying, of which only five had to be on their Service type, the wonder is that so many survived. Alas, however, some did not even get as far as their first operational patrol.

In 1962 some 500 of the R.F.C. and R.N.A.S. met at Lancaster House at the Jubilee Party of the R.F.C. Very brisk most of us looked and very pleased we were to see each other. You could almost catch the whiff of burnt castor oil in those august precincts... It was a notable party.

THE MEN

Without the air mechanics, the "Ack Emmas" as they were always called, no squadron could have operated. Generally speaking they were a splendid lot of chaps in their khaki jackets, of the kind always known as "maternity jackets", and their forage caps and the flight sergeants with a four-bladed propeller above the chevrons on their sleeves. The mechanics would cheerfully work all night in a freezing canvas hangar (for of course there was no "black-out"), changing a mainplane or fitting a new engine. When the aeroplanes for which they were responsible had been in a scrap they would gather round and proudly count the bullet holes and shake their heads over a damaged longeron or main spar, very much as their successors did a quarter of a century later. Mercifully the breed does not change. My batman was a dear old gentleman called Davies. He was an old soldier of the best type and I loved him dearly, except on the occasion when, arriving back in my Nissen hut late one cold night, I found that he had turned up my oil-stove too high and everything was about an inch deep in smuts! I did not love him at all then.... It is a great joy at unit reunions in these later days to meet again those good fellows who worked so hard to keep the aircraft in the air. On such occasions time goes into reverse and behind the old faces you can see the young men you knew so long ago; and I never cease to wonder, with humility, at the esteem in which the ground crews held and, it seems still hold their more fortunate comrades who flew the aeroplanes they maintained.

THE MACHINES

The Sopwith Camel was a small, open-cockpit biplane, usually fitted with a 130 and later 140 h.p. Clerget rotary engine. It had a top speed, low down, of about 110 m.p.h. It was extremely manoeuvrable and very light on fore and aft control. The rotary engine had considerable gyroscopic effect, so that you required full left rudder on both vertical turns. It was armed with two Vickers guns, which fired through the propeller. These were subject to a number of stoppages, most of which could not be rectified in the air. They would also freeze up unless fired periodically. A Camel was a very cold little aeroplane and it had the endearing habit of soaking your right foot in engine oil. We wore, at first, leather flying coats and later a lined, wind-proof combination suit called a Sidcot suit. On our feet we wore thigh-length, sheepskin boots and on our heads a fur-lined helmet with a chin piece and masked goggles. To leave off your chin-piece was to court a frostbitten chin, despite the whale oil with which most people smeared the exposed parts of their faces. Under the gauntlets we wore a pair of silk gloves. We had no parachutes, which did not come into general use until about 1924.

Our opposite numbers among the enemy flew the Albatros D.V and the Pfalz. Both these were biplanes with streamlined, monocoque fuselages and powered with 180 – h.p. Mercedes engines, water-cooled, which must have made them warmer than the Camel. Neither was anything like so manoeuvrable as the latter, but they were much faster, both level and in a dive. They carried two Spandau machine-guns, firing like ours through the propeller. The Fokker Triplane, which appeared early in 1918, was comparable with the Camel in performance, except that it climbed better. I only met them two or three times.

THE 4TH APRIL, 1918

In the thick fog of dawn on 21st March, 1918 the Germans launched their last great offensive of the war, against the Fifth

Army front, east of St. Quentin, and by the beginning of April had pushed us back to within a dozen miles of Amiens. A short sector of the so-called Line went through the village of Warfusée l'Abancourt, about a mile east of Villers-Bretonneux, and ran between the Amiens – St. Quentin road and the River Somme. It was held by an assorted collection of 500 kite balloon section men, G.H.Q. clerks and batmen, drivers, Labour Corps men and in fact anyone who could hold a rifle, all raked together by a certain Brigadier-General Carey and thrown into the line. As many squadrons as could be spared, our own among them, were withdrawn and hurried to the Somme, where they operated from any fields big enough to be used as landing grounds, to help to stem the field-grey tide.

On the 4th April the Germans attacked again, in what was to be their penultimate push in that sector and drove us back as far as the aerodrome at Villers-Bretonneux. The battlefield as seen from the air, presented a remarkable spectacle and looked more like a field day than a battle of the First World War. Clouds were at about 1,000 feet and the air between them and the ground was thick with aircraft of all descriptions, Camels, S.E.5's, Dolphins, Bristol Fighters and R.E.8's, but very few of the enemy. The "Line" consisted of men lining a hedge beside a road, while the Germans lined the opposite bank of another road, forking off at an angle. Further on, men lay in extended order across a grass field and, near by, others were furiously digging rifle-pits. Behind this thin khaki line, stretcher-bearers were carrying off the wounded, riderless horses were galloping about, and a few hundred yards in rear, an anti-aircraft battery was firing level over open sights like a field battery. Crashed aircraft lay around in many fields and over all hung a pall of smoke from the burning village of Villers-Bretonneux. The Germans captured the place later and that was about as close as they got to Amiens. It was close enough.

On the evening of the 6th April, I was flying at 2,000 feet and was just crossing the line where it ran across the aerodrome at Villers-Bret, when I felt a blow on the calf of my right leg, as if I had been hit very hard with a cricket stump. Some Boche soldier had let fly with his rifle and by a fluke hit me, but I don't suppose he knew how lucky he had been, for I was able to fly back to my landing ground without difficulty. When I was taken to a Casualty Clearing Station, in pouring rain later that evening, the first person I saw was my sister, who had been out as a nurse since 1915!

Appendix 2

1917 ～ Aircraft Flown ～ 1946

Maurice Farman Shorthorn.
De Haviland 1, 5, 9, 9A, 53. Moths, Tiger Moth, Leopard Moth, Hornet Moth.
F.E. 2B, 2D.
S.E. 5, B.E. 2C, Martinside F4.
Avro Mono, Lynx, Tutor, Anson.
Sopwith Pup (80 & 110 Le Rhone), Camel, Snipe, 1½ Strutter, Triplane, Cuckoo.
Bristol Scout, Monoplane, Fighter, Bulldog, Blenheim.
Bisley, Beaufort, Beaufighter.
Siddeley Siskin.
Blackburn Shark, Skua.
Armstrong Whitworth Atlas; Auspeed Oxford.
Miles Magister, Mentor, Monarch, Master I, II, III.
Witney Straight (dual); Bolton Paul Defiant.
Gloster Gladiator, Meteor (dual) (1943).
Fairey IIID (Seaplan), Gordon, Swordfish, Battle.
Vickers Virginia (as 2nd pilot), Vildebeeste, Wellington VIII, XI.
Supermarine Southampton, Spitfire, Walrus,
Hawker Horsley, Osprey, Hart, Hart Trainer, Hind,
P.V.4, Fury, Hurricane.
Handley Page Hampden.
North America Harvard, Mitchell (as 2nd pilot),
Douglas Marauder (as 2nd pilot); Republic Thunderbolt.
Beech craft, Percival Proctor, Provost (dual).
Ju 87B (Stuka).
Dragon fly (helicopter) (dual) (1949).
Saunders Roe Skeeter (helicopter) (dual) (1950).
Kirby Kite (glider).
Falcon III (glider).

E.M.K

This list of aircraft flown 1917-1946 was given to the author by his grandfather – Guy Knocker, 2nd Lieutenant RGA attached RFC 1917-18; Group Captain RAF (retired) – in 1968 inside a three volume pictorial history of the RAF
"Fifty Years On … (still flying right wing low!)"

Appendix 3

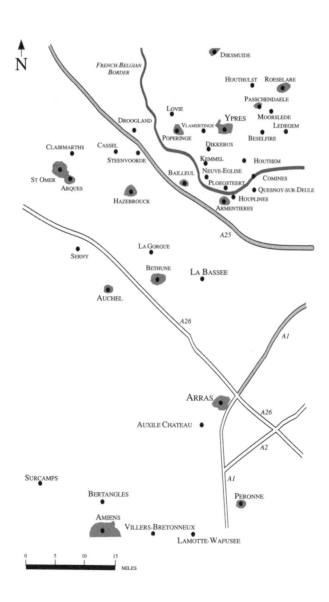

Table of Place Names mentioned in the diaries of
2nd Lieutenant Knocker

Original Spelling	Corrected Spelling	Location	Notes
Armentieres		11 miles S Ypres	
Arques		2.5 miles SE St Omer	
Auchel		8 miles W Bethune	
Audrique			No Trace
Auxi Le Chateau		25 miles NE Amiens	
Bailleul		10 miles SW Ypres	
Barck	See Berck		
Beilangle	See Bertangles		
Bercelere	Beselare	6 miles E Ypres	
Berck		7 miles SW Etaples	
Bertangles		5 miles N Amiens	
Billers Bret	Villers Bretonneux	12 miles E Amiens	
Break			No Trace
Bruay			No Trace
Cassel		11 miles NE St Omer	
Conteville		15 miles NE Amiens	
Clair Marais	Clairmarais	3 miles NE St Omer	
Claor			No Trace
Comminel	See Comines		
Commines	Comines	8 miles SE Ypres	
Dickebush	Dikkebus	3.5 miles SW Ypres	
Dixmunde	Diksmuide	12.5 miles N Ypres	
Dooglandt/Droglandt	Droogland	7 miles W Poperinge	
Hauberge			No Trace
Hazebruck	Hazebrouck	13 miles E St Omer	
Hollebeke		4 miles SE Ypres	
Holthulst Forest	Houthulst Forest	9 miles N Ypres	
Honplines	Houplines	11 miles S Ypres	
Houltem	Houthem	6 miles SE Ypres	
Kemmel		5.5 miles SW Ypres	
La Bassee		7.5 miles E Bethune	
La Gorgue		21 miles SE St Omer	
Ledignan	Ledegem	10 miles E Ypres	
Lovee	Lovie	3 miles N Poperinge	
Maricourt Wood		21 miles S Arras	
Marie Capell	St Marie Cappel	11.5 miles NE St Omer	
Marquise			No Trace
Mont Rouge			No Trace
Moorslede		8 miles NE Ypres	
Morceuil	Moorsele	12 Miles E Ypres	
Neuve Eglise		8 miles S Ypres	
Peronne		26 Miles S Arras	
Poldernock Ridge	Polderhoek Chateau	S Ypres	

Polygon Wood		3.5 miles E Ypres	
Proven		4 miles NW Poperinge	
Quesnoy	Quesnoy Sur Deule	11 miles SE Ypres	
Rouen		44 miles E Le Havre	
Roulers	Roeselare	12 miles NE Ypres	
Scholer			No Trace
Seille			No Trace
Serny		11 miles S St Omer	
Steenvoorde		14 miles W Ypres	
Sur Camps	Surcamps	15 miles NW Amiens	
Thexy	Thezy-Gilmout	8 miles SE Amiens	
Vert Fallon			No Trace
Vlamertinge		3 miles W Ypres	
Warfusee	Lamotte-Warfusee	14 mile E Amiens	

Note: Some of the places named do not appear to exist according to the current data available.

Index